D0095176

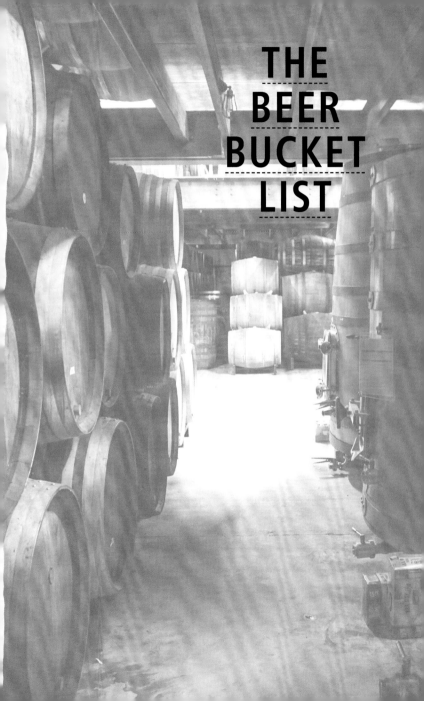

THE
BEER
BUCKET
LIST

THE
BEER
BUCKET
LIST

A TRAVEL-SIZED GUIDE TO OVER 150 OF THE BEST BEER EXPERIENCES ON THE PLANET

Mark Dredge

DOG 'n' BONE

This edition published in 2019 by Dog 'n' Bone Books
An imprint of Ryland Peters & Small Ltd
20–21 Jockey's Fields   341 E 116th St
London WC1R 4BW   New York, NY 10029

First published in 2018 by Dog 'n' Bone Books.

www.rylandpeters.com

10 9 8 7 6 5 4 3 2 1

Text © Mark Dredge 2019
Design © Dog 'n' Bone Books 2019

The author's moral rights have been asserted. All rights reserved. No part of this publication may
be reproduced, stored in a retrieval system, or transmitted in any form or by any means, electronic,
mechanical, photocopying, or otherwise, without the prior permission of the publisher.

A CIP catalog record for this book is available from the Library of Congress and the British Library.

ISBN: 978 1 911026 98 3

Printed in China

Editor: Caroline West | Design concept: Eoghan O'Brien | Reformat design: Jerry Goldie |
Illustrations: Stephen Dew
Photography credits: See below

Key: t=top; b=bottom; l=left; r=right; m=middle; c=center

p2 tl, tr, mc Matthew Curtis; mr, bl, br Mark Dredge; p6 Matthew Curtis; p8 Matthew Curtis; p9 Shawn Patrick Ouellette/Portland Press
Herald/Getty Images; p11 Brianna Soukup/Portland Press Herald/Getty Images; p12 Matthew Curtis; p13 Mark Dredge; p14 iStock; p15
Jessica Rinaldi/The Boston Globe/Getty Images; p17 Lonely Planet Images/Getty Images; p19 Spencer Platt/Getty Images; p21 Scott
Eells/Bloomberg/Getty Images; p23 Mark Dredge; p24 George Rose/Getty Images; pp27–30 Mark Dredge; p31 Anthony Tahlier/Corridor
Brewery and Provisions; p32 Mark Dredge; p33 Band of Bohemia; p34 John Gress/Corbis/Getty Images; p35 Chris Sweda/Chicago Tribune/
Getty Images; p36 Found Image Press/Corbis/Getty Images; p37 Raymond Boyd/Michael Ochs Archives/Getty Images; p38 Gary Porter/The
Washington Post/Getty Images; pp41–42 Mark Dredge; p43 Luke Sharrett/Bloomberg/Getty Images; pp44–46 Matthew Curtis; p47 Mark
Dredge; p48 Matthew Curtis; p49 Mark Boster/Los Angeles Times/Getty Images; p50 Lonely Planet Images/Getty Images; p51 Matthew
Curtis; p53 Justin Sullivan/Getty Images; p55 Ken James/Bloomberg/Getty Images; p56 Matthew Curtis; p58 Hemis/Alamy Stock Photo;
p60 George Ostertag/Alamy Stock Photo; p61 Felix Choo/Alamy Stock Photo; p63 Jay Reilly/Aurora/Getty Images; p65 Hemis/Alamy Stock
Photo; p66 Kaz Ehara/Toronto Star/Getty Images; p67 Connie Tsang/Cask Days; pp68–73 Matthew Curtis; p74 LatitudeStock—David
Williams/Gallo Images/Getty Images; p75 Print Collector/Getty Images; pp76–78 Matthew Curtis; p79 FourPure; p81 Andrew Errington/
Getty Images; p84 SSPL/Getty Images; p85 RDImages/Epics/Getty Images; p87 Patti Nickell/Lexington Herald-Leader/MCT/Getty Images;
p89 Jon Lewis/Alamy Stock Photo; p90 Matthew Curtis; p92 ToniFlap/iStock; pp93–96 Matthew Curtis; p98 Mr Standfast/Alamy Stock
Photo; p99 Stephen McCarthy/Sportsfile/Getty Images; p100 Fishman/ullstein bild/Getty Images; p103 UIG/Getty Images; p104 Matthew
Lloyd/Bloomberg/Getty Images; p105 Alan Copson/Getty Images; p107 Artur Widak/NurPhoto/Getty Images; p108 Barry Mason/Alamy
Stock Photo; p109 John Baran/Alamy Stock Photo; p110 Tibor Bognar/Corbis Documentary/Getty Images; p112 Forster/ullstein bild/
Getty Images; p113 Bruce Yuanyue Bi/Lonely Planet Images/Getty Images; p115 Mark Dredge; p117 manfredxy/iStock; p118 Andrew
Bain/Lonely Planet Images/Getty Images; p119 Bob Pool/Getty Images; p121 Jon Hicks/Corbis Documentary/Getty Images; p122 Florian
Gaertner/Photothek/Getty Images; p123 Leber/ullstein bild/Getty Images; p124 Mark Dredge; p127 Pilsner Urquell; p128 Cultura RM
Exclusive/UBACH/DE LA RIVA/Getty Images; p129 Matej Divizna/Getty Images; p131 Westend61/Getty Images; p132 Anibal Trejo/
Shutterstock; p133 Birrificio Italiano; p134 Jumping Rocks/UIG/Getty Images; p135 Baladin; p136 Philippe Lissac/Corbis Documentary/
Getty Images; p138 Fred de Noyelle/Corbis Documentary/Getty Images; pp140–141 Matthew Curtis; pp142–143 Mark Dredge; p145
William Van Hecke/Corbis/Getty Images; p147 Matthew Curtis; pp148–149 Mark Dredge; p150 Krzysztof Dydynski/Lonely Planet Images/
Getty Images; pp151–153 Mark Dredge; p155 Werner Dieterich/Getty Images; p157 Mark Dredge; p159 Yadid Levy/robertharding/Getty
Images; pp160–161 Mikkeller; p163 Gerard Puigmal/Getty Images; p164 Dean Conger/Corbis/Getty Images; pp166–168 Mark Dredge;
p171 Andrew Watson/Getty Images; p173–174 Mark Dredge; p175 Peter Harrison/Getty Images; p177 Simon Shiff/Melbourne Good
Beer Week; p178 Loop Images/UIG/Getty Images; p181–182 Tim Cuff/Alamy Stock Photo; p185 Mark Dredge; p187 Robin Bush/Getty
Images; p188 Matthew Curtis; p190 Mark Dredge; p191 Matthew Curtis; p192 Wibowo Rusli/Lonely Planet Images/Getty Images; p193
Mark Dredge; p195 Hoang Dinh Nam/AFP/Getty Images; pp197–201 Mark Dredge; p202 Kim Won-Jin/AFP/Getty Images; p204 Mark
Dredge; p205 Brent Lewin/Bloomberg/Getty Images; p207 Pradeep Gaur/Mint/Getty Images; pp208–209 Kiyoshi Ota/Bloomberg/Getty
Images; p210 Volksblad/Gallo Images/Getty Images, p211 Johnny Greig/Alamy Stock Photo; p212 Mujahid Safodien/AFP/Getty Images;
p215 Menahem Kahana/AFP/Getty Images; p217 Mario Tama/Getty Images; p218 Iarigan - Patricia Hamilton/Getty Images; p221 Bruce
Yuanyue Bi/Lonely Planet Images/Getty Images

Contents

Introduction

The Beer Bucket List is a collection of essential world beer experiences. It's the most important old breweries and the industry-changing new ones; it's the greatest world beer bars and pubs; the unmissable beer festivals; the most delicious destinations for beer and food; the must-visit cities to go to drinking; the unexpected, the unusual, the unknown, the classics, the most famous, the best. And out of a global search it's wonderfully become a local celebration of the world's beer diversity.

The author adding another tick to the list.

You can use *The Beer Bucket List* as a drink-before-you-kick-it list, if you like, but you might need to live forever to complete it. I haven't completed my own beer bucket list yet and that's mainly because I'm adding things quicker than they're being ticked off.

While I searched the world for beer experiences, I was continually surprised by what I was finding: the hop-growing region of North Patagonia; the Middle East's first brewpub in Batroun, Lebanon; the super high-end breweries in Western Australia's wine-growing region; the cities in India with 25 brewpubs; the increasing number and quality of Thai beers coming out of a country in which it's effectively illegal to brew; the community Zoigl brewhouses of northeast Bavaria. In fact, the more I looked the more I found. And not just a few unexpectedly located bars with a few taps, but genuinely unique things that show just how craft beer and local beer cultures are found everywhere.

My challenge was working out what counted as being worthy of going on a bucket list for the serious beer lover. It couldn't just be a bunch of nice pubs and cool breweries which you should go to if you're passing. It had to be definitive, selective, and had to go further than what's in your glass—it's about the travel, the discovery, the experience.

Some beer things are unequivocal beer bucket list ticks. They are the wonders of the beer world, where the equivalent of the Northern Lights would be the Pilsner Urquell cellars or Munich's Oktoberfest. Some ticks are more specific, like swimming with sharks or running a marathon, in that it takes a certain kind of person to want to do them—drinking Lithuania's farmhouse ales is one such example, as is having a pint in the Arctic Circle. Sometimes a tick is earned by going somewhere because that's the only place, or the best place, you can drink a certain beer or beer style: Czech Polotmavy, Vietnamese *bia hoi*, West Midlands Milds—that's the same as going to Israel or Italy or Peru to eat the local food.

There are quirks of the beer world that few people know about, like the Belgian bar that only opens for a few hours on Sunday morning and only sells sour beer, or there's the pub in northern England that serves all its ales directly from wooden barrels. Then there's the personal side of a bucket list where going to a favorite brewery allows you to taste something beyond just the ingredients used in the recipe.

There have been countless brilliant surprises while I've been working through my own beer bucket list and I now have new favorite bars, breweries, beers, and beer cities, and I'm more excited by the world of beer than I've ever been before. It also excites me that I've still got a lot more beer to drink before I even get close to completing my list. Until then, this is *The Beer Bucket List*, and these are the world's essential beer experiences.

TOP 10 BEER BUCKET LIST TICKS

- See the Burton Unions at Marston's Brewery, England (see page 85)
- Drink in the Pilsner Urquell brewery cellars in Plzen, Czech Republic (see page 126)
- Visit the brewing Trappist monasteries in Belgium (see page 138)
- Go to Cantillon in Brussels and drink Belgian Lambic (see page 147)
- Go to Oktoberfest in Munich (see page 111)
- Drink Zoiglbier in Oberpfalz, Germany (see page 114)
- Drink Guinness in Dublin, Ireland (see page 106)
- Visit Sierra Nevada Brewing Co, Chico, while on a California road trip (see page 54)
- The Great American Beer Festival (see page 46)
- Go to The Mussel Inn, Onekaka, New Zealand (see page 180)

1

Chapter 1
North America

Drink Allagash Brewery's White

MAINE'S MOST-LOVED BEER

In 1995, when Rob Tod opened a brewery in Portland, Maine, that only made a cloudy, Belgian-style White Ale, people thought he was bonkers. He started brewing this beer because he wanted something different and unique that you couldn't already get. Trouble was, there was probably a reason why you couldn't get it in Portland: no one wanted it. Or they didn't—yet. But Rob persevered through a tough decade and now Allagash White is Portland's—and Maine's—beer.

White is smooth and creamy; the spices—curaçao, orange peel, and coriander seed—play in the background; and there's some fruity yeast. It's gentle with underlying power and depth, a versatile beer that's sessionable yet complex, familiar yet exciting, and the ultimate beer for food.

Allagash Brewery runs free tours around their impressive facility. You can't buy any beer to drink there, though; instead, everyone who visits gets a 3-oz (85-ml) pour from each of the four taps. The beers change and you can come in every day, if you wish, and get the four free pours. It's a nice, generous approach to the tasting room and one that encourages people to visit, but then also to go into town to drink Allagash beers in the bars.

To reflect their love of Belgian-style beers, Allagash installed a coolship in 2007 and produce a small range of spontaneously fermented beers to go alongside an extensive barrel-aging program. These are all very good. The coolship beers are comparable to the best Belgian Lambics, while the barrel sours are complex, elegant, and nuanced.

You walk into Allagash and it's warm, friendly, and welcoming. The simple generosity of offering a few good beers for free is

Make sure you sign up for a free tour at Allagash.

something you don't see in many places, so visit the brewery, go on the tour, have your beers, then head into town and drink some more Allagash White—it's a wonderful, pioneering beer and you should raise a pint to Rob Tod for his focused dedication and the way in which he gave Portland, Maine, its most important beer.

The Lowdown

WHAT: Allagash Brewing Company

HOW: Open every day, from 11am to 6pm (www.allagash.com).

WHERE: 50 Industrial Way, Portland, Maine 04103, USA

LOCAL TIP: **A Brewery Secret...**

You get four small pours of beer at Allagash, but, if you look closely, you'll see there's another tap. Ask your bartender about the "fifth tap."

Drink in Portland, Maine

THE OTHER BEERVANA

America is flanked by two Portlands, one in Oregon (see page 58) and one in Maine; two lighthouse beer destinations, two beacons of brewing. Oregon's Portland is known as Beervana, but I think you can safely say there's a Beervana on each coast because Portland, Maine, is a must-visit beer destination.

Great beer cities have certain features in common. They're usually built on the foundation of some long-standing brewers, alongside a drive of new breweries that are typically established in regenerating neighborhoods, with most opening their doors so you can drink the beer where it's made. There'll be at least one classic or legendary pub that's been around for decades, probably creating the city's early interest in beer or at least giving people the beer they didn't realize they wanted yet, and then there'll be some standout pubs and bars that sell beer from all over the town, state, country, or world. Add good food, easy accessibility and travel, and a strong community feeling, and that's how beer-city destinations pull you in. Both beery Portlands have all these things. Here's the key stuff to know about the one in Maine.

The classic brewers include **Allagash** (see page 9), **Shipyard** (86 Newbury Street, Portland, Maine 04101), and **Geary's** (38 Evergreen Drive, Portland, Maine 04103), the latter two specializing in British-style beers.

There are more than a dozen new or newer breweries that you should definitely try and get to. **Bissell Brothers** (4 Thompson's Point Road, Portland, Maine 04102) produce some exceptional beers in the zeitgeist style of New England IPAs. Their Swish DIPA is sensational, a wowing beer that's fresh and tangy like juice, intensely aromatically hopped, slick and smooth and satisfying to drink, with a fullness of body that pushes the juicy hops forward, then, importantly, leads to a clean and dry finish (something that's often missing in this kind of brew). Bissell's current location is their second home, as they started out in the space left vacant by the Maine Beer Co. (see page 12) when they moved to nearby Freeport. These

two breweries are Portland-important for an additional reason: the brewing space they once used is across the street from Allagash and that industrial complex now has (at the time of writing) three breweries: **Foundation, Austin Street**, and **Battery Steele** (all at 1 Industrial Way, Portland, Maine 04103). All are open to the public, but have limited hours, so check ahead before visiting—you'll want to go to these breweries when you visit Allagash. It's a beer hub on the edge of town and also close to Geary's.

Downtown Portland has the rest of the best breweries and it's possible to walk or get short cab journeys or ride-shares between them all—opening hours aren't consistent, so check ahead before visiting. **Liquid Riot** (250 Commercial Street, Portland, Maine 04101) is an essential stop by the waterfront in the center of town. It's a huge corner brewery, distillery, and restaurant—the food is good and the beers are varied and very tasty. **Oxbow Blending & Bottling** (49 Washington Avenue, Portland, Maine 04101) is a cool space—a big, open drinking area in an industrial unit. They have barrels and also a space to blend the beers, but no brewkit there (that's an hour north-east from Portland). Beers include the excellently hoppy Luppolo dry-hopped lager and a range of Saison-inspired beers, including Farmhouse Pale Ale, which has fruity hops meeting fruity-spicy yeast. **Rising Tide** (103 Fox Street, Portland, Maine 04101) is an industrial space that's popular with locals. Their Ishmael is a good Altbier-ish kind of Amber that makes a nice change from all the IPAs you'll have been drinking.

For something a little different, go to **Urban Farm Fermentory** (200 Anderson Street, Portland, Maine 04101). They make beer, cider, mead, kombucha, and jun, all on a small scale and all using local and foraged ingredients. Some beers are hop-free, while others contain Maine-grown hops; they use kombucha and jun cultures in some of their beers, while the fruits and spices in the beers are all handled subtly. It's a fascinating exploration of fermentation and you shouldn't skip it.

Across the bridge in South Portland, there's **Foulmouthed Brewing** (15 Ocean Street, South Portland, Maine 04106). I didn't love their beers or the food—I think I went on a bad day, as a lot of the locals said I should go. **Fore River Brewing** (45 Huntress Avenue, South Portland, Maine 04106) was one of the places I didn't manage to get to, as was **Bunker Brewing** (Unit D, 17 Westfield Street, Portland, Maine 04102), which is out near Bissell. And, almost opposite Urban Farm Fermentory, is **Lone Pine** (219 Anderson Street, Portland, Maine 04101), which opened soon after I visited.

The classic pub in town is **The Great Lost Bear** (540 Forest Avenue, Portland, Maine 04101), which is, for me, the quintessential old American beer bar, the kind of place that's the complete opposite to bare bricks and back-bars lined with identical tap handles. This pub has old brewery neons, mirrors, and signs on the walls, old beer cans, and lots of knick-knacks and tat collected over the years; it has the right kind of darkness, over-friendly service (edged with a little I-don't-actually-care), music from a couple of decades ago that you know all the words to, TV screens that never shift from the sports channels, belly-busting bar food, lots of different spaces (meaning you can hide in the back somewhere or head to the bar and sit next to a local for a chat), and all accompanied by 70-odd draft lines, mostly from Maine. The Bear has been an institution since 1979 and you have to go.

The go-to geek bar is **Novare Res Bier Café** (4 Canal Plaza, Portland, Maine 04101), which is hidden down some backstreets and feels like a bunker. It has a lot of Maine drafts and many guest brews, including some lesser-seen European imports. The bottle list is excellent if you love Belgian and Belgian-style beers,

Bissell Brothers have earned an enviable reputation for impressive IPAs.

including some of the hard-to-find Allagash catalog. I preferred drinking in the **King's Head** (254 Commercial Street, Portland, Maine 04101) and at the **Mash Tun** (29 Wharf Street, Portland, Maine 04101) for their local beer ranges, cozier spaces, and less nerdy atmospheres, so head to those for a different and—for me—better experience.

Portland is famous for its great seafood. **J's Oyster** (5 Portland Pier, Portland, Maine 04101) is a little shack by the water, old-timey, well worn by locals and tourists, and an institution in town. There are oysters, of course, but get a lobster roll with an Allagash White for a proper Portland lunch. Across town is **Eventide** (86 Middle Street, Portland, Maine 04101), the modern evolution of the seafood shack, which has a list of oysters from both Maine and other states, served with a flavored ice. Their decadent lobster roll is like a buttery sponge topped with brown-buttered lobster and there are a dozen local beers on tap.

Portland, Maine, is definitely a destination for beer lovers and it has all of the attributes you could want from a complete beer city. I still can't make up my mind whether I prefer the beer beacon of Portland in Oregon or Portland in Maine, though I do crave Allagash and Bissell beers and wasting hours in the Bear after having amazing seafood for lunch…

Maine Beer Co.

BREWING GREAT BEER AND GIVING BACK TO THE WORLD

Around 16 miles (26km) from downtown Portland is Freeport, where you'll find Maine Beer Co. They started out in the hot-spot brewing incubator a block from Allagash—in fact, they created that space in 2009—and are now revered for their wonderfully hoppy ales and commitment to their mission statement: "Do What's Right."

With their charitable ethos, Maine Beer Co. are going out of their way to validate the saying that beer people are good people.

The beers are in the hazy, hoppy style and are elegant, clean, and balanced—and so hoppy they'll make you say "wow" out loud. Lunch is a great example of a powerful IPA and big beer that's incredibly drinkable and fresh, all with bitterness, balance, and a bright flavor through the middle, while Mo is a tropical-scented Pale Ale that's lush and lovely.

The Maine Beer Co. follows "1% for the planet" by donating 1% of gross profit to environmental non-profits. Their motto also encourages them to be as sustainable as possible: they are very low-waste and solar panels off-set their energy use, helping them as they head toward being off-grid. And they donate money to a whole range of different charities and not-for-profit organizations, with the goal of creating a sustainable relationship between their beer and our planet.

Their "Do What's Right" mission statement is built on three pillars: producing outstanding beer, giving back, and smiling every day. That smile sums up the whole place perfectly. Maine Beer Co. do everything right.

The Lowdown

WHAT: Maine Beer Co.

HOW: The tasting room is open Monday to Saturday, 11am–8pm, and Sunday, 11am–5pm (www.mainebeercompany.com).

WHERE: 525 U.S. Route 1, Freeport, Maine 04032, USA

Go to Hill Farmstead Brewery

THE FABLED BREWER OF SOME OF THE WORLD'S BEST BEERS

It's not easy to get to Hill Farmstead. Or, at least, it's not quick to get there and you can't just "pop in for a pint." You have to plan ahead, you have to know that you'll be driving down country lanes for miles, you have to know that there'll likely be a long line when you do get there. But it's all worth it because they genuinely brew some of the world's best beers (and there's a great view while you wait to get a drink).

What makes their beers so good is an elegance, depth, and clarity of flavor that few others can achieve. Their Pale Ales, IPAs, and DIPAs are hazy and have a pleasing roundness, with an abundant fresh fruitiness from the hops, but it's always in balance, always exceptional, and there's something taut and yet restrained about these beers. Their Saisons are extraordinary for their lightness and yet unrivaled depth, a dance of ethereal yeast and playful, teasing bubbles. Very rarely do you find beers that are perfect; at Hill Farmstead, it's very rare that they aren't perfect.

The farmstead in North Greensboro, Vermont, has been in Shaun Hill's family for over 220 years. It's now where he brews in a smart, modern brewery, far away from anything apart from views of the land. To see this facility on the Hill family's farmstead, this beautiful barn brewery with its wide-ranging views, to have the anticipation of the journey and to arrive into beer-geek bliss, is an essential world-beer experience. The beers might be

It's one of the more remote breweries you can visit, but it's well worth the effort to get there.

hyped up, but it's not the fan-boy, squealing kind of hype that fad brewers receive; this is the venerable respect that only a handful of the world's greatest brewers can live up to. It's a pilgrimage beer destination.

LOCAL TIP: **Be Patient**

After the long car journey to Hill Farmstead, you will most likely be in need of a beer. Unfortunately, unless you're there on a rare quieter day, you're going to have to stand in one of the long lines made up of with beer lovers desperate to get their hands on the latest limited releases. Don't panic, it's worth the wait.

The Lowdown

WHAT: Hill Farmstead Brewery

HOW: Open Wednesday to Saturday, 12–5pm (www.hillfarmstead.com).

WHERE: 403 Hill Road, Greensboro, Vermont 05842, USA

Visit Yuengling Brewery

AMERICA'S OLDEST BREWERY

Yuengling Brewery's beers might not excite most drinkers, but the brewery has a worthy and relevant place in the Beer Bucket List for its history as America's oldest brewery still in operation and for being one of its largest breweries today.

Established in 1829 by German émigré brewer David Gottlieb Jüngling—who vaguely Americanized his surname to Yuengling—as The Eagle Brewery, it's been in the same family ever since, with the fifth-generation David due to pass it on to the sixth-generation in coming years. Their Traditional Lager is the beer to try, a toasty, simple brew with some caramel-y malts and a definite grassy hop character. An eagle on the label makes reference to the original brewery's name.

The Yuengling Brewery tour is a gap in my Beer Bucket List and so, not having been, I don't know the full details, but the website promises a look around the hand-dug cellars, where the beer was once stored, and a walk around a site that has lived through so much American history (37 different US presidents have served during Yuengling's timeline). Plus, the Pottsville location of the brewery has been active since 1831, which is an impressive fact (the original Eagle Brewery burnt down in that year and was rebuilt at a different location).

The Lowdown

WHAT: Yuengling Brewery

HOW: The brewery runs tours on Mondays to Fridays, 10am–1:30pm (roughly on the hour), and on Saturdays, 10:30am–1pm (April to December only on Saturdays). For more details, visit www.yuengling.com.

WHERE: 501 Mahantongo Street, Pottsville, Pennsylvania 17901, USA

Drink at The Alchemist

BECAUSE NOT MUCH TOPS A HEADY

Go to Vermont to drink beer. Focus on the north of the state, where there's Burlington, a lakeside town with some top breweries and bars; south of there is Fiddlehead Brewery and also Hill Farmstead (see page 13); in Waterbury is Prohibition Pig, a brewpub with Hill Farmstead taps and often beers from Lawson's Finest (another must-drink brewery), including their exceptional Sip of Sunshine. The Prohibition Pig is important, as it was here that The Alchemist's beers were born and where John and Jen Kimmich brewed until the pub was drowned by Tropical Storm Irene in 2011.

John and Jen Kimmich at their brewery.

The storm came through at what was already a turning point for The Alchemist, a soggy serendipity (or perhaps an omen if you've read the book with the same name as the brewery) that led them to turn even further than originally planned. They'd been brewing in the pub since 2003 and making a Double IPA called Heady Topper since 2004—that beer got a lot of attention every time it was released. By 2011 the Kimmiches had decided to build Alchemist Cannery, a 15-barrel brewery and canning line not far from the pub, where they would just brew and can Heady Topper. They filled the first cans two days after the pub flooded, while still assessing the damage and before realizing that the pub had to close.

So their focus changed by necessity. The pub was no more and all their attention went into perfecting Heady Topper, a beer that was already close to perfection for most drinkers. It's a Double IPA of vibrant fruitiness, upliftingly tropical but not sweet; there is mango and

pineapple and some savoriness at the edges, plus a dry bitterness to balance the full, hazy body. It's only available in cans (apart from in one bar, Hen of the Woods, in Waterbury), all their hoppy stock is turned in a week to ensure freshness, and it's only sold within a short radius of the brewery.

From being a small-batch brew in a small pub basement, the beer has gone on to grow the Cannery and, in 2016, build a new brewery in Stowe, Vermont that you can visit (all the Heady is still brewed in Waterbury, by the way). At Stowe they brew Focal Banger IPA, Crusher Imperial IPA, and Beelzebub Imperial Stout, plus others, and you can visit and get three samples (one each of the three main hoppy brews) to taste and buy four-packs to take away.

Heady Topper is one of the world's best IPAs, a beer that's sought after around the world, but one you need to travel for if you want to drink it fresh. Go to Stowe, have some tasters, and buy fresh four-packs, before heading to Waterbury to drink in the **Prohibition Pig** and the **Blackback Pub**, working your way through their excellent beer lists. Then find somewhere to go and drink the cans of Alchemist beers as fresh as possible, ideally with a wonderful view of the Vermont countryside. Some Beer Bucket List ticks are as simple as drinking fresh beer near where it's made, and this is one of them.

The Lowdown

WHAT: The Alchemist

HOW: Open Tuesday to Saturday, 11am–7pm (www.alchemistbeer.com).

WHERE: 100 Cottage Club Road, Stowe, Vermont 05672, USA

Drink at Brooklyn Brewery

THE BOROUGH'S FLAGSHIP
BEER DESTINATION

Brooklyn Brewery is important for brightening its borough and returning brewing to the neighborhood, as well as for being a must-visit beer destination—and a must-visit for everyone, from locals to beer geeks to city tourists.

Blaring beats on the stereo, bold and bright designs all around, and the kind of atmosphere that's formed by shared bench seating and great brews are what to expect at Brooklyn Brewery. There are around 14 taps, plus special bottle pours, with some brews only to be found in the taproom. When you enter, you'll swap dollars for tokens, with most beers costing one token (US$5) and some being as much as four tokens.

Have a Brooklyn Lager. It's a beer you'll no doubt already know, but this is the place to re-acquaint yourself with it and to understand how it was able to build the brewery. Sorachi Ace is a favorite of mine, a beer that's spicy, zesty, lemony, and peppery, with a creaminess running through it all and ending with a long dryness. And always look for some of the super-rare bottles to share.

On Fridays they run free brewery tours and there'll be a line of people outside before the doors open. The tour is worth going on. It lasts for 30 minutes and is loud and fast, though don't necessarily expect to learn how to become a brewmaster—instead you'll hear fun stories about the brewery and its history. There's a pizza truck outside for when you get hungry.

Brooklyn Brewery has been at the heart of the New York craft beer scene since its inception in 1988.

The Lowdown

WHAT: Brooklyn Brewery

HOW: Free brewery tours on Fridays (at 7pm and 8pm) and the brewery opens on Saturdays and Sundays (from midday, with free tours half-hourly). From Monday to Thursday, there are paid-for tours at 5pm (www.brooklynbrewery.com).

WHERE: 79 North 11th Street, Williamsburg, Brooklyn, NY 11249, USA

Brooklyn Beer Crawl

Go to **Other Half** (195 Centre Street, Brooklyn, NY 11231) for their exceptional hoppy beers—this is the most essential Brooklyn beer-stop, even if the location means basically standing up in a cramped-in space, wedged at the open end of their brewhouse. (FYI: the brewery is opposite a McDonald's if you want to know what world-class IPAs taste like with chicken nuggets.) **Threes Brewing** (333 Douglass Street, Brooklyn, NY 11217) is a fun space, with great beers and barbecue food. Closer to Brooklyn Brewery is **Greenpoint** (7 North 15th Street, Brooklyn, NY 11222), which is another fun brewpub with good beers. **Tørst** (615 Manhattan Avenue, Brooklyn, NY 11222) is the go-to, beer-nerd bar.

McSorley's Old Ale House

A MUST-VISIT MANHATTAN INSTITUTION

There's an article from *The New Yorker*, available online, which describes in beautiful detail what it's like to drink in McSorley's, a Manhattan pub that opened in 1854. It was published in 1940 and brought a new focus to this old tavern. In the story you can feel the deep character of the place; you can sense how it's remained unchanged for decades; you almost blow the dust from your screen as you read it and hear the roaring chorus of drunk Irish men from a century ago. Read the piece before you go, as you'll realize that nothing about this place has changed and there's nowhere quite like it.

If you go during busy times, then you'll have to wait outside. Step inside and it's literally spit and sawdust. The staff—dressed in old-style uniforms—are so busy and disinterested that you'd better be ready to order from the moment you walk in, but also ready to wait your turn. There are two beers: pale and dark. Order a beer and you'll get two glasses—order three pales and you'll get six glasses. Got it? Each are poured with a thick, Czech-style foam into small, chunky, robust glasses that can withstand the staff grabbing them half-a-dozen to a hand and drinkers crashing them together when saying cheers. The beers are decent, without needing colorful tasting notes, and evoke old-timey tastes; think Amber-ish lager with some richer malts and a rougher finish, with the dark a midpoint between a Schwarzbier and a Porter. But you aren't really there for the liquid; it's the liquid history that matters.

It's Manhattan's oldest continually operated saloon and began as an Irish working-man's bar. Supposedly Abe Lincoln and John Lennon drank there. It's inspired poems, paintings, and plays. It survived Prohibition, though you can't imagine them ever not selling alcohol. Their philosophy of "Good Ale, Raw Onions, and No Ladies" lasted until 1970 when females were finally allowed inside—but only after an order from the court (a women's restroom was only added in 1986 and it wasn't until 1994 that the first female worked behind the bar). The male restrooms, by the way, are marvelous, and no matter how many beers you've had, you can't possibly fail to hit the huge urinal. It's a Top 10 Pub Restroom Tick, if anyone is interested in completing that list...

The bar is packed and raucous, almost as if people behave differently there, as if they have a pass to act like riotously drunk Irish men. You'll be packed inside, sharing tables stacked with beers. It's certainly touristy, but almost in the way that Katz's Deli, another local institution, is. People come here for something unique and they get it. There's a resistance to change, but that makes it feel as though you're stood drinking in a lively bar over 150 years ago, which creates an inimitable beer experience. It's a pub of cultural, social, and historic importance, a time-machine drinking experience that'll make you wish time travel was actually possible. As well as all of that, it's just a damn fun place to have a few glasses of beer.

The Lowdown

WHAT: McSorley's Old Ale House

HOW: If you want a calmer experience to take it all in properly, go on a midweek afternoon. If you want the full madness, then go on the weekend (www.mcsorleysoldalehouse.nyc).

WHERE: 15 East 7th Street, New York, NY 10003, USA

The walls of McSorley's are heavy with the weight of tall tales and lively discussions from the thousands of drinkers who have passed through its doors.

Go to the Home of Extreme Beer

DOGFISH HEAD: ONE OF MY TOP BEER BUCKET LIST TICKS

I had the idea for *The Beer Bucket List* when I was thinking about some of the world breweries I wanted to drink at, but had never visited before. There were many in the US and Dogfish Head was at the top of the list.

A decade ago, as I was just getting interested in beer and looking beyond the local selection, Dogfish Head was the ultimate symbol of difference. It was an "extreme" side of things that most appealed to me, the way in which they were brewing beers unlike anyone else— beers toward the extremities of brewing in terms of strengths and ingredients—but also how they made their Ancient Ales or how they barrel-aged beers or used unusual ingredients. The idea of "Off-Centered Ales" made them the antitheses of boring British beer and I was desperate to drink them. Finally, I've now been there.

The brewery is not the most convenient place to get to, being around a three-hour drive from the nearest major airport, but it's worth the effort. A steampunk treehouse stands in front of the vast brewery and leads you into the bright, glass-fronted tasting room. Inside, anyone who visits can get four 3-oz (85-ml) tastes of any beers on tap and there'll be around 20 taps to choose from. You can also buy pints and additional tasters, or get growlers filled. Next door is a store selling bottles, growlers, and merchandise, and there's also a food truck. The tasting room is where you begin. You go, have a beer or two, go on the tour, and then move to their pub, **Dogfish**

Head Brewings & Eats (320 Rehoboth Avenue, Rehoboth Beach, Delaware 19971).

This is where Dogfish Head started in 1995, brewing on a tiny kit (then the smallest commercial brewery in the country) and only after changing local legislation—it was The First State's first brewpub. It's now a classic, all-American, all-star quarterback of a bar, the kind of place you've seen in a hundred movies, but never quite experienced in real life, somewhere with soul, characters, stories. There are 25-plus taps of Dogfish beers, including rare vintages and brewpub exclusives. The food is also really good and you'll want to eat it.

I started with a 60 Minute IPA—I might initially have been drawn to the extreme beers, but I wanted their hero brew first. It's a 6.0% ABV American IPA and has that proper old-school, citrus peel and pith quality. It's a classic beer that deserves attention and, by the end of the night, it's what I wanted to drink more of, going through the extremities and back to the grounding of this fine IPA. There's also 90 Minute, their 9.0% ABV Double IPA and one that shares a family resemblance with the 60 Minute. It's deep gold, with a toasty malt sweetness that smothers the ABV; there are hops all through it, but not the bursting, vibrant kind of modern hops—it's more oily and rich with flavor and bitterness. These were beers I had loved reading about years ago; I loved the story of Sam Calagione, the brewery's founder, developing a machine that was capable of adding hops continuously to these IPAs for 60 or 90 minutes. It's very easy to fall into the trap of getting complacent about important older breweries, focusing

THE BEST BEER HOTELS

- Hotel Oberpfalzer Hof, Windischeschenbach, Germany (see page 114)
- Hotel Purkmistr, Pilsen, Czech Republic (see page 130)
- Dogfish Inn, Lewes, Delaware
- Brewhouse Inn and Suites, Milwaukee, Wisconsin (see page 36)

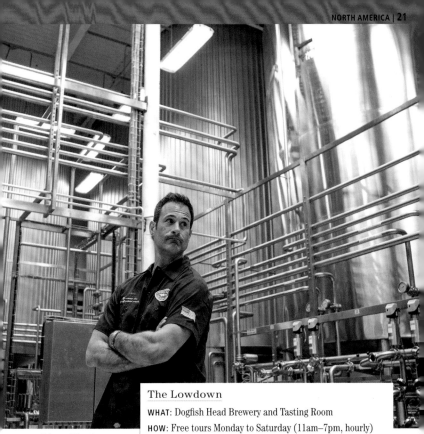

Dogfish Head founder Sam Calagione.

The Lowdown

WHAT: Dogfish Head Brewery and Tasting Room

HOW: Free tours Monday to Saturday (11am–7pm, hourly) and on Sundays (12–7pm, hourly). Go on a Saturday for a special tour that gives extra details and gets you into the steampunk treehouse (www.dogfish.com).

WHERE: 511 Chestnut Street, Milton, Delaware 19968, USA

more on the newcomers, but Dogfish Head has to be considered as one of America's most important breweries.

After the IPAs, I wanted some of the extreme beers. Palo Santo Marron, their 12.0% ABV Brown Ale, is aged in 10,000-gallon (45,000-liter) vessels made from Paraguayan Palo Santo wood. It's like a truffle, deep with dark fruits and chocolate, caramel, and vanilla. The wooden barrels—there are two—are the largest ones made in the US since Prohibition. World Wide Stout was also on when I visited. It's a monster Imperial Stout, high-teens in ABV, thick, rich, and voluptuous, and yet with the smooth drinkability of a bold red wine.

Dogfish Head was right at the top of my must-visit Beer Bucket List destinations. It was one of the original breweries that showed me how interesting and different craft beer could be and it's now rightly regarded as a classic American craft brewery. It's an essential stop, where you should plan on visiting the tasting room before going to Brewings & Eats and staying and drinking there all night long. (And if you're in need of a lie down after all that great beer, you can get a room at the Dogfish Inn, just a short cab ride away in the nearby town of Lewes.)

Asheville, North Carolina

AMERICA'S BEST BEER CITY?

It wasn't that I'd fallen out of love with beer; I was just feeling a bit unmoved by it, weary of it. I'd been to a lot of breweries in the preceding weeks and was jaded from traveling and drinking too much, and I wasn't quite ready to go on a crawl of seven more breweries in an afternoon. But then I wasn't quite ready for Asheville.

No one has ever said anything bad about Asheville as a beer town, so I knew it was supposed to be good. What surprised and delighted me was the very high quality of the beers, the variety of breweries, and the general sense that "Beer is great!" But, most of all, I loved the spaces and environments: the breweries are huge, open, bright spaces, mostly in the center of town, and mostly with outdoor space (the North Carolina sunshine helps). They usually have the brewery stainless on show, are all within a few blocks of each other, and are brewing on significant kits—not pots and pans in the back of a small bar. They take beer seriously in Asheville.

The star brewery is **Wicked Weed Brewing**. They have two locations in town and two production facilities out of town (although you can't visit those). There's the original Pub (91 Biltmore Avenue, Asheville, North Carolina 28801), which has a large restaurant space upstairs and a more casual space downstairs where you can drink in view of the tanks—all the "clean" (as opposed to "wild" or sour) beers on tap in the pub are brewed in the pub. A few blocks away is **Funkatorium** (147 Coxe Avenue, Asheville, North Carolina 28801), where they mature barrels of wild and sour beers and have them all on tap. Both stops are essential. Pernicious IPA was the best IPA I drank in four months of dedicated book research (and I drank a lot of IPA in that time). Amazing for its brightness, dryness, big aroma of citrus and tropical fruits, pineapples, and peaches; for its depth of hop flavor; and for its sharply clean bitterness that made me never want to drink any other IPA ever again. They also make some of the best sours I've drunk and some of the best barrel-aged stouts, including BA Milk and Cookies, which is grown-up chocolate milk that'll make you giggle like a little kid. I liked it there a lot.

Here are some other breweries, bars, and restaurants in town—take a deep breath…

Burial Brewing (40 Collier Avenue, Asheville, North Carolina 28801) is the place to go to drink more great IPAs. There's an industrial, dark, dive-y vibe inside; they have a large, German-style outside space and the most curious brewery mural you'll ever see of Sloth from the Goonies hugging Tom Selleck.

Go to **Asheville Brewing** (77 Coxe Avenue, Asheville, North Carolina 28801) for huge and excellent pizzas and a brewpub that feels as if it's the real heart of the town.

Catawba Brewing (32 Banks Avenue, Asheville, North Carolina 28801) is a huge space, with room inside and out, food trucks, an open sight of all the tanks, and a large beer list—try their Farmer Ted for what realistically seemed like a faithful reinvention of an American Cream Ale. Plus, go to Buxton Hall BBQ next door for whole hog meats and local brews.

Twin Leaf (144 Coxe Avenue, Asheville, North Carolina 28801), opposite Funkatorium, has some good lagers and Belgian styles of beer, plus typical American brews (though I didn't rate the US styles as highly as the European brews).

Green Man (27 Buxton Avenue, Asheville, North Carolina 28801) was busy with older drinkers when I went. It felt like the kind of place these people had been hanging out in for years (it's been open since 1997, so they probably have been). It had proper locals and a proper drinking bar; it was a place for a pint and not somewhere to sip samples. I loved their ESB for its rich maltiness, brown bread, cherries, and dry finish.

Hi-Wire (197 Hilliard Avenue, Asheville, North Carolina 28801) has a good vibe, with the brewery sitting behind the bar and the beers tasting decent (a vague description, but I think I'd been to a few breweries by this point and my notes descended into useless doodles, which I assume means the beers were good or I'd have written bad stuff about them…)

Bhramari Brewing (101 South Lexington, Asheville, North Carolina 28801) makes food-inspired beers, or beers with edible ingredients, and, while many of them sounded interesting, I didn't love any of the beers I drank there (they were mostly just odd or possibly a combination of what was ill-conceived or just badly delivered), though other reviews have been more positive.

On the edges of town you've got the recent transplants of **Sierra Nevada, Oskar Blues**, and **New Belgium** (please search for their addresses online—I'm bored adding them

The taplist at Wicked Weed's Funkatorium.

and you all know how to Google)—all have built impeccable, inimitable sites with huge tasting rooms and are wonderful environments in which to sit and drink beer. Opposite New Belgium is **Wedge Brewing Co.** (37 Paynes Way, Asheville, North Carolina 28801) in a shared creative space. **Highland Brewing** (12 Old Charlotte Highway, Asheville, North Carolina 28803) was the first in town and their British-style brews are nice. If you want to go to the original pub in town, then it's **Barley's** (42 Biltmore Avenue, Asheville, North Carolina 28801, which is just up the street from Wicked Weed's pub. There's 20-plus mostly local taps in this old-school pub, which also serves pizzas. If you want bottles to take home, then go to **Bruisin' Ales** (66 Broadway, Asheville, North Carolina 28801)—it's a world-class beer store. And I've probably missed a bunch of places from this list; there's that much good beer in Asheville.

I spent three days in Asheville and still didn't get to all the places I wanted to visit. I'd happily go back any time. It was the kind of place that got me excited about beers and breweries again, primarily for the way you can visit so many superb locations, all within the space of a few blocks, and also for just how big and professional those breweries are. Asheville stayed with me long after I left and it's the place I've recalled most fondly to people asking me about my recent beer travels. I loved it in Asheville.

Which is the Best American Beer City?

You always see the same dozen or so names on the "Beer City USA" lists. The Portlands, San Diego and San Francisco, New York, Denver, Chicago, and Seattle, plus small cities such as Burlington, Asheville, Boulder, Bend, Grand Rapids, and Minneapolis. But which one deserves the title of "Best Beer City?"

I've been to all of them, except for Seattle and Minneapolis (those places are next on my list!), and all are brilliant in their own way. Personally, I always prefer the smaller cities, the places where it's easy to walk around, and where there's a close-knit culture. For its mix of high-quality breweries, excellent drinking spaces, and general beer vibe, I think Asheville is the must-visit beer destination in the US. The closest big-city contender is San Diego, but it doesn't win on account of being so big and because everything is so far away—you need to hire a lot of cabs to get around and visit everywhere.

Local street art welcomes you to one of the world's greatest beer cities.

Go to Cigar City Brewing

AND ATTEND HUNAHPU'S DAY

Forget the theme parks, Cigar City is Florida's finest attraction. The tasting room pours over 20 taps of their own beers, including classics such as Jai Alai IPA, plus limited-release specials, many of which either use something uniquely from Florida or inspired by the city's stories. Just getting to the brewpub is on the Beer Bucket List, but every year they hold an event that pulls in beer geeks from all around the world.

Hunahpu's Day is an annual event held on the second Saturday of March to release Cigar City's imperious Hunahpu's Imperial Stout. The beer is a Mayan monster, a 10.2% ABV brew that's thick with dark chocolate, vanilla, mocha sweetness, and fragrant cinnamon, which contains a background fruitiness and bite from the two different chilis used in the brewhouse. It's a ticketed event that has become one of America's must-visit beer festivals, with over 100 other breweries attending and pouring their own beers. The list becomes ever more impressive each year.

Both Cigar City and Hunahpu's Day are both still on my Beer Bucket List. Florida, in general, deserves some good beer attention, as it's emerging as one of America's most interesting states for new brews. And Cigar City is the place to begin—it's also only a 20-minute drive to the theme parks if you want to do both in one day...

The Lowdown

WHAT: Cigar City Brewing

HOW: The tasting room opens Sunday to Thursday (11am–11pm) and Friday to Saturday (11am–1am). Brewery tours are also available on Wednesday to Sunday, from 11am (www.cigarcitybrewing.com).

WHERE: 3924 West Spruce Street, Tampa, Florida 33607, USA

TEN GREAT TAPROOMS AND BREWERY BARS IN AMERICA

- Russian River Brew Co, Santa Rosa, California (see page 52)
- Stone World, Escondido, California (see page 49)
- Pizza Port Ocean Beach, San Diego, California (see page 48)
- Jester King, Austin, Texas (see page 26)
- Wicked Weed, Asheville, North Carolina (see page 22)
- Dogfish Head, Rehoboth Beach, Delaware (see page 20)
- Sierra Nevada, Chico, California (see page 54)
- Bell's Eccentric Café, Kalamazoo, Michigan (see page 42)
- Avery Brewing, Boulder, Colorado (see page 44)
- Cigar City, Tampa, Florida

Jester King—the Ultimate Farmhouse Brewers

A GENUINE APPROACH TO SEASONAL BREWING

The old ideals of brewing seasonally and using local ingredients have long been replaced by year-round brewing and consistent beers, even at the famous and classic Belgian farmhouse breweries, thus removing that essential seasonal element. At Jester King, just outside Austin, Texas, they've brought those fundamentals back and are making them mean something genuine again; this is one of the only breweries where the terms "seasonal" and "farmhouse" mean anything substantial and real.

To Jester King, the words "farmhouse" and "seasonal" mean beers that grow uniquely in a particular time and place. Land, air, and the changing seasons dictate the beers they make and they have no interest in seasonal trends; when an ingredient is ready, they'll brew with it and then when the beer's ready, they'll release it. Everything has its own timeframe, which is managed by nature's calendar and not a release schedule.

It's a holistic approach and much more detailed than my simplified distillation of their philosophy. Central to it all is their yeast. This was captured and cultivated from the land on which the brewery sits (a 58-acre/23-hectare ranch) by picking herbs and fruits, and by allowing the different microorganisms to flourish or fade away. That mixed culture of yeast and bacteria has been evolving since they first started using it, always moving in different directions, and also changing with the seasons:

in summer, when it's warmer, the yeast is worked harder and produces more fruity esters and spice; in winter, the yeast is more chilled out and that allows the bacteria to produce more acid. It's a natural, seasonal variation, which the brewery embraces.

Jester King's use of hops is particularly fascinating: every beer they produce includes a proportion of aged hops, which the brewers store in a barn located on their ranch for a few years to allow them to dry fully (theoretically these hops should give no bitterness, yet beers brewed with only the old hops come back with a recorded IBU). The hops are a flavor element in Jester King beers—although rarely a prominent one—and instead fulfil the additional role of being a "lever" in the beer; the antibacterial properties of hops can change a beer's profile by manipulating its microbial properties. Simply: more hops means less acidity. The hops are also a gatekeeper for good and bad bacteria, allowing the good through and removing the bad, where they later combine with the acidity and pH level to repeat the process of removing negative bacteria.

They use as much Texas grain as possible. They have their own well water, which has a high mineral content. It isn't necessarily flawless brewing water, but it's the

The Lowdown

WHAT: Jester King Brewery

HOW: Ideally, you need a car to visit, but that means having a designated driver. You can use ride-share apps in Austin (but not Uber at the time of writing) and it'll cost between US$30–50 each way. The brewery bar is open on Fridays (4–10pm), Saturdays (12–10pm), and Sundays (12–9pm). There are often brewery tours, so just ask at the bar (www.jesterkingbrewery.com).

WHERE: 13187 Fitzhugh Road, Austin, Texas 78736, USA

Jester King manage to produce seasonal beers that do justice to the brewery's stunning rural backdrop.

water they have and so that's what they use. They have an orchard (peaches, plums, and blackberries to begin with, more to follow) and farm their land. The fruit is important, as they change what they brew depending on what's just been harvested. And while all the beers vary, they also all come from the well-attenuated, hop-bitter, and yeast-forward school of Saisons and pale Belgian ales, which gives them a consistent base.

There's also a coolship in the brewery that they can use from December to February when the Austin air is cool enough to brew spontaneously fermented beers. They began this project in 2012 and started releasing these beers—called SPON—three years later, using the traditional production method of Gueuze and producing something similar and reminiscent of the classics, but with a unique flavor profile that gives more lemons, tannins, fruit pith, and leather.

The majority of the Jester King beers are sold on site and that's how they want it to be: drink beers with a flavor that is a unique reflection of the place and time, in the location in which they were brewed. The space is also spectacular, being set in so much quiet, rural, rolling ranch land. There's a pizza restaurant next door, too. You'll see as many kids and

dogs running around as you'll see beer geeks repeatedly running back to the bar—and this bar has numerous drafts, the latest releases, guest beers, wine, and cider, plus a large bottle selection, some of which, like SPON, is only available in the brewery and has to be drunk there.

Jester King have reinvented the idea of farmhouse beers and seasonality, and made it mean something once more. To drink their exceptional beers at the brewery and to be surrounded by the nature that shaped those beers is a special thing.

BBQ and Beer in Austin

BECAUSE I ALSO HAVE A FOOD BUCKET LIST

Soon after 10am there are 100 people in front of me in the line at Franklin Barbecue. We're waiting for the best smoked meat in Austin, Texas. They open at 11am but, whether you arrive at 8am or midday, you're going to have to wait about three hours. That's just how it works here.

People have deckchairs. There's country music on the stereo. Six-packs are being passed around—beer for breakfast before the brisket. The young couple in front of me has a case of Modelo ("It tastes like a warm taco!" she says). They're here on vacation—they came straight from the airport and they're talking about what else is on their Barbecue Bucket List (I immediately *get* these people). The older couple behind me are arguing over how much meat to order ("We need at least 2lb of brisket and 1lb of sausage," he says). Staff come around regularly, letting you know how long the line is ("You'll be eating around 1:30pm"), how much meat is left ("There's plenty of brisket and turkey, no pulled pork, maybe some ribs, but no promises"), asking if we want to buy beers while we wait (of course we do).

The line is fun. People make friends. Every so often there's a waft of intense smoke in the air. A sweetly woody smoke. It's almost unbearable when you're hungry and there's still two hours until you will eat. As you get closer to the door, the smell is less of wood and more of meat. Incredible meat.

The three-hour wait is part of the experience of going to Franklin Barbecue. The excitement and anticipation grow while you're there. Everyone else is in a good mood; they're hungry and ready for great meat. And the meat *is* great. It's incredible what can be done with just an amazing piece of meat, plus salt, pepper, smoke, and a lot of time. They also sell a dozen Austin craft beers to go with the food, which allows me to put Franklin Barbecue in this book. It's the ultimate beer-and-barbecue experience, especially if you have a few breakfast beers in the line and a local IPA with your food—I love how the bitter citrus works with the big, senses-smouldering smoke.

My food bucket list and beer bucket list tend to overlap and combine in most places I visit. I'm a flavor tourist, always wanting whatever's local—and in Texas, that's barbecue.

As you can see it's worth the wait, particularly when accompanied with a can of local IPA.

The Lowdown

WHAT: Franklin Barbecue

HOW: Open Tuesday to Sunday, 11am until they sell out, usually by 3pm (www.franklinbarbecue.com).

WHERE: 900 East 11th Street, Austin, Texas 78702, USA

A strong Germany-inspired line up at Live Oak.

The Best of Austin, Texas

If you've gone all the way to Austin to drink beer (and eat barbecue, obviously), there are a few more must-visit stops in town. **Live Oak Brewing** (1615 Crozier Lane, Del Valle, Texas 78617) is set on 23 acres (9 hectares) of land, with outside seating for around 1,000 people and space to wander around. They brew straight-up, excellent versions of classic German beer styles—they are some of the best lagers and wheat beers I've had outside of Germany. I love their Pilz for its dry bitterness and lift of Saaz hops, plus the roundness of malt; the sort of subtle caramelized sweetness that the more astute beer nerds will taste comes from the decoction mash Live Oak use. Their Big Bark Vienna lager is bready and biscuity with stone-fruit freshness. And their flagship Hefeweizen is smooth, creamy, dry, and refreshing—both are good antidotes to those who've drunk too many IPAs. It's right by the airport, so make it your first or last stop.

The ABGB—or **Austin Beer Garden Brewery**, although everyone just calls it by the acronym (1305 West Oltorf Street, Austin, Texas 78704)—is a cool, outside-inside space with a range of great lagers, as well as some ales. It's a favorite spot with locals. All I need to say about **Banger's** (79 Rainey Street, Austin, Texas 78701) is that is has 100 beers on tap, 30 different kinds of homemade sausages, and a huge beer garden. Nearby, and also on Rainey Street (at number 61), is **Craft Pride**, which has a Texas-only beer board and probably the best tap list in town.

Chicago's Beer and Food

THE WORLD'S BEST CITY FOR BEER AND FOOD

Belgium has an embedded culture of *cuisine à la bière*, and beer and food are ever-present together, making it a great destination for eating and drinking with a beer focus. But I think Chicago is just as—if not more— exciting to visit because there's a newness to the city's beer and food possibilities. It's at the progressive, evolving end of what great beer and food can achieve together (and it's where you'll find the world's first Michelin-starred brewery—see page 32).

Cruz Blanca (904 West Randolph Street, Chicago, Illinois 60607) is a brewery taquería, a casual, Oaxaca-style, smoky-alley kind of place with a shiny silver brewkit beside the wood-fired grill. The beers use stories of the European move to Mexico and this is a narrative line that draws them into present-day Chicago. There are a lot of European beer styles, thanks to that background, including Pastry War, a nutty, toasty Vienna Lager, plus there are IPAs, a few Belgian-inspired brews, strong Barley Wines, Brown Ales, and a lot more. They're brewed with local ingredients where possible and food is sourced in the same way—

The beers at Cruz Blanca work exceptionally well with the tacos served at the taproom.

a poster in the restaurant tells you where all the ingredients come from. The food is very good (as you'd expect at a venue from top chef Rick Bayless), with dinner-plate-sized, handmade corn tacos arriving with a range of fillings. On Saturdays they run brewery tours— book online in advance to get on one.

Forbidden Root (1746 W Chicago Avenue, Chicago, Illinois 60622) focuses on botanic brews, using wood, leaves, flowers, roots, fruits, piths, peels, and herbs and spices, plus some intriguing beers based on old-school spirits and sodas. All the beers I had were good, integrating the botanicals in novel, balanced, deft ways to give pours you rarely find elsewhere. The food uses a lot of fresh green ingredients and is very good—not so much cooked to match specific beers but providing a broad menu for the wide beer variety. That's the new focus of beer and food, and it's not prescriptive pairings—it's high quality all round to appeal to every taste. Start with a flight, so you can try a few of the botanical brews.

Corridor Brewery & Provisions (3446 N Southport Avenue, Chicago, Illinois 60657), in West Lakeview, combines a wide-ranging beer list, such as IPAs and funky Saisons, with a menu of Midwest food, including pizzas, salads, and sandwiches, all moving toward a much better quality of eating. The venue is smartly casual; the silver tanks are lined up down one side; and there's banquette seating, bare bricks, and lots of wood. It's not a brewery with a restaurant and neither is it a restaurant with a brewery; Corridor is a midpoint on a Venn diagram of brewing and cooking, which is greater than the sum of its parts.

Beer and food offerings at Corridor Brewery & Provisions.

These are just three good examples of the beer and food in Chicago, and it goes much farther and way deeper than anywhere else I've visited. The exciting thing is how well considered the beer and food are together. It goes way beyond fried, yellow bar food to produce dishes that reflect a similar level of care and attention as that which goes into the brewing process. This in turn elevates the beers in positive ways. The result is a city where the beers and food are broadly better than anywhere else.

Band of Bohemia

THE WORLD'S FIRST MICHELIN-STARRED BREWERY

Band of Bohemia is the world's first Michelin-starred brewery. Situated in an old warehouse, it's designed like a Fibonacci spiral with a mix of materials and natural elements: wood, brick, glass, stainless steel, fire, and water. There are leather bar stools and velvety private booths. It's plush and comfortable; open collar. There's informally formal service with a friendly smile. The 10-barrel brewery is behind the bar, with serving tanks sending the beer straight to the taps. The brew space leads through—physically and creatively—to the open kitchen.

There are five beers on tap, each with a foodie inspiration or basis and a mix of edible ingredients. Kitchen and brewery work together, with the food reverse-engineered to match the beers; the brewer makes something new, details the beer to the chef, who then has a few weeks to come up with the right dishes. Neither the kitchen nor brewery are restricted to particular cuisines or styles, and instead come up with flavor combinations that work, with menus that change constantly.

There's a finesse and precision to the beers, with a subtle use of spices, fruits, teas, flowers, and herbs. Taste them properly and you know these guys really understand food and beer together, as all the beers hit a food-friendly sweet-spot, a range between 6.0–8.0% ABV, giving enough depth without being too much, all with a rich texture and a round, wine-like softness. Plus, they all have a clean dryness with low bitterness; they are considered beers, beers brewed to be drunk both with food and also just by the pint (and the bar seating is ideal for simply having a few beers). Have the beers with food and follow the suggested pairings, that's where you'll find the experience is elevated. It's not just that they work very well, or that they make you think more deeply

Not your standard taproom food.

GREAT AMERICAN BEER AND FOOD PAIRINGS

- Loaded nachos go with a good lager, like a taut Pilsner or doughy Helles—you want something that's light but which can lift the heavy cheese and salsa.

- Garlic cheese fries is a California bar snack and it calls for a West Coast IPA. Garlic and hops are best buddies, the salt loves the booze and bitterness, and the cheese enhances the malt.

- Wings in tangy hot buffalo sauce need a good chocolate-y Porter to smother them in fire-fighting malt sweetness.

- Cheeseburger always goes with IPA. Don't bother ordering anything else. Hops love cheese, juicy meat, and all the sweet condiments.

- Mac 'n' cheese goes with a malty Pale Ale, the old-school kind, the one with a round, caramel-y body of sweetness and a powerful bitterness.

- Chicken tenders with Double IPA. I genuinely don't know if this is the best pairing, all I know is that I've only ever had chicken tenders with DIPA and it's always a wonderful combination.

- Wood-fired pizzas want a dark lager (or a gentle Stout), something toasty with malt and dry to finish, where that malt darkness matches the singe on the edge of the crust.

- A bowl of chili wants a Milk Stout, something to cool down the heat and add a smooth, sweet, cocoa quality that enriches the chili.

about beer and food. It's actually simpler than that: you can drink great beer with great food that's designed to go with it.

The front men of Band of Bohemia are Michael Carroll and Craig Sindelar. Michael started as a chef and baker, including three years at Chicago's three Michelin-starred Alinea restaurant, before going across town to brew at Half Acre—he's the Band's head brewer. Craig is the wine guy and a whole lot more. He was Alinea's head sommelier for almost a decade before he and Michael banded together with the goal of elevating brewery food beyond typical brewpub fare. It's this fusion of a fine-dining pedigree with a chef-trained, brewery-raised consideration for beer that makes the culinary brewhouse work. Band of Bohemia is the first brewery to get a Michelin star and, as of spring 2018, they are still the only ones.

The Lowdown

WHAT: Band of Bohemia

HOW: Open Tuesday to Sunday (times vary, so check the website first), but closed Mondays (www.bandofbohemia.com).

WHERE: 4710 N Ravenswood Avenue, Chicago, Illinois 60640, USA

Band of Bohemia represents a new chapter in the relationship between beer production and food appreciation.

Goose Island's Barrel Program

A WONDER OF THE BEER WORLD

It's the smell that hits you first, a knockout, heavyweight hook to the olfactory bulb, a wallop of wine, a slug of bourbon, the sweet, sweet wood, the unmistakable fizzy, fuzzy fruitiness of fermentation, that deep, eternal, preternaturally attractive aroma of sugars magically turning into alcohol. As you walk through this warren of wood, this temple of barrels, you'll never quite figure out or comprehend how big it is, how many barrels there are, how much beer is stored in them, how much life these barrels have lived, how many people have tasted something which previously lived within them, whether this is a wine, a whiskey, or another beer, or even how long ago those seeds sprouted and started growing into trees, which are now living a new life as casks filled with beer.

In 1992, Goose Island filled six Jim Beam bourbon barrels with Imperial Stout as a special for the brewpub's 1,000th batch—they were probably the first brewery ever to use ex-whiskey barrels to age beer, a significant credit in the history of craft beer. They've since gone on to turn their barrel house into the largest of its kind—around 140,000 square feet (13,000 square meters) with tens of thousands of barrels—and have also added wine and other alcohol barrels to their stable. There are beers containing coffee, fruited brews, soured ales, beers aged in rare and very old bourbon barrels.

Bourbon County Brand Stout is the most famous one produced at Goose Island—an intense behemoth of thick, rich dark beer with the deep, deep depth of bourbon, vanilla, wood, and cherries.

The stout is aged for 8–12 months in oak barrels, where the variences in Chicago's climate—cold winters and hot summers—help draw out the flavors of the wood.

The Barrel House, or The Staviary, is insane. It's also not particularly easy to visit. To gain access you will need to look up events months in advance, befriend brewery employees, walk past in the hope of catching a whiff of the heavenly insides, or do whatever you can to get in. And, when you're there, take a few minutes to just breathe in, to deep-inhale the headiest air your lungs ever have joyously taken in. I think breweries smell good, but a warehouse with tens of thousands of barrels filled with strong ale is one of the most intoxicating aromas in the world of beer.

The Lowdown

WHAT: Goose Island Beer Company

HOW: The Tap Room is open Thursday to Sunday (opening times vary each day, so check the website in advance). You can also book a tour of the production brewery (www.gooseisland.com).

WHERE: 1800 West Fulton Street, Chicago, Illinois 60612, USA

Once the barrels are blended, the result is a truly world-class stout.

Lagunitas Brewing Company, Chicago

If you want to see what craft beer can do, how big it can be, just how impressively massive, then go to Lagunitas (2607 West 17th Street, Chicago, Illinois 60608). It's the largest and most open craft brewery I've been to, one which pulls you in through a glowing backlight corridor of a psychedelic trip to a bar of US$5 pints, which keeps you there with an elevated walkway around the whole, wowingly huge, spaceship-like brewery, and one which kicks you out with glassy eyes and a goofy smile.

Lagunitas was bought by Heineken in 2017 and it'll probably soon be the largest craft brewery in the world. That means the Chicago brewery is only going to get bigger and more extraordinary. Go there, get a pint of IPA, and walk around looking over at the stainless-steel city beneath and all around you.

Milwaukee's Old Lager Breweries

A REMINDER OF THIS ONCE-GREAT BREWING CITY

If I had a time machine and could go any where in history to drink a few beers, then Milwaukee in the late 1800s would be high on my list. When émigré brewers came to the US Midwest from Germany, they made their German-style lagers and served them in German-style surroundings—this created the beginning of a new beer culture in America.

These brewers often started out small, but some grew into enormous companies. Milwaukee had some of the largest breweries in the country, all making ranges of Euro-styled lagers, with famous names like Miller, Pabst, Blatz, and Schlitz, making Milwaukee a great brewing city, a city that had beer flowing through it, and brewery buildings on every corner. The greatness didn't last forever and almost all the breweries closed or moved away, but that's now changing as old brewing spaces are reopening and the city is re-engaging with its beer past.

The best of this is happening with the long-shuttered Pabst brewery buildings. Pabst was once the world's largest brewery—and in living memory, hitting their peak in 1977. Their story began with Jacob Best, who started The Empire Brewery in 1844, which later became Best and Company. When Best died, his fourth son Phillip took over (two of his other sons opened Plank Road Brewery, which later became Miller Brewing). Phillip had two daughters and one of them was married to a steamboat captain called Frederick Pabst. Best liked Pabst and convinced him to jump ship and turn into a beer baron. Pabst became perhaps the greatest of the great beer barons of that time and, on his death in 1904, he was one of the richest men in the world.

After Pabst's peak in 1977 they somehow went from being the largest brewery to closing their Milwaukee brewing operations within 20 years (though the beers continued to be brewed in other USA facilities). When those Milwaukee buildings were shut, they stayed shut for a decade or more, and it was only from 2007 onward that they were revived. Now 16 of the 28 original brewery buildings remain and many are open, with the whole area in the middle of a mega renewal.

Best Place (901 W Juneau Avenue, Milwaukee, Wisconsin 53233) is the spot to visit for much more of this history—both for Pabst specifically and Milwaukee brewing in general. The building was once a school but, as Pabst was expanding, they took over the space and turned it into their headquarters (the store is a must-visit for anyone who loves old brewery memorabilia and beer glasses).

A vintage postcard celebrating Milwaukee's brewing history.

Across the street is the most impressive of the buildings, which housed the old brewery and has been turned into **The Brewhouse Inn & Suites** (1215 N 10th Street Milwaukee, Wisconsin 53205), where you can see the kettles prominently on display in the lobby. Around the block from here is a modern brewpub in an old Methodist church from the 1870s. It's been over 20 years since Pabst beers were brewed in the city and now **Pabst Milwaukee Brewery** (1037 W Juneau Avenue,

Milwaukee, Wisconsin 53233) is making them again. They have a mix of resurrected Pabst brands (some from decades ago) and also new brews. You can also get the classic Pabst Blue Ribbon on tap, but it's not brewed there.

The most well known of Milwaukee's old brewers today is **Miller Brewery**, thanks to their endurance and prominence in the city, and it's a good tour to go on if you're in town (4251 W State Street, Milwaukee, Wisconsin 53208).

Frederick Miller arrived in the USA in 1854 and, so they say, brought yeast that traveled with him for around a year before he reached Milwaukee and took over the Plank Road Brewery (I asked the tour guide how Miller kept his yeast alive, but they didn't know…). He opened a beer garden and it was a catalyst for cultural change: a bright, lively space in which to drink his bright German lagers. On the tour you'll see the brewhouse, which was added in 1886. By 1903 High Life—"The Champagne of Beer"—had become their main beer. The brewery was also responsible for creating the light beer category when they released Miller Lite in 1975—it was, as they say on the tour, "the most popular new beer of all time."

The tour takes you through the handsome old brewhouse on the huge campus, a site

The Plank Road Brewery was bought by Frederick Miller for US$2,300.

that includes 79 buildings over 82 acres (33 hectares) in the city, and you'll get to see the packaging and distribution, with half a million cases being filled and dispatched every day. You'll see the Plank Road Brewery house, which is there as a reminder of Miller's history, and after that you head to the old brewery tunnels that were dug by the Best brothers. The tour ends in the tasting room with three beers. Whether you like Miller beers or not, it's a key brewery in American history for its place in the development of beer culture and for being the one that outlasted all the other great names in this once-great brewing city.

Is the Miller Brewery a Beer Bucket List tick? I have to constantly check with myself whether I think places are worthy of the list or if they're just interesting places to visit if you happen to find yourself nearby. If you're interested in American beer today, then knowing about its early beginnings, or at least its image-defining, teenage growth spurt, then Milwaukee is an important point of reference. It's also the most deeply ingrained beer city, the one with the most beer history.

More to Milwaukee than Miller

If you go to Milwaukee, then it'll probably be for craft beer, not Lite beer. And rightly so, as it's a good city for drinking, with a lot of new breweries opening—though there are too many for me to mention more than a couple here. Go to **Lakefront Brewery** (1872 N Commerce Street, Milwaukee, Wisconsin 53212), ideally on a Friday for their famous fish-fry, and do the tour if you can as it's drunken, lively, loud, and fun. Across the river is **Like Minds Brewing** (823 E Hamilton Street, Milwaukee, Wisconsin 53202), which is a food-focused brewery doing great things in both the kitchen and brewhouse, especially with brett-fermented IPAs. **Sugar Maple** (441 E Lincoln Avenue, Milwaukee, Wisconsin 53207) is the best bar for sampling the widest range of beers.

The Beer Time Machine?

If a time machine existed to take me drinking, then there are a few places I'd love to go. Old Milwaukee would definitely be one of them. I'd probably try and hang around for a few decades into the turn of the 20th century. One of the great moments I'd fly back to would be Pilsen in November 1842, to be able to drink one of the first ever glasses of golden lager. It would also be amazing to drink in busy London pubs in the early 19th century, a time of Porter and the beginnings of Pale Ales, smoggy, smoky taverns, and a Dickensian novel of a bar crawl.

Pabst beers have been drunk in Milwaukee for over 170 years.

Drink your Way Around Grand Rapids

THEY CALL IT "BEER CITY"

In 2012, Grand Rapids emerged as a surprise newcomer to share the title of "Beer City USA" with Asheville, North Carolina. The following year, the Michigan city won the title outright and it's an accolade they've enthusiastically grabbed hold of. It is a great beer city, one that is made brilliant by being compact, but dense with delicious beers, and by a strong local beer community.

Founders Brewing (235 Grandville Avenue SW, Grand Rapids, Michigan 49503) will almost certainly be your first stop in town. A big, bright beer hall, with glass looking through to the brewhouse, it has the ambience of a long-standing brewery; places aren't built like this now. It's old tavern in style: wooden, bar seating, loads of taps, classic bar food, a store on the side. You probably don't need me to tell you to start with an All Day IPA, which is a modern phenomenon of a beer, a seasonal that turned into the top-seller within a few years, and the beer which we can reasonably say kick-started the Session IPA trend. Its rich pale malts aren't sweet and have the important job of hoisting the citrusy, orangey, floral hops forward. It's got the all-day-long, refreshing quality, but also a demanding kind of bitterness that keeps you interested. Later on, you'll want to try their big stouts, which they're also famous for, including the Breakfast Stout and anything aged in a bourbon barrel.

The rest of Grand Rapids is a big brewery crawl, where you can walk, bus, or grab a cab to anywhere you want to go, with nowhere being more than 10–15 minutes away. My favorite stop for beer was **Creston Brewery** (1504 Plainfield Avenue NE, Grand Rapids, Michigan 49505). It's in what looks like an old-timey diner or too-bright hotel lounge bar, which is a little odd but you can overlook this for the very good brews. I loved their Lookout Hill ESB for its deep, deep maltiness, the kind that's like eating a whole tin of the best cookies you've ever had (they use locally produced Pilot Malt House grains).

Brewery Vivant (925 Cherry Street SE, Grand Rapids, Michigan 49505) is one of those places that's often featured on those "you won't believe what this brewery used to be" lists, as it's in a converted old funeral home. The stained-glass bar backdrop makes the whole room bright with color. The beers all have a Belgian-farmhouse inspiration and they're all very good. Out near Vivant is **Elk Brewing** (700 Wealthy St SE, Grand Rapids, Michigan 49503), where they play with a lot of different ingredients and serve them in a simple taproom. They also have a second, larger facility in Comstock Park (700 Wealthy Street SE, Grand Rapids, Michigan 49503). Nearby is **East West Brewing Company** (1400 Lake Drive SE, Grand Rapids, Michigan 49506), a small kit run by the same owners as the Indian restaurant next door. They have an uncurried brewpub menu, but this is effectively a curry house brewpub, since you can bring in the Bombay Cuisine food to go with your beers.

There are two **Harmony Brewing** venues in town. The original brewpub (1551 Lake Drive SE, Grand Rapids, Michigan 49506) is out east and has wood-fired pizzas and a cozy local vibe, while Harmony Hall (401 Stocking Avenue NW, Grand Rapids, Michigan 49504) is west and has a sausage menu, reflecting the fact that the building it's in was once a sausage factory. There's a cheese IPA bratwurst served with bacon jam—if you don't order it, then you're an idiot. Beers varied but were mostly good, and there's a lot on tap to choose from.

New Holland's main brewery is 30 miles (50km) away, but they've opened a huge, modern brewpub in GR called **The Knickerbocker** (417 Bridge Street NW, Grand Rapids, Michigan 49504). This has a large central bar and loads of seating space, primarily with a sit-down food focus and a locally sourced menu. I recommend eating there, as they've worked hard on how the food and beer work together—I had a golumpki, a meat-stuffed cabbage and far tastier than "meat-stuffed cabbage" suggests (it's also a nice combination of GR's old German heritage and Michigan's agriculture and farming). All the New Holland beers are there, plus some specials and brewpub-only beers. I love The Poet Oatmeal Stout, while Madhatter is the classic kind of Midwest-style IPA that's all oranges.

In the center of town you've got **The B.O.B.** (20 Monroe Avenue NW, Grand Rapids, Michigan 49503), a fun, multipurpose Big Old Building which is the kind of place you'd probably end your night at if you're a local and then regret the last few beers you drank… You've got a brewery there, plus bars, restaurants, a comedy club, and a nightclub. They have a good Peanut Butter Porter and I find any peanut butter beer hard to ignore—I love it in the same way that I love pineapple on pizza.

Grand Rapids Brewing Co. (1 Ionia Avenue SW, Grand Rapids, Michigan 49503) has a large corner space with the seating pushed tightly together. There are 17 or so taps of house beers, with the expected spectrum of styles. Down the street is **HopCat** (25 Ionia Avenue SW), a much-celebrated brewpub chain. I didn't get the hype myself. The house beers were limited in range and quality, while the rest of the list—albeit enormous and very good—were guest beers. I also didn't get hooked on their crack fries. Still, the tap list is massive, if that's what you want.

To the north of town there's **Greyline Brewing Company** (1727 Alpine Avenue NW, Grand Rapids, Michigan 49504), a modern space off the main street. Their nitro Oatmeal Stout is good and they make some ace IPAs. There's also **The Mitten Brewing Co.** (527 Leonard Street NW, Grand Rapids, Michigan 49504), a baseball-themed

brewpub in an old firehouse—it's a great building to look at. I largely liked all the beers I tried there, without anything jumping out especially.

Grand Rapids is a Beer City and it has claimed many similar titles in the last few years. It works as a beer city because it's varied and interesting, easy to navigate, and there are some high-quality beers on tap. But, most of all, it works because the people who live there and work in beer really love, support, and celebrate it.

Founders (below) is one of the names that draws people to Grand Rapids, but spots like Harmony Hall (above) convince beer lovers to stick around the town for a few days.

Bell's Brewery's Eccentric Café

GET HOPSLAMMED

Bell's Brewery, in Kalamazoo, is a familiar hug of a tasting room. You know the sort: old wooden surroundings, big and spacious yet cozy, and decades' worth of breweriana knick-knacks on the walls. You'll find comforting food, a 30-tap beer list with names you'll know from this famous brewer, names you'll be desperate to drink, plus some new ones which you'll want to know about, and service that's new-best-buddy friendly.

Two Hearted is their essential beer. It's one of those all-time-great IPAs, one that's been around for years but which continues to taste modern, new, and exciting. Imagine all the possible flavors of orange in the world and that's what Two Hearted tastes like. Orange blossom, marmalade, candy, candied peel, freshly squeezed juice—and all from just Centennial hops. It's bitter and just-sweet and the old-school epitome of high drinkability.

You might want to time your visit to coordinate with the early-year release of Hopslam, their terrifyingly tasty 10.0% DIPA which is intense, powerful, and wonderful. It's one of those beer names that people just know; they've heard of it and they want to drink it.

Bell's celebrated their 30th anniversary in 2015. Any American craft brewer that's in its 30s is worthy of attention. They were there at the beginning and they continue to do things that get both beer geeks and general drinkers excited. Bell's are one of America's great craft brewers and The Eccentric Café and General Store is one of America's great tasting rooms.

A glass of Bell's Two Hearted in all its golden glory— a beautiful demonstration of the incredible flavor profile offered by Centennial hops.

The Lowdown

WHAT: Bell's Brewery's Eccentric Café

HOW: The café is open Monday to Wednesday (11am to midnight), Thursday to Saturday (11–2am), and Sundays (11am–midnight). The General Store is also open for extended periods every day of the week. You can also tour the brewery at Kalamazoo, with tours running on Saturdays and Sundays, on the hour from noon till about 4pm (www.bellsbeer.com).

WHERE: 355 E Kalamazoo Avenue, Kalamazoo, Michigan 49007, USA

Visit the Budweiser Brewery in St. Louis

FOR THE MOST BEAUTIFUL BREWERY YOU'VE NEVER SEEN

The one thing I didn't expect on walking into the Budweiser brewhouse in St. Louis was for my dropping jaw to crash into the opulently mosaicked tile floor while I was looking up at chandeliers and Victorian architecture. It is the most beautiful brewery you've never seen.

In many ways, this is a museum. Or it's the ornate front door and priceless treasure of a colossal gray machine. Most readers will scorn or just not read this entry. They'll automatically overlook it as being the "other" dark side of light beer that they've moved on from, that they dislike and don't even consider. But they *should* consider it because it's important, both right now and in the past.

The story of Budweiser and Anheuser-Busch is one of my favorites in the history of beer. I wrote 3,000 words about it for my book, *The Best Beer in the World*, and I could've written 30,000 more. The short version is that, in 1876, the Anheuser-Busch brewery wanted a new beer to add to their already broad range of Central European-style lagers. They wanted something lighter and more refreshing than their amber-ish lagers and were vaguely inspired by the beers of what's now the Czech Republic. They couldn't exactly replicate that beer using their own ingredients—primarily for the higher proteins in the six-row malts—so they added rice to give it a lighter color and drier body. It was a new kind of beer for Americans, a new kind of American Lager, special for its use of American malts, rice, and European noble hops, and it suited a new taste for lighter beers served in glasses.

Of greater historical importance than the world-dominating brew that we know Budweiser went on to become, the Anheuser-Busch brewery was pioneering and at the forefront of American brewing at the end of the 19th century. They were among the first to bottle their beers on a large scale, the first to set up distribution networks outside their city, including building train lines to transport it and dotting those lines with ice houses to keep the beer cold before refrigerated trucks, and they were the first to use the new process of pasteurization to stabilize their beers. Altogether this eventually—20 years after its first release—made Budweiser America's first national beer brand.

If you're in St. Louis—and you should go, as it's a good beer city—then visit the brewery and book a tour. You'll see the famous Clydesdales stables, the enormous conditioning tanks, the brewery buildings from the late 1800s, and the remarkable brewhouse. Most remarkable, or perhaps sad, is that the brewers don't get to work in this space; they brew from an office in front of computer screens because that's how big beer is brewed nowadays. But within that huge brewing behemoth there's this beautiful brewhouse that brews millions of bottles of Budweiser every day.

Forget your preconceptions of Budweiser and take the brewery tour—you'll see this titan of the beer world in a new light.

The Lowdown

WHAT: Budweiser Brewery Tours

HOW: Tours run daily throughout most of the day, although opening times differ slightly in June and August, so check out the website first (www.budweisertours.com).

WHERE: 12th and Lynch Street, St. Louis, Missouri 63118, USA

Colorado Essential Beer Experiences

Here are just a few suggestions for beer-related things to do if you're visiting Colorado, one of the great American beer states.

- **Drink a Fat Tire at New Belgium Brewing Company** (500 Linden, Fort Collins, Colorado 80524): Before IPA was everywhere and every brewery's flagship beer, everyone had to have an Amber, the kind of beer that called "Come over here" to the lager drinkers and eased them into this new thing called craft beer. Fat Tire is one of the most successful and best examples of American Amber and, while you'll also want to try the brewery's excellent IPAs and sensational sour beers, you should begin with a Fat Tire.

- **Have an IPA at Odell Brewing Co.** (800 E Lincoln Avenue, Fort Collins, Colorado 80524): The brewery is a few blocks from New Belgium and only a fool wouldn't go to both breweries (book a tour at each place, too). Odell IPA is an American classic.

- **Avery Brewing in Boulder** (4910 Nautilus Ct N, Boulder, Colorado 80301): This is a place where you'll definitely get drunk because you'll want to drink a dozen different beers, they'll all be great, and then you'll want to order a dozen more.

- **Go to Oskar Blues Brewery and drink Ten Fidy** (1800 Pike Road, Unit B, Longmont, Colorado 80501): Just drink whatever versions of it they have. Then grab some cans of any of their beers and drink them after going on a long hike or mountain bike ride or something suitably outdoorsy. That's the Colorado thing to do.

A well-stocked Colorado bar with Left Hand, Odell, Avery, and plenty more local breweries on tap.

- **Have a Helles or Kellerpils at Prost Brewing Company** (2540 19th Street, Denver, Colorado 80211): Enjoy a steinful of South Bavarian lager with skyline views over downtown Denver. Try and take a look at their beautiful copper brewing kettles. Lager lovers also have to get to **Bierstadt Lagerhaus** for their Slow Pour Pils (2875 Blake Street, Denver, Colorado 80205).

- **Go to Falling Rock Tap House** (1919 Blake Street, Denver, Colorado 80202): A cult and classic craft beer bar with no crap on tap. There's an eyes-popping-out-of-your-head 100 taps (I've seen the cellar and it's ridiculous)— and you'll want to drink most of them. Bar food is enormous and there's loads of it, but I always just have chicken tenders, fries, and a Pliny. It's one of my personal Cult Beer Bar must-dos.

- Have one of Crooked Stave's **exceptional brettanomyces-fermented beers** (3350 Brighton Boulevard, Denver, Colorado 80216); drink **Left Hand Brewing Company's Nitro Milk Stout**, one of America's great dark beers (1265 Boston Avenue, Longmont, Colorado 80501); and find a **Yeti Imperial Stout at the Great Divide Brewing Company** (there are two great locations in Denver, so check out the website at www.greatdivide.com).

- Want to see the **largest brewery in the world?**: Go to Golden and have a free tour of the vast MillerCoors facility there. Times vary, so check the website first (www.millercoors.com).

- Head up, way up, 10,152ft (3,100m) up, to **Leadville**: And drink at **Periodic Brewing** (115 E 7th Street, Leadville, Colorado 80461). This is the highest brewery in America (and almost the highest-elevated brewery in the world).

TOP US BREWERY TOURS

- Allagash, Portland, Maine (see page 9)
- Anchor Brewing, San Francisco, California (see page 50)
- Sierra Nevada, Chico, California (see page 54)
- Dogfish Head, Milton, Delaware (see page 20)
- New Belgium, Fort Collins, Colorado, or Asheville, North Carolina (see page 22)
- Anheuser-Busch, St Louis, Missouri (see page 43)
- Jester King, Austin, Texas (see page 26)
- Lakefront Brewery, Milwaukee, Wisconsin (see page 38)

The Great American Beer Festival

DRINK THOUSANDS OF BEERS ONE OUNCE AT A TIME

Imagine a room. Probably the biggest room you've ever been in. It's about the size of 10 soccer pitches. You've paid around US$80 to get into this gigantic room for four hours. You've been given a small plastic glass with a fill-line denoting 1oz (30ml). As you stand staring in awe at the sheer scale of this space, packed with people, you need to figure out how to work through some of the 3,500 beers in front of you, one ounce at a time. This is the Great American Beer Festival.

Your ticket gets you unlimited 1oz pours of beer. An ounce is one giant gulp, two big tastes, or three little sips. But three little sips of over three thousand beers is an impossible feat… In glorious Yankee grandeur, the GABF is really great in many ways: the space is so huge you need the map to orient yourself and you'll still get lost; the beer selection is unrivalled and overwhelmingly incredible, with hundreds of the best breweries pouring amazing brews; and the atmosphere of a thousand lively conversations rises into an electrifying roar.

There are negatives: sips are different to drinks, meaning it's difficult to get a decent taste of longed-for beers; the food isn't very good, which is probably why people bring homemade pretzel necklaces with them to snack on (it took me three days of searching for the pretzel necklace stand to realise people made their own…); you'll need to queue for rare beers and this could take a long time for the small sample; and there's also an inevitable frat party drunkenness toward the end as the people who pounded the Imperial IPAs at the beginning of the session feel their impact. But these are minor issues. No other world beer event is like the GABF. Go at least once in your life.

ESSENTIAL WORLD BEER FESTIVALS

- Great American Beer Festival, Denver, USA
- Great British Beer Festival, London, UK (see page 97)
- Great Australian Beer Spectacular, Melbourne, Australia (see page 176)
- Mikkeller's Copenhagen Beer Celebration, Copenhagen, Denmark (see page 160)
- Oktoberfest, Munich, Germany (see page 111)
- Independent Manchester Beer Convention Manchester, UK (see page 95)
- Annafest, Forchheim, Germany (see page 116)
- Beavertown Extravaganza, London, UK (see page 76)

The Lowdown

WHAT: The Great American Beer Festival

HOW: GABF take places annually around late September/early October (www.greatamericanbeerfestival.com)

WHERE: Colorado Convention Center, 700 14th Street, 14th and Stout Streets, Denver, Colorado 80202, USA

Delicious American beer, 1oz at a time.

White Labs, San Diego

WHERE YEAST GEEKS FIZZ WITH EXCITEMENT

San Diego is synonymous with hops. Hops are the superstars of craft beer and San Diego is their Hollywood. But in many ways yeast, which so rarely gets the headline billing, is the real hero; it's the studio, the production, the sound design, all wrapped up in one, and beer wouldn't even exist without it. And in San Diego, away from the hollering hops, you'll find the world's best destination to better understand yeast and get a full focus on fermentation.

White Labs, one of the world's foremost yeast suppliers, plumbed in a 20-barrel brewhouse into their global headquarters and bought loads of small fermenters. The idea was to brew a base beer and then separate the wort into a few different fermenters, adding a different yeast to each, then serve the beers side-by-side in the 32-tap tasting room, meaning you can taste what different yeasts will do to exactly the same brew.

This is a geeky beer stop where you'll want a few small glasses to sip rather than a couple of pints to sink. The differences that yeast presents can be dramatic in the same beer in terms of taste, aroma, and appearance, and it's beer-brain expanding, making you think while you drink. It's rare that

San Diego is where you'll find the headquarters for White Labs, and is a must-visit for any beer geek and homebrewer with even a passing interest in the effect of yeast and fermentation.

a beer experience can be so educational and informative, while also being fun, and it's unmissable if you're in San Diego. Hops might be the megastar today but without the yeast, the hops wouldn't even have a stage upon which to sing and shout and get all the attention.

The Lowdown

WHAT: White Labs San Diego

HOW: Open daily 12–8pm (6pm on Sundays).
Check the website for information on tour times
(www.whitelabs.com)

WHERE: 9495 Candida Street, San Diego, CA 92126, USA

West Coast IPAs in San Diego

THE HOPPIEST BEER CRAWL

The West Coast is the best coast for IPAs. West Coast really just means San Diego, which is the epicenter of the kind of IPA that's known for being bright, powerful, bitter, and big with citrusy aromas. It's altered from the angry early origins of a decade ago, when these beers were called things like Hopocalypse and Palate Wrecker, and everything was so bitter there was a chance your body would reject it as poison before you could swallow. The evolution has seen a mellowing, a shifting of weight, keeping the lean, tight, dry, and strong golden bodies, Cali-toned with no excess chub of chewy, caramel-y malts, and changing that ruinous bitterness into bigger, juicier aromas and a better overall balance.

IPAs dominate disproportionately in San Diego, but complaining about that is like moaning that the sun shines too much there, because when you're in San Diego you want the sun and you also want all the IPAs you can get. There are over 100 breweries in and around the city, and every bar will have a range of IPAs on tap as well. You've got exciting new breweries and established old favorites, and each one has at least a few different IPAs—Session, a straight-up IPA, a Double IPA, a seasonal, possibly one with fruit or wild yeast. To drink all the IPAs in San Diego is to go on the hoppiest, happiest beer crawl in the USA. And that's simply what this entry in The Beer Bucket List is: go to San Diego and drink as much IPA as possible.

I'm not going to give specific IPAs to try because there are too many and we all like different things from an IPA. However, on my last trip (March 2017), my three favorite IPAs were Pizza Port Ocean Beach's Jetty IPA, Fall Brewing's Green Hat, and Societe's The Pupil, although half a dozen more feature in the *Other Essential California Craft Beer Experiences* entry (see page 57).

With so many great and varied IPAs available, picking the best one in town is a near impossible task. Just don't drink them from jars because that's ridiculous.

Stone Brewing World Bistro & Gardens

FENG SHUI AND IPA

Stone Brewing World Bistro & Gardens, in Escondido, San Diego County, is one of the most remarkable beer gardens and brewery venues in the world. It's a beautiful, tranquil, one-acre space; there are water features, ponds with koi carp, natural stones, a running brook, an open-air patio, fruit trees, herb gardens, and plant life all around. It's a heavenly, almost-oxymoronic contrast to their gargoyle-faced brand, and history of being Arrogant Bastards and ruining you with heathen-ly hops.

Order IPAs. Have a Go To Session IPA, an Enjoy By, a Ruination Double IPA, and feel an angry surge of sedating hops flow through you while surrounded by the harmonizing *feng shui* of the gardens. Eat here, too, as it's some of the best food you'll find in any brewery anywhere in the world, with all the ingredients being sustainably sourced—they are the largest restaurant purchaser of local, small-farm, organic produce in San Diego County.

Also go to **Stone's Liberty Station** location (2816 Historic Decatur Road, San Diego, California 92106), which is vast, immaculate, slick, and smart, a sprawling garden with ponds, plants, and water features. It was once the US Navy's mess hall in the Naval Training Center and has been transformed into an oasis of calmness and Cali cuisine, where they have the Stone line-up, plus Liberty Station specials.

Both of these venues, plus the one in Berlin, Germany (see page 121), are extraordinary spaces and with almost no equivalents in the beer world. The 3D reality of their wonderful spaces can only be experienced in real life. The Escondido location, in particular, is an unmissable world Beer Bucket List destination.

The Lowdown

WHAT: Stone Brewing World Bistro & Gardens

HOW: Open daily from 11am, with regular tours throughout the day—book in advance (www.stonebrewing.com).

WHERE: 1999 Citracado Parkway, Escondido, California 92029, USA

Don't be fooled by the serene setting, Stone still produce riotous IPAs.

The Anchor Brewery Tour

VISIT THE ORIGINAL AMERICAN CRAFT BREWERY

Anchor was America's first craft brewery; it was a craft brewery before anyone even knew or used the words "craft" and "brewery" together. The significant part of the story of this venerable San Franciscan brewer took place in 1965 when Fritz Maytag bought a controlling share of the failing Anchor Brewery, rescuing it from otherwise imminent bankruptcy.

One of America's most handsome brewhouses.

The Lowdown

WHAT: Anchor Brewing

HOW: There are 90-minute tours two or three times a day throughout the week. Book months in advance to avoid disappointment (www.anchorbrewing.com).

WHERE: 1705 Mariposa Street, San Francisco, California 94107, USA

The brewery's history tenuously leads back to 1871, when a German brewer, Gottlieb Brekle bought an old saloon and plumbed in a brewery. In 1896 Brekle sold the brewery and the name changed to Anchor. From then on it passed to multiple owners, burnt down twice, shuttered through Prohibition, then reopened and moved location half a dozen times until Maytag took it over. Maytag moved it again a few years later—this time to Potrero Hill, where it's been ever since—and tried to transform its tumultuous wellbeing and then-terrible reputation.

Between then and now a lot happened and for much of the early years of craft brewing Anchor were at the forefront; the sole point of reference for new small brewers, especially for those in California. Steam Beer is the flagship brew, a style they've kept alive and which has become a unique American invention—it's a lager brewed at a warm temperature with a specific yeast that's evolved to suit this method of production. If we want to know what US beers tasted like 100 years ago, then this is one of the closest brews for telling us the answer.

Alongside Steam they effectively brewed the first IPA with their Liberty Ale, though they did it before modern IPAs were a thing. And they brewed Old Foghorn Barley Wine in 1975, the same year that the first American Light beer was released (see page 37). In 2010, Maytag retired from the brewery and sold it to Bay Area booze entrepreneurs Keith Greggor and Tony Foglio, who are continuing the traditions of this historic brewery and also building a new site near the Giants' baseball stadium.

You should visit the brewery on Potrero Hill. You begin and end in the taproom. The impeccable brewhouse next to the bar has three copper vessels, which were built in Germany in 1956. You'll see the impressive open fermentation room; you'll smell the intoxicating hop room; there's the cellar, packaging area, and a walk down a hall of fame-style line of photos and beer history, which takes you back to the taproom for a flight of beers. Tours sell out months in advance, so plan ahead.

Once you're done at the brewery, you should find an old bar somewhere in town and sit down with a pint of Steam Beer. It's a key beer in America's craft beer history.

Drink in San Francisco's Toronado

AND CONSIDER THE CULT BEER BAR

It was 2010 and my first stop in San Francisco had to be Toronado. This was my first beer trip to the USA and this was perhaps the most famous American beer bar I could name, or at least the most infamous in this city—a dark dive bar on the other side of the world that promised beers I'd never tasted before, beers I'd only ever imagined being able to drink, in a bar with a fearsomely great reputation.

I walked in from the rain and stood for minutes staring at the beer board over my head. I already knew what I wanted—Russian River's Pliny the Elder—and I'd decided I wanted that beer weeks before, but I couldn't stop looking at all the other beers I could order. I could drink any of them. All of them. I'd read about this place. I knew that I had to be prepared, to know my order, to place it, to give them cash, leave a tip, and not faff about. It was a cash

Toronado is a craft beer institution and you must not leave without ordering at least one beer from Russian River Brewing Co (see page 52).

transaction, coarse, curt, and exactly what I'd expected—it somehow felt like the real deal and that I'd arrived in American craft beer.

I've been back many times since and I'm still overawed by the beer list and the bar, and I still always order a Pliny, though I still spend ages ogling the beer board. Toronado has a pull about it, an intangible, unavoidable magnetism, and it has a comfort of sorts, a kind-of familiar routine in a place that isn't home. I know there are better places to drink, yet I can't stay away. It's the draw of the cult beer bar. The kind of place you hear or read about before visiting. Then you go and have a great time and you always return, somehow feeling that you must, hoping for a repeat of that first great hit.

The Rake is London's Toronado. **Zlý Časy** is Prague's. There's **Rattle n Hum** in Manhattan and **Barcade** in Brooklyn. There are cult beer bars all around the world. People who don't drink in those places regularly know the names and tell others to go there when, in reality, they aren't the best places to drink anymore. They are carried along on old reputations from when choice wasn't there. Not that any of this is bad and I won't stop going to Toronado when I'm in San Francisco, because visiting long-standing and famous beer institutions like that is definitely a Beer Bucket List tick.

The Lowdown

WHAT: Toronado Pub

HOW: Open daily, 11:30–2am (www.toronado.com).

WHERE: 547 Haight Street, San Francisco, California 94117, USA

Go to Russian River Brewing

BECAUSE EVERYONE WANTS TO DRINK PLINY
AT THE BREWERY, RIGHT?

One thing you see when you travel the world drinking beer are collections of empty bottles. Whether it's a bar, bottle store, or brewery, there'll be bottles left over from tastings, like trophy brews that've been enjoyed over the years. If ever you see these lined up, you can guarantee there'll be a tall brown bottle with a green label and a red circle in the middle; there'll always be a Russian River Pliny the Elder. It's a simple measure of the beer's lure.

Russian River Brewing in downtown Santa Rosa is the type of place that will have you feeling butterflies of anticipation on your first visit (and probably subsequent ones). Not many other breweries can do that. There's an "I've made it" kind of joy when you see the sign hanging on 4th Street, a relief and excitement, an excitement that grows when you step inside and see the colorful chalkboard beer list. You'll probably want to order everything—and you can, as they offer a tasting tray of all the draft beers. But don't get this because, by the time you've drunk the whole thing, you'll be too pissed to have pints of all the beers you really want. It's like having an all-you-can-eat buffet and then ordering a few main courses and some desserts.

I always want a Blind Pig, then a Pliny, then some Belgian beers, and then probably some of the beers you can only get on tap there. These are among the most revered beers in America; the hoppy pale brews have come to define the industry's upper-level of quality,

to define their own kind of terminally dry, bitter, and exaggeratedly aromatic IPAs that others have copied since. The Belgian styles, in particular the barrel-aged sours, can surely be credited with starting the craze for quality sour American beers and they are still among the best being brewed in the country. If you can time your visit to get Pliny the Younger, then you'll get to drink one of the world's most-hyped and hunted-after Triple IPAs (although personally I'd prefer a six-pack of Blind Pig over a small glass of Younger).

In late 2018, Russian River opened a new taproom and brewery (which also offers tours) in Windsor, 10 miles (16km) north of Santa Rosa. This adds another Beer Bucket List tick because you'll obviously want to visit both the new brewery and the original downtown brewpub. Take some Pliny home to your mates and friends who work in local breweries and bars. They can add this much-wanted trophy to their empty bottle collection and you can tell them how it's even better fresh.

The Lowdown

WHAT: Russian River Brewing Company

HOW: Open daily, from 11am–midnight (www.russianriverbrewing.com).

WHERE: 725 4th Street, Santa Rosa, California 95404 and 700 Mitchell Lane, Windsor, California 95492, USA

LOCAL TIP: Beer then Wine?

Not content with being home to some of the best beers on the planet, the Russian River Valley also produces some world-class wines in the form of Pinot noirs and Chardonnays. Beer lovers might want to pay particular attention to the natural wines produced in the area. The low-intervention techniques used will be familiar to those who appreciate naturally fermented beers with their dryness and funk.

Pouring Pliny the Younger, the brewery's triple IPA, which is released as a special once-a-year beer every February.

Sierra Nevada Brewery

DRINK PALE ALE, ONE OF AMERICA'S MOST IMPORTANT BEERS

This should be a pilgrimage for beer lovers. It's the Beer Bucket List equivalent of getting to one of the Seven Wonders of the World. Sierra Nevada is a brewery of monumental importance, an original craft brewer, the brewery which can be credited with giving us the archetypal American Pale Ale, the brewery which has built one of the most modern and yet timelessly handsome brewhouses, the brewery focused on a sustainable approach to beer, and also one that is always at the forefront of new technology. I could write this entry about each of those points, or all of those points, but I'm focusing on drinking a pint of Sierra Nevada's Pale Ale at the brewery in Chico. That's the essential Beer Bucket List tick.

Sierra Nevada Pale Ale is probably your favorite brewer's favorite beer and it's probably the most important American craft beer ever brewed. It's the classic American craft beer and as important today as it was when first released in 1981.

American Pale Ales were barely a thing before Sierra Nevada decided to brew an adapted version of an English ale recipe, one with a toasty, toffee-ish malt body, and then to add a newly released American hop called Cascade, including a decent dry-hop to emphasize the floral, grapefruity Cascade aroma. We take this kind of beer for granted now, even overlook it as being old-fashioned, but there was almost nothing else like it in America all those years ago, certainly not in a commercial brewery. Today, it's both an important classic and a great modern Pale Ale.

When you get to the brewery, there's a range of tours available, including the regular one (which is free) and includes a generous amount of beer at the end. The brewhouse is the kind that makes you coo, with old German-built copper kettles being the star attraction, although just as unforgettable is the hop room, an undeniable entry on the Top 5 Best-Smelling Things in Craft Beer list, where huge bales of whole-flower American hops are broken apart by hand.

After the tour, go to the taproom where you can pick from the 19 beers on tap and a food menu of pub classics. Have a pint of Sierra Nevada Pale Ale because it will be at its freshest and you might also get two options: the regular draft-style Pale Ale, which is 5.0% ABV, or a bottle-strength version that's only found there. You should probably get both.

Sierra Nevada is an essential brewery to visit. It's one of those places that demands you dedicate at least a day to it. Don't make other plans, don't try and visit other breweries or bars. Just go on a brewery tour and then sit in the taproom for as long as possible, drinking as many beers as possible. There are few places that are more important, or greater to visit, than Sierra Nevada's Chico brewery.

Sierra Nevada Pale Ale cans ready to be shipped from the warehouse.

The Lowdown

WHAT: Sierra Nevada Brewery

HOW: Free 90-minute tours run Monday to Thursday, 10am–6pm; Friday to Saturday, 10am–7pm; and Sundays, 10am–6pm (www.sierranevada.com).

WHERE: 1075 East 20th Street, Chico, California 95928, USA

Having opened in 2013, Modern Times quickly established a well-earned reputation for exceptional beers.

Other Essential California Craft Beer Experiences

- Go to **Firestone Walker Brewing Company** (1400 Ramada Drive, Paso Robles, California 93446) and drink as many beers as possible. Add the Firestone Walker Invitational to your must-visit beer festival list.

- In San Francisco you need to go to **Cellarmaker Brewing Co.** (1150 Howard Street, San Francisco, California 94103) for a taste of the best IPAs, then head over the street to **City Beer Store** for a great range of draft and bottled beers. And go to see the Giants play baseball, as it's a great stadium with great beers on tap.

- Across the Bay is **The Rare Barrel** (940 Parker Street, Berkeley, California 94710) for wonderful sour beers. Also go to **Faction Brewing** (2501 Monarch Street, Alameda, California 94501) for the great view back to the city while drinking amazing hoppy ales. (**St George Spirits** is next door if you want something different to drink.)

- Visit **Admiral Maltings** (651 W Tower Avenue, Alameda, California 94501), which is a micro-malting with a bar on site. They floor-malt small batches of local barley, so forget the hops for a few hours and focus on the grain.

- If you want proper good lagers in California, then go to the taproom at **Moonlight Brewing** (3350 Coffey Lane, Santa Rosa, California 95403). Their small tasting room is open Friday to Sunday. Drink everything.

- Drink **Bear Republic Brewing Co.**'s Racer 5 at the brewery (345 Healdsburg Avenue, Healdsburg, California 95448). This is a personal one for me—a favorite beer and a classic American IPA.

- Visit **Lagunitas Brewing** (1280 North McDowell Boulevard, Petaluma, California 94954). They have an outside space at the brewery and that's good, but the Upstairs Bar is the legendary place—the essence of Lagunitas' hoppy, hippy vibe and a stoner's bedroom of a bar where no one leaves sober.

- Go to **Boonville Beer Festival**, the annual festival that has run for over 21 years. There's live music, good food, arts and crafts, and 80-plus breweries (entry tickets get you unlimited tasters). It's set in the hills and redwoods of Anderson Valley and is organized by **Anderson Valley Brewing**. (www.avbc.com).

- **Beechwood BBQ & Brewing** (210 E 3rd Street, Long Beach, California 90802) is where to go for low and slow barbecue, plus a lot of exceptional beers on tap.

- **Modern Times**' Lomaland Fermentorium (3725 Greenwood Street, San Diego, California 92110) is a must-visit in San Diego. At the forefront of new brewing and a vocal supporter of independent craft brewing, Modern Times do everything well. Get some cans of cold-brew coffee for the morning after. In North Park there's also their Flavordome.

- **Pizza Port Brewing Company**'s Ocean Beach destination (1956 Bacon Street, San Diego, California 92017) is a definite on my Beer Bucket List. I love it there. By the beach, chilled out, unreal tap list, great pizzas. All of the four Pizza Port brewpubs, plus their Bressi Ranch brewery, should be on your list to get to.

- **Alesmith Brewing Company**'s IPA is another of those American IPAs that I personally can't resist. Their taproom is huge and impressive, though not as atmospheric as others. Still, the beers are excellent—the IPA is wonderful, and you can't skip the Speedway Stout (www.alesmith.com).

Visit Portland, Oregon

GO TO BEERVANA

There are 70 breweries in Portland, Oregon, plus over 30 more in the surrounding metro area. The quality of beer there is almost a moot point; in Portland, bad beer can't succeed because the drinkers are too smart, too beer-aware, and too surrounded by great brews to accept anything other than very good.

To go with that high quality you've got the great combination of quantity and accessibility, where you're always essentially in the middle of a potential beer crawl. To add to the quality and quantity of breweries, you've also got the variety: if you want the all-star American brewpub and its list of IPAs, then you've got it. If you want Belgian Saisons, then there's a brewery specializing in those. A gluten-free brewpub, breweries focusing on lagers, English ales, sour beers; there's tradition and innovation side by side. There are great locations and locations with great variety: old music halls, big beer gardens, and industrial estates. And there's good beer everywhere. Growler fills in gas stations and pharmacies; if there's not a bar or brewery on the corner of the block, then there's probably a liquor store, bowling alley, or restaurant with a huge beer selection. It's

Wall decorations at Hopworks Urban Brewery Bikebar, just one of the many beer-focused places in Portland worthy of a visit.

arguably the city with the greatest beer range and greatest density of beer.

If I have to suggest a few names, then **Breakside Brewing** (www.breakside.com) is essential for the best of everything, especially their much-loved IPA. They have three venues in town, so figure out which is best for you. Go to **Cascade Barrel House** for super sours (939 SE Belmont Street, Portland, Oregon 97214); **Hair of the Dog** for strong and aged ales (61 SE Yamhill Street, Portland, Oregon 97214); and **Widmer Brothers** for the original Portland brewer (959 North Russell Street, Portland, Oregon 97227). Then try and go everywhere else—and there are a *lot* of places to go.

That's the obvious attractions for the beer tourist. For the locals, beer runs deeper. Walk around the city and you'll see brewery T-shirts worn like sports shirts. Everyone has their local, everyone knows about beer, everyone has their favorites. Craft beer is the casual and much-loved fabric of life in Portland and Oregon. The weather helps, too: it rains a lot, it's a bit miserable for a lot of the time, so people look for indoor activities and that leads many straight to a taproom or pub. Then, when the sun does shine, everyone rushes to the beer gardens. The weather (wet winters and springs, sunny late summers) also helps in another way because Oregon is the second-largest hop grower in the country.

There are many great US beer destinations, many places calling themselves "Beer City USA" or marketing themselves on their beers. I've already suggested that the other Portland, the one in Maine, could also be a Beervana (see page 10) and I've put Asheville, North Carolina (see page 22) as my top USA beer destination, but few others can challenge the overall prominence of Portland, Oregon. It is Beervana.

Bend Beer City

If you're going to Portland, Oregon, then add an extra day or two to your trip and go to Bend, another great American Beer City. There you'll want to go to **Boneyard** for their insane IPAs and DIPAs, then get down to **Crux Fermentation Project**, ideally to see sundown over the Cascade Mountains, while you drink lagers, hoppy USA brews, and Belgian-inspired Saisons. Another great-view brewery is **Craft Kitchen & Brewery** overlooking the Deschutes River. The food is barbecued, the beers are freshly brewed, and it's all designed to be shared and enjoyed in a cool, communal space. **Deschutes Brewery & Public House** is downtown and huge. A classic drinking space where you should start with now-classic beers such as Black Butte Porter or Fresh Squeezed IPA. From here, there are more than a dozen other places to drink great beer. And plan on going to (or from) Bend via Hood River so you can stop at **pFriem Family Brewers** to drink their eclectic range of elegant, excellent brews (707 Portway Avenue, Hood River, Oregon 97031).

Drink Bale Breaker's Field 41

THE BREWERY IN HOP FIELDS

America is the biggest grower of hops in the world and Yakima, in Washington state, is the world's largest hop-growing area, accounting for around 75% of US hops. It's these hops which brewers around the world are demanding and using in a large number of beers, where they shine brightest in IPAs and hop-forward brews, showing off their citrusy and tropical aromas, their deep oily flavor, and a powerful bitterness.

Visit Yakima toward the end of summer and the landscape is rolling green as the bines grow upward along tall trellises and give the air a sticky, heady, leafy aroma, all with some stunning mountain scenery around you. And right in the middle of the hop fields of Loftus Ranches, one of Yakima's longest-running and largest hop farms, is **Bale Breaker Brewing Company**, flanked on three sides by Cascade hops—the hop which effectively kick-started craft brewing. Come here to drink beer surrounded by hops, where you can sit outside with the greenest of brewery views.

Have Field 41, which is Bale Breaker's Pale Ale, hopped with those Cascades and Simcoe, and named after the field in which the brewery was built. Topcutter IPA and Bottomcutter DIPA are their other flagship brews, and these are some of the tastiest, hoppiest beers in the hoppiest part of America.

The Lowdown

WHAT: Bale Breaker Brewery Taproom

HOW: The taproom is open from Tuesday to Sunday. Brewery tours take place on the fourth Saturday of the month during the summer (www.balebreaker.com).

WHERE: 1801 Birchfield Rd, Yakima WA 98901, USA

The Ones that I Still Need to Tick Off

MY AMERICAN HIT LIST

I haven't completed my Beer Bucket List—if anything, the list is growing longer—and there are still many great American places that are high up on my to-do list. Here are some of them.

• One day I want to walk down to the beachfront and go to **Pelican Brewery Company** (33180 Cape Kiwanda Drive, Pacific City, Oregon 97135). I'll order a pint and sit with one of beer's best views: a view over the Pacific Ocean and out to Haystack Rock. It's one of those places that you can almost feel, smell, and taste when you look at the pictures. A place with a majestic, magnetic pull; a pilgrimage pint to drink by the sea at sunset.

• **De Garde Brewing** (6000 Blimp Boulevard, Tillamook, Oregon 97141) let nature choose their brewery location in Tillamook, Oregon, west of Portland. Specializing in wild and spontaneous fermentation, yeast is vital to them, so, when they were working out the best location for their brewery, they placed wort along the cool Oregon coast, analyzed their fermentations, and discovered that the best came from Tillamook. Their beer ferments in coolships and is then transferred to wooden barrels, where it stays for between three months and three or more years. Their beers are almost exclusively sold in the taproom, which is clearly the best place to go to drink them. It's stories such as this, and breweries like this, which are progressing craft beer in new directions; it's single-minded and dedicated to specific styles and processes, and these places currently appeal to me the most. It's the next development of American craft brewing.

• **Scratch Brewing Company** (264 Thompson Road, Ava, Illinois 62907) is a brewery and farm, and their focus appeals to me in a similar way to De Garde's. They brew an ever-rotating range of beers using home-grown and foraged ingredients, including flowers, tree barks and saps, roots, mushrooms, and fruits, which change according to season and availability— they also have a couple of people specializing as farmers and foragers, working between the brewery and the kitchen. Food is sourced locally and includes house-baked bread and pizza. And you can drink the beers sitting in the forest, which is like their own walk-in grocery store. There aren't many—or any—breweries like Scratch that source ingredients so widely from their land. The brewery is open Thursday to Sunday, but check ahead for opening times.

Pelican Brewery has three spots in Oregon, but it's the original beach front brewpub in Pacific City that's worthy of the beer bucket list.

• **New Glarus Brewing Co.** (2400 State Highway 69, New Glarus, Wisconsin 53574). If you've had their fruit beers, then you'll know why I want to go, but I also just want to have a pint of Spotted Cow, their Wisconsin farmhouse ale that's brewed with Wisconsin malts.

• **Suarez Family Brewery** (2278 U.S. 9, Hudson, New York 12534), in rural Livingston, has the kind of focus that gets my attention: clean and long-fermented unfiltered lagers; mixed-fermentation, farmhouse-style ales; and "crispy little beers" that are bright, light, lively, and fresh. Every photo that I've seen of their beers has made me immediately want to drink them—having a glass of their lager at the brewery is right at the top of my "I-want-to-drink-that-right-now" list.

• **Spencer Brewery** (167 N Spencer Road, Massachusetts 01562) is American's only Trappist monastery that makes beers. You can't visit the brewery (but you can visit the abbey) and that makes me want to go even more.

• **Fat Head's Brewery, Cleveland** (24581 Lorain Road, North Olmsted, Ohio 44070). I've been to their brewery in Portland, Oregon (which is now closed), and the beers were amazing, especially Head Hunter IPA. But I want to go to the original brewery in Cleveland, just to sit there and drink too much of their beer. While in Cleveland I'll also go to **Great Lakes Brewing** (2516 Market Ave, Cleveland, Ohio 44113) because I really like their beers—they make excellent lagers and their Porter is in the upper tier of world Porters (www.greatlakesbrewing.com).

• Then there are the two couldn't-be-more-different, non-contiguous states of **Alaska and Hawaii**. Both have loads of beer and amazing sights to see. To drink the Smoked Porter at the **Alaskan Brewing Company** (5429 Shaune Drive, Juneau, Alaska 99801) is a must-do beer thing for me. There's the Great Alaska Beer and Barley Wine festival held in January in Anchorage (perhaps the only reason to go to Alaska in January), which is also where you can drink at **Anchorage Brewing Company**, **Midnight Sun**, and **Broken Tooth**. In Hawaii, you're drinking good beer in paradise. All the main islands have breweries and they all seem to brew American styles, with many having a local twist, such as adding fruit or coconut. **Maui Brewing Co.** (605 Lipoa Parkway, Kihei, Maui, Hawaii 96753) and **Kona Brewing Co.** (Pawai Pl, Kailua-Kona, Hawaii 96740) are the best known and there's a lot more to go with them. An Hawaii island-hopping beer tour sounds like a decent vacation to me.

• And I think drinking a local beer in each American state should definitely be on the Beer Bucket List.

A brewery in Hawaii, that's about all you need to know as to why the Kona brewery is on the list.

Craft Beer in Tijuana

AN UNEXPECTEDLY BRILLIANT BEER DESTINATION

I think I expected to be shot at or forced to be a drug mule as a minimum encounter in Tijuana. My prepare-for-the-worst expectations may go some way to explaining why I would now put Tijuana—and Baja California in general—on a must-visit list of beer destinations. And not just because I survived; it's because Tijuana is developing its own beer culture in unique settings.

Having crossed the border from San Diego (way easier than my movie-life mind made it out to be—just ride the Trolley to San Ysidro and follow the signs), then navigated the no-man's land between the border and downtown, a wasteland of cheap pharmacies and ramshackle taco joints (just get a US$5 cab at the station—it's easier), we finally found ourselves walking down Avenida Revolución in search of **Norte Brewing Co.** (Calle 4TA, 22000 Tijuana, Baja California). "Search" being the right word, since you won't see it—or any signs of it—from street level. Basically, turn right down Fourth Street, from Avenida Revolución, and, a little way along, on your right, is multi-story car park. Trust me when I say that you enter the car park and find the elevators on your left. Go to the

fifth floor, turn left as you come out, and you'll pretty much walk into the brewery. It's worth the search because the beers are some of the best you'll find—try the Session IPA and Amber Ale, which is a neat update of Mexico's love of Vienna-ish Amber lagers. There are also huge windows that give you a view over the whole of downtown TJ. It's an exceptional place.

A block away—you can see its rear-side from Norte—is **Mamut** (Calle 3RA, 22000 Tijuana, Baja California). This is a large, second-floor brewing space with decent kit, plus a big restaurant and a nice terrace where you can sit and enjoy the beers and the view over the busy street below. Further down Avenida Revolución, between 6th and 7th, **Teørema** and **Lúdica** breweries have a co-tasting room (1332 Avenida Revolución, 22000 Tijuana, Baja California), with Teørema brewing in the back and Lúdica bringing their beers over from their nearby brewery. And this is all good enough reason to make the trip down from San Diego. But there's something even better.

Plaza Fiesta (Calle Paseo de Los Héroes 10001, Zona Urbana Rio, 22010 Tijuana, Baja California) is an open-air "craft beer galleria," although "colectivo" is also a good name. The Plaza opened in 1980 as a mall. It became a hot-spot for nightlife in the late 1990s, but things turned nasty and it earned the nickname of Plaza de Balazo—the Bullet Plaza. This saw the nightclubs move out, bars close and re-open, and then close again. It wasn't until 2015 that things picked up, thanks to El Tigre Bar, who swapped hardcore punk bands for a tap list of Lúdica brewery beers.

There's a quirk in Mexican licensing that makes it expensive for a brewery to have its own bar or tasting room, but the breweries

Go to Ensenada

Tijuana isn't the only Baja California hot-spot and it's worth heading farther south to Ensenada, where they hold an annual Craft Beer Festival (www.ensenadabeerfest.com) in March, which features around 100 Mexican breweries, mostly from Baja Mexico (where most of Mexico's brewers are based). They also have a Colectivo of their own at Baja Brews—a beer garden with views over the ocean, a couple of restaurants, live music, and many Baja breweries pouring their own beers (see www.bajabrews.com for more details).

GREAT TACO AND BEER PAIRINGS
(I LOVE TACOS AND BEER)

- **Carne asada with Dunkel lager**: The lager's toasty, just-roasted malt flavor and refreshingly clean finish are perfect against the spice.

- **El pastor with Pale Ale**: This comes off a huge spit of pork, is carved like a doner kebab, and is excellent with a Pale Ale, especially one that's heavily on the tropical-fruit side, to pick out the pineapple that tops the meat.

- **Baja fish tacos with IPA**: This is a classic San Diego brew and food combo, with the citrus in the hops bridging across to the fresh lime on the fish.

- **Mission-style tacos and Saison**: This dish of small, double-layered corn tacos with grilled meats, chopped white onion, cilantro (coriander), salsa, and lime calls for a Saison that's dry, lively, and feisty.

Beer and tacos. Enough said.

can all share the same license in the Plaza. So the owners of El Tigre spoke to other breweries and many moved in, opening their own taprooms, so turning Plaza Fiesta into Plaza Cerveza. Today the Plaza Fiesta is a maze of bars and restaurants over two levels. Each is the size of a shipping container or two, stacked and packed inside a tight space, a little like a small mall or food court.

Each taproom is different and pours beers from the brewery that runs it. **Fauna** is a local favorite. It's upstairs in a basic space with 12 or so taps, including some guest beers. The house beers are very good. Next door is **Paralelo 28** who brew their beers on a small kit out the back of the bar. Everything is good—clean, fresh, balanced. **Border Psycho** is opposite and their beers are more diverse and adventurous, with DIPAs, Imperial Stouts, Black Saisons, and more, but their Cream Ale is a good refresher if you want something simpler. **Insurgente** is on the corner and that's a clean, bare, Nordic-like space, with a range of great beers. **El Depa** pours the Silenus brews. And there are many others, too. You can walk from taproom to taproom, with each offering something different. More than the beers and the spaces, the bar staff were all great and informative on my visit; there was a real energy from them.

There's an obvious and expected link to San Diego, with a number of TJ brewers also working in SD. Yet, while there is that link, and there are plenty of IPAs, there are more Pale Ales and even dark beers in this area, a sign that Baja California is turning in its own direction.

Tijuana massively surpassed my expectations. It's a new beer destination with cool breweries, good beers, fun taprooms, and the unique Plaza Fiesta (which opens every day, from 5pm), plus a scene that's young and exciting, and creating a genuine local beer culture. Go!

Drink at Dieu du Ciel!

IS THIS CANADA'S BEST BREWPUB?

Two biology post-grads walk into a bar. Jean-François Gravel and Stephane Ostiguy are lab partners at Montreal's McGill University, one working on a Master's and the other toward a PhD—and they like to drink beer. They like it so much that together they start making their own at home, led by Jean-François who had already been homebrewing for a few years. Then in 1998, just two years after first meeting, they open Dieu du Ciel! as a brewpub on the edge of the city center. Their chemical, biological, and creative curiosity leads them to brew experimental beers, to play around with different yeasts, hops, and other ingredients, and this marked them out as different from day one. The figurative translation of their name is a common exclamation you'll hear when people drink their beer: "Oh my god!"

Today the brewpub looks like it's 20 years old. There are too many chairs and tables wedged in irregularly; there's not enough space to move around; the little brewery is packed to the side of the busy bar; and it will be busy, because a lot of people love this place. (In 2006 the brewpub was joined by a second space in Saint-Jérôme—259 rue de Villemure, Saint-Jérôme, Quebec J7Z 5J4—where a larger brewery was installed. You can also drink there.)

The beers are an even mix of Belgian and American-style brews, and it'll help if you can read both French and English if you want to properly understand the beer board. The beers are exceptional across that board. If you want an IPA, then have Moralité, which is *très fruité*,

juicily smooth, and dryly bitter. And it'd be a mortal sin to skip Péché Mortel, their highly regarded Imperial Stout infused with coffee—it was one of the original beers that got them attention and continues to be world-class today, especially on tap in the pub where it's served on nitro, giving it even more body, richness, and deliciousness.

Two biology post-grads walk into a bar. Or, more accurately, they walk into a lab and then into a bar, where they leave their white coats behind on the way to walking into their own brewpub and then into their production brewery. There's no punchline and it's no joke that the bar they end up eventually walking into became the best brewpub in Canada.

LOCAL TIP: **A City of Brewpubs**

Given the fact that Dieu du Ciel! is one of the best brewpubs in the world, you'll want to spend a good few hours in there. But when planning your visit to Montreal, be sure to leave plenty of time to check out some of its other gems. Start with a stroll (and end with a stagger) down Rue Saint-Denis and the nearby streets and you'll find excellent brewpubs like **Le Saint-Bock, L'Amère à Boire,** and **Le Cheval Blanc**.

The Lowdown

WHAT: Dieu du Ciel!

HOW: www.dieuduciel.com

WHERE: 29 Laurier Avenue West, Montreal, Quebec H2T 2N2, Canada

Dieu du Ciel is known for its Péché Mortel Imperial Coffee Stout, which makes perfect sense as it's so good.

St-Ambroise Oatmeal Stout

If you're in Montreal, then don't miss **McAuslan Brewing** (5080 St-Ambroise Street, Montreal, Quebec H4C 2G1). Based in the St. Henri district, they've been at the forefront of Quebec brewing since they opened in 1989. They offer brewery tours on Thursdays, Fridays, and Saturdays at their visitor center, and then you can go next door to **L'Annexe St-Ambroise Pub** to drink some more. I think their St-Ambroise Oatmeal Stout is one of the best versions of this great style you'll find.

Drink the Unibroue Beers

AT LE FOURQUET FOURCHETTE

You can't visit the Unibroue brewery in Chambly, Quebec, which is a shame as they are one of Canada's top and original craft breweries, having made beer since the early 1990s. They brew in the Belgian style with a top-quality range of classic beers, including Blanche de Chambly, their zesty-spicy Witbier, and La Fin du Monde, their big hit and Canada's most-awarded beer—this is a boozy, ripe, and rich Tripel. Unibroue were one of the breweries that introduced a taste for Belgian beers to emerging American and Canadian drinkers.

The best place to drink these beers is down the road from the brewery at **Le Fourquet Fourchette**, close to the imposing Fort Chambly. Walk in and you'll be stepping back in time. It's all dark wood, like the bowels of an intricately carved old ship. Wooden barrels hang over the bar. You've got the main dining hall, the more intimate Chasse-Galerie Tavern, and The Abbey Hall, which looks just like an old abbey hall (even though it's never been one) with its arched, cloistered ceiling. If the weather is good, you can sit outside overlooking the Richelieu River; if the weather isn't good, then huge west-facing windows give you the same great view without getting cold or wet.

The name of the restaurant means brewing mash "rake" and fork and that's the essence of what you'll find—beer and food. There are a few taps of Unibroue and the rest of the beers are in bottles, most of them 26fl-oz (750-ml) corked bottles. The food is very good and smart, featuring beer in many of the recipes and showcasing some Quebecoise dishes. There's a suggested beer match for every plate, something the brewery is particularly focused on, and it's one of the better, most-considered beer venues for matching dinner and drink, where you can work through the elegant and powerful range of Unibroue's beers. The brewery is now owned by Sapporo, but that should be of zero concern because of the ongoing quality of these fine beers.

The Lowdown

WHAT: Le Fourquet Fourchette

HOW: www.fourquet-fourchette.com (For more on the brewery, visit www.unibroue.com)

WHERE: 1887 Avenue Bourgogne, Chambly, Quebec J3L 1Y8, Canada

The best of beer and food at Le Fourquet Fourchette.

Drink at Canadian Beer Festivals

ALL THE GOOD BEERS TOGETHER IN ONE PLACE

Canada has over 700 breweries spread around its great expanse. To drink from the best of them in one place, put **The Great Canadian Beer Festival** on your must-visit list. It takes place annually in Victoria, British Columbia, in early September, and celebrated its 25th festival in 2017. Each of the 60-plus breweries attending brings a bunch of their best and most interesting beers. Tickets go on sale in July and sell out quickly (see www.gcbf.com for more details).

Cask Days is Canada's celebration of cask-conditioned ale. In late October every year, the organizers fill an old factory in Toronto with over 400 casks of ale made by over 200 different brewers, with many breweries supplying something new and unique for the much-celebrated event. The venue is graffitied, urban, and cool. There's good coffee and great food. The crowd is young. There are cask beer festivals every week all around the UK and almost all of them could learn something from Cask Days about how exciting and interesting a festival like this can be. Check out www.caskdays.com.

Cask Days is a super example of how to present a traditional product in a modern light that appeals to all types of beer lover.

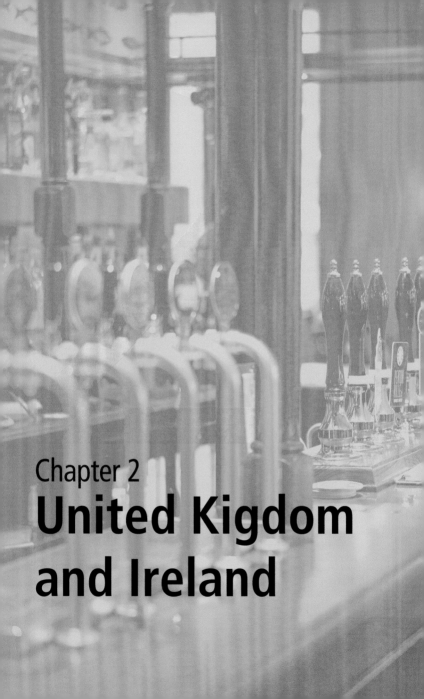

Chapter 2
United Kigdom
and Ireland

Tour Fuller's Griffin Brewery
—the Oldest Brewery in London

AND DRINK THEIR WONDERFUL LONDON PORTER

In 1845, John Bird Fuller, Henry Smith, and John Turner created a partnership of brewers and took over the Griffin Brewery in Chiswick, on the banks of the River Thames. Fuller, Smith, and Turner, now known just as Fuller's, is London's oldest still-operating brewery—and it's a liquid icon of the city, especially their best-selling beer, London Pride.

Go on the public tour of the Griffin Brewery, it's a wonderful place to explore. It's part museum and part working brewery, often side by side, and you'll walk all around, past copper tanks from the 1800s and dented old mash tuns, as well as the current stainless-steel tanks and robot-powered kegging area. The tour ends in the Hock Cellar where you can taste everything they have on cask and keg—you'll have a choice of around 16 beers. Start with the four members of the "Pride Family." This makes up around 75 percent of the brewery's output and includes Chiswick Bitter, London Pride, ESB, and Golden Pride. London Pride is their bestseller and it's a marvelously malty ale, with a toasty-biscuit depth and a deep, peppery hop bitterness. What's most fascinating about these four beers is that they're all brewed with exactly the same ingredients—pale ale malt, chocolate malt, and crystal malt, plus English Target, Challenger, Northdown, and Golding hops, the latter giving the aromas, plus Fuller's distinctively marmalade-y yeast. Simply put, the difference is essentially the amount of water used, the aging time (the stronger the beer, the longer the aging), and that Chiswick and ESB are both dry-hopped. Try them all and see if you can spot the family resemblance.

Next to the casks you'll find their next-generation beers, including Frontier, an ale-lager hybrid (it's an ale yeast with a cold maturation and a zesty New World hop aroma) that's become their second bestseller, despite only being released in the summer of 2013. There's also Black Cab Stout, Montana Red, and Fuller's IPA, which is a proper English-style IPA that's robust with tangy English hops.

There's also a store selling bottles, and you should look for Past Masters, a series of one-off historic brews based on retired Fuller's recipes—they're a liquid time machine. Buy a couple of bottles of Vintage Ale as well—one to drink now, one to enjoy in a few years.

If you're lucky, you'll get London Porter on cask. It's inspired by the great Porters of London's past (but it probably doesn't taste like an 18th-century dark ale). Although only introduced in 1996, it's already one of the defining beers of the style: so smooth, so rich with dark malts, but not bitter like coffee; you'll get caramel and cocoa, yet it's never too decadent that you couldn't drink a few. The intensity of malt is what makes this beer special; there's a roundness that's like a warm cuddle compared to the cold kick of a kegged IPA. You usually find it in bottles and on keg, but try the cask version, as it's world-class.

The site is still known as the Griffin Brewery (the griffin is the mythical creature that's regarded as the guardian of great treasures). Look at the Fuller's logo and you'll see a griffin protecting a cask of ale. The brewery is definitely one of beer's best treasures and the ales made there are legendary.

The Lowdown

WHAT: Fuller's Griffin Brewery Tour

HOW: Monday to Saturday (11am–3pm, hourly). Tours last up to two hours, including drinking time (www.fullers.co.uk).

WHERE: The Griffin Brewery, Chiswick Lane, London W4 2QB

The Best of British Cask Ales

PLUS HARVEY'S SUSSEX BEST VERSUS
TIMOTHY TAYLOR'S LANDLORD

A perfect pint of cask ale is almost unbeatable in the beer world—and perhaps only rivalled by German Helles poured straight from a barrel. The greatest cask ales have body and texture, a fullness of flavor but still some soft subtleties. They need to be balanced in malt and hop, even if the beer is rich or powerful. And, when the ale's been kept impeccably, there's a zingy, vibrant quality that somehow feels alive in your glass.

Walk into most proper British pubs and you'll see hand-pulls on the bar. Curved wooden handles, a colorful badge attached to the front, and a hidden "engine" that's directly linked to a cask of ale in the pub's cellar. That beer leaves the brewery before it's ready for drinking and undergoes a small secondary fermentation, allowing a gentle carbonation to develop that quite literally brings it to life and gives it a lift of aroma and flavor. The pub needs to store the ale properly and prepare the cask to be served a few days after it arrives there, timing this moment so that the ale reaches its perfect freshness.

Most breweries make cask ale and it's available around the whole of Britain, though a few standout beers dominate their different areas, with two beers in particular celebrated as regional classics that you must try: Harvey's Sussex Best in the south and Timothy Taylor's Landlord in the north. Both beers are frequently available; they are much loved and often well kept—they are traditional British pub ales and I wanted to visit their hometowns to understand them a bit better.

Harvey's Sussex Best is brewed in the lovely town of Lewes, in Sussex. Lewes is worth visiting, if you can, for the old town center, castle, and hilly cobbled streets, plus almost every pub serves Harvey's beers, with their classic Best being a must-have. This is an auburn-colored ale, deep with teacake-like malts that give sweetness before the earthy, fruity bitterness of English hops comes through. That lingering, dry bitterness makes you crave the immediate malt sweetness and creates the kind of drinkability for which these beers are famous. In many ways, Sussex Best is actually like strong black tea—malty, floral, tannic, and bitter, with some added sweetness. That flavor somehow makes it comforting and also wonderfully British. The Brewers Arms, in Lewes, is a perfect place to drink it or, if you're in London, then go to The Royal Oak, in Borough. This is a Harvey's pub that feels like your grandmother's living room—old sheer drapes (net curtains),

Situated by the banks of the River Ouse, Harvey's Brewery dates back to 1790.

well-worn wooden floors, and faded rugs; it's cozy and calm, with old family portraits on the wall. There's a familiarity to it and the Best is the perfect fit.

Timothy Taylor's Landlord is a "classic strong Pale Ale" that's intrinsically Yorkshire, but it goes beyond England's biggest county and is a favorite of many drinkers. The beer is brewed in Keighley (pronounced Keef-lee), about 20 minutes from Leeds. It's amber-gold in color, the malt is a little sweet with some toffee flavor and toastiness, the hops are floral, but it's all very subtle. The joy of this beer is the smoothness and rounded texture (the soft local water is very significant here), and there's something incredibly satisfying and unchallenging about it, as if you know after one mouthful that you're already about to order two more. It's easy-going, reliable, and just good—it is what it is and fits the no-nonsense Yorkshire temperament very well. Keighley isn't a big place, but a train goes there directly from Leeds, so it's worth jumping off and walking a few minutes down the street to the Boltmakers Arms, a cozy little pub with a wood-burning fire in winter and a great pint of Landlord all year round. Stay on that train and head to Skipton for The Woolly Sheep Inn for another excellent Landlord, plus some good pub food. Or there's one Timothy Taylor pub, the Town Hall Tavern, in central Leeds.

Both Sussex Best and Landlord were first brewed in the mid-1950s; they are both classics and both much loved, typically with

a bit of a north-south divide, but these two are dramatically different drinks. You have a feeling that the general drinker should fall on one side or the other: the richly malty, deeply and dryly bitter Sussex Best or the smooth, malty, fruity Landlord. Me? I'm having a pint of best.

FIVE BRITISH CASK ALE BUCKET LIST TICKS

- Pint of Adnams Bitter or Broadside near the brewery in Southwold, Suffolk.

- St Austell's golden, zesty Tribute overlooking the sea in Cornwall.

- The much-loved Thornbridge Jaipur, which shows how well a modern powerful IPA works when served in the traditional way.

- A warming pint of strong, smooth, malty Theakston's Old Peculier after a long walk in Yorkshire.

- An 80/- (80 shilling) in an old Scottish pub, to taste the popular style of years ago (and keep it thriving today).

LOCAL TIP: The Best Cask Ale City in Britain?

Ask 100 British beer-lovers which is the best city in the country for drinking cask ale and you'll probably get a dozen different responses, but certain places are mentioned consistently. The criteria that make a city great for cask ale are a good variety of pubs—including one or two flagship pubs—the excellent condition of the beer across many different pubs, some very good local breweries, ease of walking around the city, and a general love of cask ale; look for a dominance of it in the pubs, which demonstrates the importance of this type of beer. The top contenders for the title of Best Cask Ale City in Britain are Sheffield and Leeds, with Manchester, York, Derby, Norwich, and Edinburgh running close behind. No one can, or will, agree on the very best, but a pub crawl around any of these places will be a very worthwhile ale-drinking experience.

Modern Cask Ales: the "Pale and Hoppy"

BRITISH TRADITIONS AND NEW WORLD ACCENTS

Cask ale is tied to many great traditions and traditional beer styles, but the way in which it can enhance subtle flavors, develop wonderful soft aromas, and kick with a deep hop flavor and bitterness means that it translates perfectly into new beer styles—and perhaps the only new British beer style created in the past decade is the "pale and hoppy session beer."

Light-colored, well-hopped sessionable ales have existed for many years, but the difference here is the use of New World hops, primarily from America, Australia, and New Zealand. The citrusy, fruity aromas from those hops can be enhanced by cask in a way that keg simply cannot replicate: there's a delicate, zingy liveliness that a keg kills. It's also something that's only properly present when the cask has been very well looked after.

Hawkshead Brewery's Windermere Pale is just 3.5% ABV, but you'd never believe that from its depth of flavor. Wonderful toasty, chewy malts and a big aroma of tropical, peachy, grapefruit-y hops make this a world-class beer. Hawkshead's Beer Hall is a must-visit place to go and drink their beers.

Bristol's **Moor Beer Co.** takes ultra-pale beers and fills them with a big hop aroma and depth of flavor. Being unfined and unfiltered, they are often lightly hazy, which adds to their texture and flavor, and you should look for Revival as being the best example of their pale and hoppies.

Burning Sky's Plateau is a light, bright golden beer that's zingy and zesty with American and New Zealand hops. It's fresh and fruity; there's a nice little roundness

of malt in the middle, then it ends really dry and bitter. It's a perfect example of this type of beer by one of the top brewers in the country.

The best cask ales can be thrilling to drink and the use of the juiciest and fruitiest New World hops gives classic beer styles an electrifying quality that's only found in British ales. The trend toward Session IPAs, which can surely look to these beers as the original iteration, makes you realize that they're thundering thrash metal compared to the elegant symphony of the best pale and hoppy session ales served from the cask.

Casks being filled at Burning Sky, in East Sussex.

Drink in some Wetherspoon Pubs

FOR SOME OF THE BEST REAL ALES

JD Wetherspoon is a chain of around 1,000 pubs across the UK and Ireland. They're famous for selling some of the cheapest drinks in town, they serve big portions of cheap food, they don't play music, and they don't always have the best atmospheres (that's a euphemism for saying they are a bit crap). However, they do reliably sell a lot of real ale and it's often well kept—in fact, nearly 300 Wetherspoon pubs are in CAMRA's *Good Beer Guide* and twice a year they hold huge real ale festivals, inviting world brewers to collaborate on one-off beers.

A big draw is that many "Spoons" (as they are known locally) are in amazing old buildings, which have been converted into pubs, often with many original features still intact or celebrated, plus there's also information throughout about the buildings' histories. There are old cinemas: The Moon Under Water in Manchester and The Coronet in North London. The Prince of Wales in Cardiff used to be a theater, while The Opera House in Tunbridge Wells is named after, well, you can guess. There are many banks: Edinburgh's The Standing Order, Beckett's Bank in Leeds, The Banker's Draft in Sheffield, and The Knights Templar in London.

Look into the Wetherspoon pub in the area you're visiting because you're almost guaranteed to be near one and that means you'll be close to a good range of cask ales.

And if you're into pub carpets, then there's a blog, which has turned into a book, about Wetherspoon pub carpets—they're famously gaudy, varied, and old-fashioned. Check out www.wetherspoonscarpets.tumblr.com.

A small selection of the cask beer on offer at a Wetherspoon pub.

LOCAL TIP: Sparkled or Unsparkled?

There are some regional differences between north and south in the way cask ale is served. In the north of England, cask ale is often poured through a sparkler. This is a small nozzle with lots of small holes (like a shower head) that screws onto the tap. The nozzle generates extra aeration and creates a thick, smooth foam when the beer is pulled through it, so producing a richer mouthfeel. In the south the tap doesn't have the nozzle, so the ale pours with a natural, often smaller, foam. Texturally they are different and drinkers have different opinions as to what's better—northerners think sparklers are better, southerners want it unsparkled.

The Best Historic Pubs in London

AND DRINK WHERE MANY GREAT PEOPLE HAVE
DRINK BEFORE YOU

For centuries, pubs have been meeting places and social spaces, somewhere to eat and drink, to find solace for an hour or friendship for an evening. London has many pubs with hundreds of years of history, more than anywhere else in the world, with notorious alumni, endless untold stories, and amazing interiors, making stepping inside feel like a trip in a time machine to stand at the bar beside ghosts of drinkers past. These are some of the best pubs that have retained their olde-worlde charms.

It's impossible not to be instantly impressed and overawed by the Dickensian darkness of **Ye Olde Cheshire Cheese** (145 Fleet Street, London EC4A 2BU), which hides down an alley off Fleet Street. Like many pubs in this part of town, it was destroyed in 1666 by the Great Fire of London and then rebuilt. But it has a history from before the flames, as a pub called The Horn existed there from 1538 and a monastery stood on the site in the 13th century.

Tread over the worn entry step and it's like walking onto the set for the latest BBC adaptation of a Charles Dickens classic: sawdust on the dark wooden floorboards,

myriad staircases taking you to snug and warm drinking rooms over different levels, and a wood fire crackling in the winter, while downstairs you sit inside vaulted cellars in the space thought to have been used originally by the monastery. When you visit, your name joins illustrious drinkers who have been there before you: Dickens, Dr. Samuel Johnson, Mark Twain, and Alfred, Lord Tennyson. The pub is now run by the Samuel Smith Brewery, so order a pint of their Old Brewery Bitter, which is still drawn from wooden barrels—just as beer would've been served when Dickens drank there.

Samuel Smith run a number of impressively antique London pubs, such as the **Cittie of Yorke** (22 High Holborn, London WC1V 6BN), the main room of which feels like a grand, old school hall or church, with a high-peaked ceiling, vast old wine vats, and a faint glow of light from outside that catches in the dusty air, to produce a whispering kind of intimacy. There's also the **Princess Louise** (208 High Holborn, London WC1V 7EP), a short walk down High Holborn, which has a traditional Victorian interior that's ornate and divided into many small drinking spaces—it's unlike any other London pub.

The Prospect of Whitby, which celebrates its 500th birthday in 2020.

The George Inn (75–77 Borough High Street, London SE1 1NH) has a fascinating 600-year history. As an inn, it was a place to rest, eat, and drink, and its location in Southwark, near the River Thames and London Bridge, made it a popular place to stop before embarking on further travels, either into or out of London, by foot, horse, or boat. Dickens definitely drank there and, in fact, mentions the pub in Little Dorrit; Churchill dined there; Pepys popped in for a pint; and, with the Globe Theatre nearby, we can guess that Shakespeare had a few pots of ale here too. Today it's a busy pub by the bustling Borough Market, but the real beauty of it is the galleried front of the building—it's London's last remaining galleried coaching inn and, since it's owned by the National Trust, the building is

Guests outside the George Inn in Southwark in 1910.

a tourist attraction in its own right. The oak beams and low ceilings inside feel cozy (when it's not too busy).

Supposedly London's oldest riverside pub, **The Prospect of Whitby** (57 Wapping Wall, London E1W 3SH) dates back to 1520. Obviously, that notorious drinker Dickens went there, and you can walk on the same original flagstone floor that he would've stood on. The bar top is made of pewter and much of the wood inside comes from old ships. Sit out back overlooking the Thames, where across the river you should be able to spot **The Mayflower** (117 Rotherhithe Street, London SE16 4NF), which is almost opposite and another historic river pub with a sea-inspired interior.

Other pubs to look for include **The Spaniards Inn** (Spaniards Road, London NW3 7JJ), in Hampstead, which has a lot of literary connections, including being mentioned in Bram Stoker's Dracula, plus John Keats, Robert Louis Stevenson, William Blake, Mary Shelley, and Lord Byron all visited and, of course, Dickens drank there too. **Ye Olde Watling** (29 Watling Street, London EC4M 9BR) was said to have been built by Sir Christopher

Wren in 1668 using timber from old ships, and he used the upstairs room to work on his designs for St Paul's Cathedral—step outside the pub, look left, and you'll see his amazing building. Then there's the wonderful anomaly that is **The Black Friar** (174 Queen Victoria Street, London EC4V 4EG), a weird wedge of a building by Blackfriars Station, which looks very old but actually isn't: it was renovated in 1905 in an Art Nouveau-style inspired by the Dominican friary that once stood there in the Middle Ages (it was technically a theme pub, but now kind of works as a history piece). It's a visual treat inside: monks all around, it's kind of cloistered in design, there's an open lounge and fireplace—and look up at the unusual mosaic-tiled ceiling.

There's something remarkable about drinking in these historic pubs. For me it's the knowledge that so many other people have passed through them over the centuries, that so many stories have been told inside, so many beers drunk, and that they all hold a rare, elemental, comforting familiarity. To become a part of that pub's story, even if just for the duration of a pint, is a rare experience.

Follow the Gamma Rays to Beavertown

FROM BARBECUE BREWPUB TO ONE OF BRITAIN'S BEST BREWERS

Beavertown Brewery is the star brewing attraction in London and started in the basement of a barbecue restaurant in Haggerston before growing into one of the world's most exciting brewers, with a rock-star appeal and an arms-open outlook that have made them many friends in the beer world. Their beers keep on getting better as well.

Beavertown's Neck Oil, Gamma Ray, and Lupuloid sit as London's front-line hoppy brews. Neck Oil is a bright and light Session IPA that's always excellent and lushly citrusy, while Lupuloid is like a bulked-up Neck Oil—bitter, dry, and brilliantly light for its punchy 6.7% ABV. Gamma Ray is a Pale Ale with a rich body of toasty malts beneath all those hops.

Beavertown brew a wide range of beers, plus there are regular collaboration brews, a barrel and sour program, and many one-off specials, making them a brewery to always look out for. They also open their Tottenham brewery every Saturday (another brewery, Pressure Drop, are located on the same estate) and regularly host different events both in and out of the brewery.

Beavertown is not just about pale ales—experimental beers using barrel-aging and wild yeasts are brewed as part of their Tempus Project series.

The Lowdown

WHAT: Beavertown Brewery

HOW: www.beavertown brewery.co.uk

WHERE: Lockwood Industrial Park, Mill Mead Road, London N17 9QP

Top London Craft Beer Spots to Visit

The Kings Arms in Bethnal Green (11A Buckfast Street, E2 6EY; www.thekingsarmspub.com) is a quiet, unassuming corner boozer, but when you get inside you'll see one of London's best-selected beer lists. I like it because it's a proper pub (not a bar) and it always has extraordinary beers. They have some superb sister pubs, including **The Axe** in Stoke Newington (18 Northwold Road, N16 7HR; www.theaxepub.com), which does a good roast dinner.

The Harp in Covent Garden (47 Chandos Place, WC2N 4HS; www.harpcoventgarden.com) has become a go-to pub for some of the best-kept cask ales in the city. Harvey's Best and Dark Star's Hop Head are always available and taste as good there as they do anywhere. There'll be a great range of other casks on, plus some good kegged beer, including a permanent line of The Kernel.

A pint of Hop Head by Dark Star at The Harp. This is one of the finest cask ales available in the UK, and a rare beer that can unite both lovers of modern craft and CAMRA members.

For one of the best beer selections, head south to **Stormbird** in Camberwell (25 Camberwell Church Street, SE5 8TR; www.thestormbirdpub.co.uk). The range is rarely rivalled for beer geeks in search of what's hopped up and hyped up. A mile or so down the road is **Hop, Burns & Black** (38 East Dulwich Road, SE22 9AX; www.hopburnsblack.co.uk), who sell beer, hot sauce, and records. They stock hundreds of bottles and some draft beer, which you can either take away or drink in. It's a cool place.

The Griffin in Shoreditch (93 Leonard Street, EC2A 4RD; www.the-griffin.com) is hidden away and worth finding for its simplicity and broad, brilliant beer list. Expect London's bigger hitters and all the classic Camden Town beers. A short walk from The Griffin is **The Old Fountain** (3 Baldwin Street, EC1V 9NU; www.twitter.com/OldFountainAles) with their mix of cask ales (Oakham Citra is always good) and British kegged beers.

The Bermondsey Beer Mile

THEY SHOULD RENAME IT BEERMONDSEY

Just south of the River Thames, and running parallel to it, is a long succession of elevated train tracks leading in and out of London Bridge station. In the arches beneath these railway lines you'll find a section running right through Bermondsey, which has become London's most brewery-populous area.

It's a unique London thing for so many breweries and bars to operate from railway arches—there are over 20 spread all around the city's rail network—and they offer relatively affordable rent, have a decent height, and keep a consistently cool temperature, so they work well as brewing spaces.

In Bermondsey, if you plot the breweries on a map they're all neatly lined up beneath those arches and one by one (starting in around 2013) they decided to open on Saturdays to serve beer direct to drinkers, putting out simple tables and building bars from old pallets stacked on empty kegs. That's when "doing The Bermondsey Beer Mile" became a thing. Since then, other bars and beery places have been rapidly moving into any vacant arch, to the extent that it's now almost impossible to complete the Beer Mile (but please don't take that as a challenge).

The Beer Mile is actually a bit closer to two miles and there's a great range of places to visit. Do bear this in mind though: most are in working breweries that set up weekly to become a temporary bar; they get very busy, so there's often nowhere to sit; they're freezing cold in winter; a lot of stag-dos come down here asking nothing more intelligent of the beer than "what's the strongest?" Plus, expect a long wait to use the temporary toilets.

It's hard to keep up to date with all the breweries and bars, but here's what was open as of the end of 2018 (this is approximately east-west): **Southwark Brewing**, **London Beer Factory's Barrel Project**, **Hawkes Cider**, **Anspach & Hobday**, **The Bottle Shop**, **Moor Beer**, **London Calling Sweden**, **Cloudwater**, **Brew By Numbers**, **uBrew**, **The Kernel**, **Affinity**, **Spartan**, **EeBria**, **Partizan**, and **Fourpure**. There's good food all around as well, especially at Maltby Street Market.

A lot of great beers are made in the railway arches at Bermondsey and it's an exciting place to experience something that's unique to London.

Brewers at work at Partizan.

The Lowdown

WHAT: The Bermondsey Beer Mile

HOW: Breweries open on Saturdays (11am–6pm), except for The Kernel which is open 9am–2pm for off-sales. Some breweries are also open on Fridays (5–10pm), offering a far calmer environment, but all the same beers.

WHERE: Railway arches between south Bermondsey and London Bridge.

FourPure taproom, before and during service.

London's Other Railway Arch Breweries

It's not just Bermondsey where you can drink beneath the railway tracks. In North London there's **Camden Town Brewery's** original location. In East London you've got **Five Points Brewing** (but go to their great pub, **The Pembury Tavern**), **London Fields**, **St. John at Hackney Brewery**, which is next to **The Experiment**, a bar shared by London's **Pressure Drop** and Cornwall's **Verdant**. Around the corner is **Deviant & Dandy** and down the street is **Forest Road's Taproom** and **Redchurch Brewery**, while a lot further east is **Pretty Decent**. In the south you've got **Brick**, **Brixton**, **Canopy**, **Bullfinch**, **Villages**, and probably others… It's hard to keep up!

The Blue Anchor, Helston

NOT QUITE BRITAIN'S LONGEST-RUNNING BREWPUB

In the 15th century, Cornwall's Blue Anchor Inn was a rest house for monks and it soon after become a beer-brewing tavern.

It has that great British tradition of being a brewing ale house, something you would find across the country hundreds of years ago, and is certainly one of Britain's oldest still-serving pubs. Although there's no evidence to support 600 years of continuous brewing, we can say beer has been made there since before the turn of the 20th century. Regardless of the specifics, beer has been central to The Blue Anchor for its entirity and it's one of those pubs which goes deeper than just its longevity. You feel a long-lived-in comfort of sorts, an awkward comfort of something built so long ago that 21st-century bottoms don't quite fit. It's ye olde stone and thatch with an 18th-century skittle alley out the back. The whole place is warm with friendly ghost stories, with reminders of centuries of

people drinking where you are now, and it's created a pub with a wonderful atmosphere. They make Spingo Ales with Flora Daze (named after Flora Days, a town-famous festival held every May), IPA, Middle, Bragget (which is hopless and brewed with apple and honey), and Special, most tending toward a sweetness familiar in ales from the Southwest, and not being much like your modern brewpub line up, and even better because of that.

The Lowdown

WHAT: The Blue Anchor Inn

HOW: Visit www.spingoales.com

WHERE: 50 Coinagehall Street, Helston, Cornwall TR13 8EL

Drink in Britain's Oldest Brewery

AND TRY A CLASSIC KENTISH ALE

Shepherd Neame *is* the oldest British brewery, but just *how old* are they?

The accolade of being "Britain's Oldest Brewery" is due to the fact that there has constantly been a brewery on their current site, in Faversham, Kent, for centuries. Until the early 2010s, the brewery thought they dated back to 1698, but their brewery historian and archivist has since managed to track a brewer to the site to at least the early 1500s. You can visit the brewery, and on certain parts of the tour you feel as if you're walking down centuries-old alleyways, with paths

The Lowdown

WHAT: Shepherd Neame Brewery

HOW: A train direct from London St Pancras to Faversham, in Kent, takes 65 minutes (www.shepherdneame.co.uk).

WHERE: The Faversham Brewery, 17 Court Street, Faversham, Kent ME13 7AX

worn by thousands of feet. The brewery building is very old, but the equipment is new, with two sides to the brewhouse: one making traditional cask ales, the other lagers and craft beers.

When the tour is over, you'll get to try some of the beers and taste Kentish Ale, for which the brewery has successfully received a Protected Geographical Indication (PGI), making it one of the few world-beer styles to have received this qualification. Kentish Ale is brewed with Kent well water; it's dry and bitter from Kent hops, plus dry-hopped with East Kent Goldings, and it's often low in alcohol and malt richness. Spitfire is their flagship brand and has the true flavor of a Kentish Ale. Plan to spend a few hours in the old market town of Faversham, too, which has some excellent traditional pubs. And if you can, visit in September when they hold an annual hop festival (see page 82).

Kent Green Hop Beer Fortnight

THE HOP GARDEN OF ENGLAND

Between the 1920s and 1960s, at the end of the summer, thousands of East End Londoners, mostly women and children, would travel to Kent's hop fields to pick the annual harvest. It was a vacation of sorts—hard labor in the late-summer sun to earn a bit of extra money.

Hops have been grown in Kent—known as The Garden of England—since the 16th century. The county has always accounted for significant amounts of England's annual hop acreage, with farmers such as Mr Golding and Mr Fuggle giving their names to new hop varieties.

Since reaching a peak in 1878, the hop acreage has dropped, but Kent is now seeing a resurgence of brewers and an interest in the local hops. Every September Kent's brewers each produce their own Kent green-hopped beers, taking the fresh hops straight from the farms and brewing with them as quickly as possible. It's a great way to celebrate both their location and the fine Kentish hops. They collectively hold a Kent Green Hop Beer Fortnight in different pubs around the county, with all the beers typically being showcased at a food and drink festival held in Canterbury (dates vary for this).

Green-hopped beers are the only truly seasonal brew, as they are possible for just a few weeks of the year and are usually best in those areas that are very close to hop farms. Kent is one of the best places to experience these annual one-off brews and the beer to look out for is Gadds Brewery's Green Hop Ale, a Pale Ale that uses lots of East Kent Goldings to add their tangy, grassy, spicy aromas.

The Lowdown

WHAT: Kent Green Hop Beer Fortnight

HOW: Visit www.kentgreenhopbeer. com for dates, breweries, and beers, plus the locations where you can drink them. Many towns in Kent are easily accessible via train in and out of London.

WHERE: Mostly East Kent, England

Hops have been growing in Kent since the 1500s.

Drink in Thanet's Micropubs

MICROPUBS, MASSIVE ATMOSPHERES

In 2005, Martyn Hillier was the owner of a small florist's in what was previously a butcher's shop, in the village of Herne, in Kent. He'd run a bottle shop in Canterbury and kept a few beers behind the flowers so he could continue selling bottled real ale, but things weren't going well. Thankfully for him, the Licencing Act of 2003 had recently been implemented, making it easier for any building to get a freehouse license to sell beer—even a tiny florist's (by tiny, I'm not exaggerating: it's one of the smallest pubs in Britain).

The idea was to set up a few casks of ale on the side and pour them for drinkers. No pub cellar, no lager lines, no expensive kitchens; just a bare simplification of what a pub is, or what it used to be. The micropub was born and it's since turned into a phenomenon, with over 300 open in Britain. The beer is served quickly, so it's fresh and there's a fast rotation through different ales, making these great places for people who want to drink a variety of good, often fairly cheap beers. Opening times are usually limited, often to a few hours at lunch and a few more in the evening, while others just open in the late afternoon, with Sundays being a couple of hours from midday.

While they are now all over the country, head to East Kent and Thanet for the home of the micropub and the greatest density of them. Bus tours have now been set up in the area so you can visit a few, or use local trains and buses to get around. **The Butcher's Arms** (29A Herne Street, Herne Bay CT6 7HL) is the obvious starting point and you'll be surprised at just how small it is—it's the definition of a micropub in more ways than being the first and the template for others to follow. **The Yard of Ale** in St Peter's (61 Church Street, Broadstairs CT10 2TU) is an old stable converted into a pub, where the cobbled floor and hay bales remind you of its past; here dogs are welcomed like local celebrities and the cheeseboard makes a great snack. Nearby is the **Four Candles** (1 Sowell Street, Broadstairs CT10 2AT), which has a microbrewery on site. **The Thirty-Nine Steps** (5 Charlotte Street, Broadstairs CT10 1LR) used to be a pet store; it's about 39 steps long, with all the beers stored behind a glass window at the back. **Fez** (40 High Street, Margate CT9 1DS) is a quirky place packed with eclectic retro randomness, where you'll have a harder time deciding which of the many different seats you'd like to sit in rather than picking your pint. A short walk away is **The Tap Room** in Cliftonville (4 Northdown Parade, Margate CT9 2NR), which has a curved wooden bar and cushion-topped stools—this is a great place to sit and enjoy some of the excellently selected ales.

LOCAL TIP: **Faversham Hop Festival**

Every year, during the annual harvest, Faversham, in the middle of Kent's hop gardens, holds a hop festival. The whole place is draped in green, with hop flowers everywhere and with people wearing garlands of hops on their head. There are processions, Morris dancers, live music, and it's all charmingly, eccentrically English. There's lots of local cask ale and Shepherd Neame (see page 80), who co-organize the event, have a green-hopped beer available, brewed with local hops.

The Lowdown

WHAT: Micropubs in Thanet

HOW: Visit www.micropubassociation.co.uk for a list of micropubs and where to find them.

WHERE: East Kent, England

Sarah Hughes' Dark Ruby Mild

CLASSIC DARK ALE MADE IN AN OLD TOWER BREWERY-PUB

The Sarah Hughes Brewery, in the Beacon Hotel, is a classic brewery-pub in the West Midlands. It's a rare and wonderful place to visit for many reasons.

The Beacon Hotel (which is a pub) was built in around 1851 and acquired its first landlord in 1852. A brewery was added later, possibly in the 1860s, but the most significant parts of this story took place in 1920 and 1921. That's when the pub's Victorian interior, which remains today, was renovated. Those years are also when the original family of owners sold the pub to Sarah Hughes who used the compensation money she'd received from her husband's death in a mining accident. Sarah started brewing beer herself and developed a recipe for a Dark Ruby Mild—a traditional local style. She brewed until her death in 1951, after which the brewery remained active until 1957 when the tanks were indefinitely emptied. The pub stayed in the Hughes family, however, and in 1987 Sarah's grandson, John Hughes, found Sarah's Dark Ruby Mild recipe and brought the brewery back to life.

Today the brewery and pub are run by John Hughes' nephew, Simon Massey. It's a traditional old tower brewery that begins in the roof with the grist case, which drops malt down into the mash tun below, with the wort flowing down into an open copper from the 1930s (that's a very rare thing to see). The floor beneath is a hop back, which is used for cooling the beer, and then the fermenters and packaging areas are on the ground floor. Trap doors run from the floor to the roof, with the malt sacks pulled up and down, instead of the brewers having to brave the steep, narrow stairs. There aren't many breweries like this any more.

Back in the bar and it's a wonder to explore the pub's preserved interior. From the front door you'll enter The Passage. On the left is The Snug, on the right is the Tap Room; there's a Smoking Room and a bright conservatory at the back. Central to all of this is a small enclosed bar which can directly serve The Passage, Snug, and Smoking Room. This has another rare feature: a "snob screen." There's a small window, around waist-height, through which you order and

The Lowdown

WHAT: Sarah Hughes Brewery

HOW: The Beacon Hotel is open daily from midday, but closes for a few hours each afternoon. To tour the brewery, call ahead and they will try to accommodate a visit—it's free, but you should tip your guide (www.sarahhughesbrewery.co.uk).

WHERE: 129 Bilston Street, Dudley DY3 1JE

receive your beer, meaning that the staff and drinkers can't see each other. All the rooms are lively with conversation and they feel like you've gone back in time with the wooden interiors, burning fires, original wallpaper that's desirably vintage, and worn banquettes. Food is the local pub staple: bread rolls with simple fillings.

They make three beers all year round and often a seasonal. There's Pale Amber, a 4.0% ABV session Bitter. Surprise is a 5.0% ABV West Midlands Bitter, made with Maris Otter malts and Golding hops, giving a sweet beginning before those hops leave a bitter finish. The most famous beer is the 6.0% ABV Dark Ruby Mild. It's moreishly malty, almost creamy; there's dried fruit, vanilla, cake, chocolate, plums, nuts, cherries... Every gulp gives you something new. It's sweet, which gives it a lovely comforting quality, a pleasing richness that you'll never get from the thrilling fireworks of an IPA, and yet it still retains a dryness that makes it easy to drink a few pints and still want more. It's a flavor you rarely get to experience with the current tastes for craft beer and, for me, it was one of those "wow" moments when I drank something remarkable that made me think differently about beer.

To summarize why drinking Dark Ruby Mild in the Beacon Hotel should be high on your must-visit list: unique interior, fascinating tower brewery, great history, and one of the world's finest dark beers—a reminder of beers from years ago which still taste excellent today.

Visit Burton-upon-Trent

AND DRINK DRAUGHT BASS IN THE COOPERS TAVERN

In the 19th century, Burton-upon-Trent was the world's greatest brewing city, built on the town's hard waters and exceptional pale, bitter ales.

Fast forward to the present day and the legendary Burton brewers of old, such as Bass, Allsopp's, and Ind Coope, have all gone, leaving only Marston's as the remaining link to the city's past (you can visit Marston's, see opposite). Yet in many ways Burton is still a great brewing city, as the skyscape is conquered by the huge Carling and Coors facilities right in the center of the town.

In the shadows of those mega-facilities, beer is deep-set in Burton's footprint: in the names of the streets and the shopping center (Cooper's Square), in the huge old buildings that would've once dominated the town, and in the many old pubs (both open and closed). There's also the National Brewery Centre and museum, and a few new small brewers. These all make Burton a place worth visiting, even if just to imagine what it might have been like in the late 19th century.

My favorite pub in Burton is the **Coopers Tavern**. To drink here is to step back to a time when Burton was at its best. There's a quiet space to the left as you enter, complete with a fireplace, while to the right, in the main bar, it feels more like a lived-in lounge with old photographs on the walls—a snapshot reminder of beer's unique place in this town's history. Keep heading through and you'll come to one of the most unusual serving areas in any pub in the country, because all the beer is packed away in the back, with standing room for just a couple of people. The pub is run by Joule's Brewery and their Pale Ale is a classic old English pale that's dry, biscuity, and floral with hops. And there are always a few modern hop-forward ales too, always kept perfectly. But you should start with a pint of the classic Burton ale, Draught Bass, now brewed at Marston's, which is gravity-poured directly from the cask.

Find somewhere to sit and imagine how this place would've been years ago when Burton was at its brewing peak and the pub was the Bass Brewery taphouse. It's a portal to yesteryear, a place to drink in history in many different ways. Some pubs are more than just pubs.

The Lowdown

WHAT: Coopers Tavern

HOW: www.cooperstavern.co.uk

WHERE: 43 Cross Street,
Burton-upon-Trent DE14 1EG

An illustration of the Prince of Wales, later Edward VII, visiting Ind Coope and Allsopp's Brewery in 1888.

Marston's Burton Union System

AND THE "CATHEDRAL OF BREWING"

The "Cathedral of Brewing" is what Marston's call their Union Room, which is home to the only remaining Burton Union System in the famous old brewing town. It is essential viewing for all brewery and beer geeks.

Burton-upon-Trent was built on barrels of Pale Ale. Every drop of its famous beer passed through wood at least a couple of times—fermentation, maturation, serving. Burton Unions were commonly used for fermentation in the 1800s, when Burton was an unfathomably large brewing city. It's an ingenious system, which was eventually replaced by modern brewing practices and equipment. All the Burton brewers tore down their Unions with the exception of Marston's, who continue to use them to brew Pedigree, their Burton Pale Ale (oddly rebranded as an Amber Ale in 2016).

The Burton Union System started as a way of separating the yeast and beer, but also had the effect of producing good fermentations, good flavor, and good, clean Pale Ales. It's a double-decker iron frame with large wooden barrels lined up side by side on the bottom layer with a large trough above them. After an initial fermentation in open tanks, the beer is fed into the wooden barrels where fermentation continues. When the forces of carbonation reach their peak, yeast and beer bubble out of the top of the barrels, up through swan-neck pipes, and collect in the trough above; the yeast and beer separate, with the beer returned to the barrels below and the yeast either drawn off for the next brews or to go to the nearby Marmite factory. When fermentation is complete, the beer moves into different vessels to mature further.

Next to the Union Room is a working cooperage, with one full-time cooper who continually repairs and maintains the barrels—this extra work is one of the reasons Union Systems became defunct.

Marston's Pedigree is the only beer that's still brewed using the Burton Union System. The way the yeast works through the barrels and trough gives Pedigree a unique flavor profile of

The Burton Union System in action.

soft stone fruits and spicy English hops on top of toasty pale malts. It's a classic English Pale Ale, the last remaining classic Burton ale still brewed in the city, and still a very good beer. I just hope that this incredible system isn't lost to modern upgrades because it's the last link to Burton's brilliant beer past and an amazing thing to see in action.

The Lowdown

WHAT: Marston's Brewery

HOW: Marston's run tours on Monday to Saturday where you'll see the Burton Union System and get to taste three of their beers (www.marstonsbrewery.co.uk).

WHERE: Marston's Brewery, Shobnall Road, Burton-upon-Trent DE14 2BG

Notable British Pub Bucket List Ticks

There are over 50,000 pubs in Britain and it can be hard to know which are good, great, or just grim. Here are some of the more notable or unusual pubs to look out for:

Want to drink in the oldest pub? Good luck trying to decipher which is *actually* the oldest, but there are some contenders: **Ye Olde Fighting Cocks** (16 Abbey Mill Lane, St Albans AL3 4HE) dates back to the 8th century, when there was pub or inn on the site, and supposedly parts of the current building are from the 11th century. **Ye Olde Trip to Jerusalem** (1 Brewhouse Yard, Nottingham NG1 6AD) is built into rock beneath Nottingham Castle and beer was probably brewed there from the 12th century, though the current pub dates from the 17th century. **The Old Ferryboat** (Holywell Front, Cambridgeshire PE27 4TG) has records dating back to the 12th century. Or perhaps it's **The Skirrid Inn** (Llanvihangel Crucorney, Abergavenny NP7 8DH), which is Wales' oldest pub, dating from 1110, and a welcome stop after a long walk over in the Brecon Beacons.

How about the smallest pub? At 12 x 7ft (3.7m x 2.1m), **The Nutshell** (17 The Traverse, Bury St Edmonds IP33 1BJ) long held that title, but **The Little Prince** (Old Kent House, 20 Market Place, Margate CT9 1ES) in Kent, opened slightly yet significantly smaller, at 11 x 6½ft (3.7 x 2m), with space for just six drinkers.

The Crooked House (Himley Road, Coppice Hill, Dudley DY3 4DA) in the West Midlands is appropriately named for how it leans heavily—one side is over a meter

Ye Olde Trip to Jerusalem dates back to 1189.

lower than the other. It can be disorienting for the first-time visitor, so watch out.

Want to drink somewhere remote? **The Old Forge** (Inverie, Knoydart, Mallaig PH41 4PL), in West Scotland, is officially mainland Britain's most remote pub. There are no roads to it, so you either have to walk 18 miles (29km) and kayak 7 miles (11km) across Loch Nevis, or wait for an irregular ferry. Another famous pub is the

Tan Hill Inn (Long Causeway, Richmond DL11 6ED)—a pub for walkers in the Yorkshire Pennines and the highest pub in Britain at 1722ft (525m) above sea level.

The Marsden Grotto (Coast Rd, South Shields NE34 7BS), near Newcastle, is a cave bar which used to be a smugglers' den. It's on the beach, part is dug into the cliff face, and there's a large elevator if you don't fancy the stairs.

Black Country Beer Crawl

EXPERIENCE TRADITIONAL WEST MIDLANDS BITTER AND MILD

Saying the words, "Who wants to go drinking around Dudley?" doesn't exactly have a big appeal for the curious beer traveler, but you should consider it as one of those interesting pockets of brewing, specializing in West Midlands Bitter and Mild, with the beer served in some traditional storied pubs.

The center of this trip should be the **Beacon Hotel** for Sarah Hughes' Dark Ruby Mild (see page 83), but there are a lot more pubs nearby, all easily accessible either by jumping on a local bus, calling a cab, or on foot (there's a few soberingly brisk 30-minute walks).

Bathams Brewery's Bitter is one of those local beer legends—mention its name to those in the know and they go glossy-eyed. But it's also a beer that a lot of people have never heard of. The best place to drink it is The Vine pub, better known as The Bull and Bladder (it was originally a slaughterhouse), which is attached to the brewery (Delph Brewery, Delph Road, Brierley Hill, West Midlands DY5 2TN; www.bathams.co.uk).

There's a small front bar on the right as you enter and a comfortable lounge to the left, with further spaces out back. It's a quintessentially old, untouched, and much-loved pub: fireplace, wooden seating, old photographs, brewery memorabilia, well-worn carpets, chatting locals, and a friendly welcome. As for the beer, the Mild is a bright ruby-brown; there's a fullness of malt flavor, a sweetish caramel flavor, and a lightly fruity aroma. You'll drink a pint of it without even noticing. Likewise with the Bitter, which shares many flavors and a similar sweet malt depth—it's golden and smooth, very light yet still full in the body, with some fruity, peppery hops. They are both characteristic of the beers from this region and that means they are sweet in comparison with other areas.

The Old Swan Inn (85–89 Halesowen Road, Dudley DY2 9PY), in Netherton, is home to the Ma Pardoe beers, which are named after Doris Pardoe who managed the pub with her husband from 1931. It's notable as a long-running brewpub, with brewing beginning in the 1860s and running through until 1993.

The pub closed in 2000, but it was revived, along with the brewery, in the following year.

Start in the front bar for the oldest part of the pub (there are two entrances—aim for the one on the right). There's a royal-red bar and patterned ceiling, complete with an old white swan, and a line of hand-pulls serving the house beers. The Old Swan Original is a lesser-spotted Light Mild. It's 3.5% ABV, and very light in color and body; where sweet malts add some chew in the middle and there's a light fruitiness—it's excellent to be able to drink this rare style. Dark Swan is a 3.9% ABV Dark Mild that's creamy and chocolatey and a little sweet, plus there are some tea tannins and general fruity aromas from the yeast. Entire is a traditional 4.4% ABV Best Bitter that has the hallmarks of the style in this area: a roundness and sweetness of pale biscuity malts, dry bitterness, and a good balance.

Holden's "Pure Black Country" beers are available in a number of their own pubs, including the Park Inn next to the brewery (George Street, Woodsetton, Dudley DY1 4LW; www.holdensbrewery.co.uk). This has been in the Holden family since 1915 when they bought the pub and the adjoining brewery—at that time they brewed dark, strong Milds, presumably similar to what Sarah Hughes would start brewing later.

Today the pub lacks the atmosphere and old feeling of the others mentioned here (there's sport on TV and flashing quiz machines), but it's a good place to try Holden beers, including Black Country Mild, a 3.7% ABV Ruby Ale that tastes like sweet tea and tobacco (my notes—bear in mind I'd had six pints when I wrote this—say "tastes like how I think my nan's curtains smelt in the late 1980s and it tastes like it's not from today"). I think this was actually a compliment,

The Old Swan Inn features on CAMRA's National Inventory of Historic Pub Interiors, thanks in part to its distinctive enamel ceiling.

as I enjoyed the beer. The Bitter is bright gold and 3.9% ABV. It's malt sweet and barely bitter, some fruity, bubble-gum esters pop out, and it's relatively dry and refreshing. A filling pub meal is good value too.

The beers of the West Midlands are almost uniquely local in how they taste. They all share a similar British malt depth and they're all low

in bitterness but high in drinkability for their sweetness—they all have a creamy fullness, which you don't taste anywhere else in Britain. More than just the beers, the pubs are worth visiting for their atmospheres, their many stories, and their place in local history.

Bundobust: the best beer and food in Britain

INDIAN STREET FOOD AND CRAFT BEER

Curry and lager are one of those clichéd British food and beer combinations, but rarely do you see great Indian food with great craft beer. Mayur Patel, owner of Indian restaurant Prashad—in Drighlington (between Bradford and Leeds)—and beer guy Marko Husak (owner of The Sparrow bar in Bradford), realized that and brought them together to create Bundobust, which I think is the greatest place for beer and food in Britain.

The idea is easy: it's vegetarian Indian street food (even the most committed carnivores won't miss the meat), cooked very well from great ingredients, served affordably, and with great beers on the side. The combinations aren't forced and there are no menu suggestions for the beers, encouraging you to experiment with the dishes and the drinks.

The vada pav is one of my favorite things to eat in the whole world. It's a spiced, fried-potato patty in a squidgy brioche bun with red and green chutneys. It's so satisfying and comforting, and there's no better veggie burger in the world. All the food is really excellent, so just order a few plates and share them with friends.

Their house beer is Bombay Dazzler, a Witbier brewed by the excellent Northern Monk Brew Co. It's made with ginger, coriander seed, and cardamom, mirroring the spices in the dishes and adding a refreshing zing to the food. If you're eating at the Leeds Bundobust, be sure to visit **The Northern Monk Refectory** (The Old Flax Store, Marshalls Mill, Leeds LS11 9YJ), the brewery's taproom. It's an easy 10-minute walk from the restaurant.

Their first restaurant was in Leeds and there's another in Manchester—both are excellent. At the time of writing in early 2019, a Liverpool branch is soon to open, with more locations and a brewery in the works.

The food at Bundobust is so good it has been recognized by the prestigious Michelin Guide.

The Lowdown

WHAT: Bundobust

HOW: Check out www.bundobust.com for their restaurants and menus.

WHERE: Manchester: 61 Piccadilly, Manchester M1 2AQ; Leeds: 6 Mill Hill, Leeds, West Yorkshire LS1 5DQ

A Sunday Roast and a Pint of Cask Ale

THE ESSENTIAL BRITISH PUB FOOD EXPERIENCE

What's the quintessential and essential British beer and food experience? That's the question I've been trying to answer. It has to be pub-based, so lager in a curry house can't count. It has to be nationwide, so not a regional specialty such as cheese cobs (rolls) and Mild in the Midlands or stew and Stout in Ireland. It could be fish and chips, but I think these should come from the chip shop and be eaten from the paper bag (though a bottle of local Pale Ale on the beach can work). A ploughman's lunch is old-fashioned now, with people more likely to get a Scotch egg or local cheeseboard. Really the only thing that definitely and definitively works is a Sunday lunch—a roast dinner—with a pint of cask ale.

Almost every good pub will serve a roast on a Sunday—and only on a Sunday (the name is literal: it's only available on Sundays and often only from 12–3pm). You'll get a choice of meats (chicken, beef, pork, and lamb, or a veggie alternative), roast potatoes, a few different vegetables, thick gravy, and probably stuffing or a Yorkshire pudding. It's a common thing for Brits to eat every week and if they don't cook it for themselves, then the pub is where they'll go to get it. And when they're at the pub, a pint of cask ale is the best option, ideally a malty Bitter with smooth, toasty grain and a dry, quenching bitterness.

FIVE PUB BEER AND FOOD PAIRINGS

- **Pie and mash with Porter:** A round, rich Porter is a great match for a pie. You need all that malt to stand up to the slow-cooked meat and gravy.
- **Fish and chips with Pale Ale:** I know I said that fish and chips should be eaten on the beach, but a lot of pubs cook this classic. A bright and zesty Pale Ale with some fragrant hops and a dry bitterness cuts through the richness of the fried fish.
- **Chicken Tikka with Golden Ale:** Curry has become a popular pub menu item and chicken tikka is one of Britain's national dishes. An easy-going, softly sweet Golden Ale is ideal.
- **Cheeseburger and IPA:** Every pub has a burger now and you want the big fruity IPA hops to add freshness and some toasty malts for sweetness.
- **Scotch egg with Best Bitter:** This common pub snack comes served with chutney or mustard on the side. I always want a good Bitter with it— the earthy hops and chewy malts match the egg and meat really well.

The Junction, Castleford

HOME OF BEERS FROM THE WOOD

Before glass bottles and steel casks, all beer was matured and served in wooden casks. It's no surprise that these were phased out: wooden barrels have to be handmade and repaired; they're expensive and heavy, difficult to clean, and everything about stainless steel is just easier. But easier doesn't necessarily mean better, and at The Junction in Castleford, West Yorkshire, you'll find the world's only pub serving a full range of ales from wooden casks.

The pub owns 180 wooden casks: some are ex-wine or whisky, some are 80–100 years old; there are various woods and sizes, and the pub sends the barrels to breweries who fill them up and return them. The pub isn't using the wooden casks to mature the beer—they are used just like regular steel casks as the method of serving.

It's been 30 years since British drinkers routinely drank ales from wooden casks and

The Junction allows us to see how wood-served beers take on new qualities, being noticeably more mellow, soft, and expansive compared with steel-cask beers.

The Junction is one of those wonderful beer anomalies. It's a place where the vision of its owners is dedicated to something that they genuinely believe in and they've created an extraordinary experience.

A pint in The Junction will give you a true understanding of the term cask ale.

The Lowdown

WHAT: The Junction

HOW: www.thejunctionpubcastleford.com

WHERE: The Junction, 109 Carlton Street, Castleford, Yorkshire WF10 1EE

Drink at Cloudwater Brewery

AND TASTE THE LATEST AND GREATEST DOUBLE IPAS

As I write this in early 2018, Manchester's Cloudwater is the most exciting brewery in Britain. They've turned the brewery into a fun taproom where they showcase their beers when they're at their freshest, while you're surrounded by the tanks in which those beers are made.

The Lowdown

WHAT: Cloudwater Brew Co.

HOW: The brewery is less than 10 minutes' walk from Manchester Piccadilly station. The Brewery Tap opening hours may extend or change, so check the website in advance (www.cloudwaterbrew.co).

WHERE: Units 7–8, Piccadilly Trading Estate, Manchester M1 2NP

A glimpse inside what is Britain's most lauded craft brewery.

Cloudwater started up in February 2015 with an Avengers-style brewing super-team and they've gotten stronger and better ever since. This is certainly a determined brewery, but what fascinates me most is their willingness to learn, improve, and share their developments and processes with drinkers—all in their drive toward achieving maximum deliciousness.

Their DIPA was the likely tipping point in this success. A powerful, juicy Double IPA, it was unlike any other beers brewed in Britain at that point. To go with its release, they published in-depth details of the brew and followed it up with more evolutions, getting more scientific, ripping the style apart and putting it back together, and always trying to improve on the processes and resulting flavors—the target for greatness is always moving and they are always hitting the bull's eye, often before anyone else realizes that the target has even shifted.

It's not just their hoppy beers—Session IPA, IPA, and DIPA—as they have an extensive barrel-aging program and some enormous foudres, plus a general approach that looks at modern seasonal beers and involves brewing to suit the time of year and their changing inspirations. Cloudwater is a brewery deserving of the world's attention.

Marble Pint at the Marble Arch Inn

GREAT MODERN BEER IN THIS CLASSIC OLD PUB

Manchester is a necessary stop on a British beer tour and the Marble Arch Inn should be where you focus your attention: it's one of the country's best pubs, serving some of the country's best beers—most of them brewed just a few hundred yards away.

The pub itself is remarkable, even if it looks like an unassuming street corner bar from the outside. It was built in 1888 and thought to have been a gin bar in Victorian times. Head to the bar, order a beer—preferably something from Marble Brewery (I recommend starting with their Pint)—and then take some time to have a good look around.

Notice that the floor is ornately tiled. You'll also notice that it isn't flat—it slopes down toward the bar. Now see where there's a large, brown semi-circle on the floor tiles—that's where the original bar was before it was removed and placed where it is today. Which door did you come in? Because there are two entrances: one at the front and one at the side. No one is quite sure why this is, but it's thought that possibly the top of the bar was for better-off drinkers, whereas the bottom one, down the slope, was for everyone else, with a curtain or glass partition through the middle of the bar—certainly there's a hole in the wall by the central door which supports this idea. Now look up at the ceiling. It's an ocher color today, but no one is sure what color the tiles were originally before they were stained through decades of second-hand smoke. One more thing: in the 1950s, and through until the 1970s, all of this was covered up, including the floor. It was only when new owners took over and started investigating that they discovered the grandeur underneath.

Once you've taken in the wonderful surroundings, focus on the beer. Marble Brewery started in the back of this pub in December 1997. Owner Jan, and then-husband Vance, took over the pub and had space out back—supposedly the options were a brewery or a karaoke room. Luckily for us, Jan hates karaoke. They brewed there until 2011 when they moved a short walk away, behind the pub (by the way, their old kit is used by the Blackjack Brewery who also brew just behind the pub). Marble make many very good beers, including Pint, a 3.9% pale and hoppy session beer that's wonderfully fruity, zesty, and peachy, and has a bold, quenching bitterness—for me, Pint in the Marble Arch is an essential world beer and pub experience. Their Manchester Bitter is fuller in malt; it's very bitter and less aromatic compared with Pint, being somehow old school yet still modern. Lagonda is their IPA, a boldly hopped brew that still keeps the great balance of British malts. Check out the keg lines as well, because you'll find a large variety of rarer brews: Imperial Stouts, barrel-aged beers, and excellent lagers.

If all of this wasn't enough, the kitchen is very good, if you're hungry, and includes classic pub food, plus 22 cheeses if you want to create your own cheeseboard (which you definitely do).

The Marble Arch Inn is a proper pub serving exceptional beers in perfect condition. The interior is fascinating and you can happily sit with a beer, just enjoying the surroundings. Unmissable.

The Lowdown

WHAT: Marble Arch Inn

HOW: www.marblebeers.com

WHERE: 73 Rochdale Road, Manchester M4 4HY

You won't find Marble's excellent Pint served anywhere better than here.

Independent Manchester Beer Convention

ONE OF THE BEST BRITISH CRAFT BEER FESTIVALS

Do you want to try the best beers from Britain's best breweries all in one place? Then you need to go to the Independent Manchester Beer Convention, or IndyMan for short.

Even overlooking the wonderful location in old Victorian baths in Manchester, this is a spectacular beer event, which takes place annually in October. It has rewritten the rules on what a British beer festival is—this is not a festival with dozens of sad-looking, dented casks lined up; it's not a room filled with old men and Morris dancers which smells of farts and pies; it's a beer event that focuses on greatness, on sampling many different beers, and being able to meet the people who make those beers, as it's the brewers who are pouring them for you.

There are interesting beer talks, good food, different spaces to explore in the wonderful venue; there are beers from Europe and the United States, as well as all the British brews, and it's just one of the friendliest, most fun, and geekiest of festivals.

The Lowdown

WHAT: Independent Manchester Beer Convention

HOW: IndyMan takes place annually in October (www.indymanbeercon.co.uk).

WHERE: Victoria Baths, Hathersage Road, Chorlton-on-Medlock, Manchester M13 0FE

LOCAL TIP: **Manchester's "Piccadilly Beer Mile"**

In London there's the "Bermondsey Beer Mile" (see page 78). In Manchester there's the "Piccadilly Beer Mile," a collection of brewers all to the east of Manchester's Piccadilly station. There's Cloudwater, Track, Chorlton, Alphabet, Beer Nouveau, Carbon Smith (and probably some others—breweries are opening quicker than I can keep up!), and on a weekend there's often a few of them open, meaning you can bounce between different brewers and taste a really interesting range of beers: Chorlton's hoppy Sours are excellent; Track make some superb hopped-up Pales, especially the Sonoma; and Beer Nouveau are interesting for how they've resurrected old beer recipes from the last century. If you're in Manchester on a Saturday, then look up each of the breweries to see which is open.

Go on a Bristol Beer Crawl

THE SOUTHWEST'S TOP BEER CITY

If you only went to King Street, where you have to walk a total of about 50 steps to get to three excellent pubs, then you'd think Bristol was a brilliant beer city. But that's just the beginning of all the great places to drink there.

Bristol works as a beer city because you've got excellent local breweries such as Moor Beer Co., Lost and Grounded, The Wild Beer Co., Left Handed Giant, Bristol Beer Factory, Wiper and True, and many more. There are great traditional pubs and craft beer bars, and it's also easy to get around the city. Plus, if you want something a bit different (and authentically Bristolian), there are loads of great local ciders as well.

You can drink in some of the breweries. **Moor Beer Co.** (Days Road, Bristol BS2 0QS), which is a short walk from Bristol Temple Meads station, brews some terrifically hoppy pale beers and pours them in a simple taproom. **Left Handed Giant** (Unit 8 and 9, Wadehurst Industrial Park, Bristol BS2 0JE) is nearby; they have limited opening hours, but a bunch of beers on tap—try their Duet or other Pale Ales, as they're very good. And check ahead to see if **Lost and Grounded** (91 Whitby Road, Bristol BS4 4AR) is open because they are one of the best new British breweries, with a cracking Keller Pils and vibrantly hoppy "special lager" called Running with Sceptres.

Go back into town and head to King Street. There's **Small Bar** (31 King Street, Bristol BS1 4DZ), which also runs Left Handed Giant, with a big range (around 30) of cask and keg beers, including lots of interesting rarities—they don't serve pints, encouraging you to sample in third, half, or two-thirds of a pint at a time. The food is good too, if you just want sandwiches, burgers, or hot dogs. Opposite Small Bar is **The Volley**, or The Famous Royal Navy Volunteer (17–18 King Street, Bristol BS1 4EF), with a huge beer list that includes lots of local brews,

The taps at The Wild Beer Co pour a mix of funky sours and fresh hoppy brews.

plus a good split of cask and keg. More good food here, too. Then just down the road is **The Beer Emporium** (15 King Street, Bristol BS1 4EF), a basement bunker bar with plenty of British and world beers. A 10-minute walk away, the excellent **Wild Beer Co.** (Wild Beer at Wapping Wharf, Gaol Ferry Steps, Bristol BS1 5WE) has a bar with a seriously good beer list and a focus on tasty food.

Elsewhere, go to **The Barley Mow** (39 Barton Road, Bristol BS2 0LF; it's in the same area as Moor and Left Handed Giant) to drink the Bristol Beer Factory beers, where you can't miss their lush Milk Stout. And don't forget the cider—you're in apple country and can drink some super scrumpies. Head to **The Apple** (Welsh Back, Bristol BS1 4SB), a cider-serving barge in the center of town.

Perhaps the best thing about Bristol in terms of the pubs is the determined focus on local products, meaning that, wherever you drink, you'll be able to find many beers that are brewed nearby.

The Great British Beer Festival

TRY 900 ALES AT BRITAIN'S BIGGEST BEER EVENT

One of the world's must-visit beer festivals, the Campaign for Real Ale's (CAMRA) Great British Beer Festival is a massive cask ale event that's held every August, in London, with around 900 beers available over five days.

Like almost all of the world's great beer festivals, it's immediately overwhelming. You're there for beer, of course, but where do you begin? Where is the best beer? How does it all work?! I've been to this festival many, many times, and I can't offer too much useful advice, I'm afraid, other than to suggest that you do a couple of laps first, figure out what's where (the restrooms/toilets, the food, etc.), spot a few beers you want to try (the festival is so big that you'll probably drink two beers a lap), and then just enjoy the fact that you're in the middle of this enormous event.

The focus of GBBF is cask ale and there are dozens of large bars throughout the huge exhibition space, all pouring different beers, plus a few regional breweries with their own bar (look out for Fuller's and St Austell, in particular). Each of the bars, which are typically grouped geographically (that part's confusing for everyone, to be honest), will have a lot of different beers and there will be a big range of styles, from classic Best Bitters to IPAs to strong Stouts—you won't find a greater variety of British beers anywhere in the world.

The beers are selected by CAMRA members from each region and often veer toward traditional and well-established breweries and styles, but you will find many of the top British cask ale brewers there. During the event they announce the Champion Beer of Britain, which immediately sees a huge line forming at that stand. And you can drink by the pint, half pint, or third of a pint, the smaller pours being a great measure for trying lots of different beers. It's a wonderful way to sample many beers you haven't had before and to revisit a few favorites.

As well as all the British cask ales, there's also a large selection of cider and perry, plus a couple of bars dedicated to international beers, primarily from the USA and Europe—you'll always find some rare treats there (although not many of the US beers fare well in casks). For food you'll find pies and pasties, mountains of pork scratchings, plus some world cuisine (but I always stick to the pies because they're excellent—the chicken balti is the best!). And if you go on Thursday, then know it's Hat Day, with people wearing all kinds of ridiculous headwear.

For the freshest and best tastes you should go earlier in the festival but, as with similar events, the fun is in the exploring, the occasional bad beer, the cheering when people drop their glass, and the chats with other beer-lovers. GBBF is big, it's fun, and there's a lot of great British beer in there.

The Lowdown

WHAT: The Great British Beer Festival

HOW: Usually held for five days in August (www.gbbf.org.uk).

WHERE: Olympia London, Hammersmith Road, London W14 8UX

LOCAL TIP: **Double the Fun**

If you're visiting GBBF, then it's useful to know that London Beer City runs at the same time and includes a packed week-long schedule of beer events all around the city. Check out www.londonbeercity.com close to the time and you'll see everything, from brewery tours to tap takeovers, beer talks, beer and food dinners, and much more.

Top 5 Beer Things to do in Wales

YOU'LL HAVE A WALES OF A TIME...

1 Watch a rugby game in Cardiff while drinking Brains' beer. At the city's major stadium, Brains have a cask ale bar where you can enjoy Cardiff's local beer. Try an SA, which is the classic Welsh ale—a smooth, malty pale beer with a subtle hint of peppery hops. Other Brains' beers include SA Gold, which kicks up the hoppiness with some zesty Cascade hops, or I like their Dark, which is a Dark Mild, nutty, smooth, and chocolatey. The city will be a mass scrum on match days so if you're not at the game, then the pubs will be busy and buzzing.

2 **Tiny Rebel Brewing** are based in Newport, about 15 miles (24km) from Cardiff. They're a modern British brewer making an excellent and varied range of beers, from their Cwtch, a Welsh Red Ale that won Champion Beer of Britain in 2015, to their excellent US-hopped Pale Ale, Fubar, to the smores-ish Stay Puft, a marshmallow Porter, plus a huge range of seasonal and limited-release beers. They have a taproom at the brewery, plus a bar in Cardiff that has over 20 beers on tap, some cask and some keg. Go and try the best of modern Welsh brewing (www.tinyrebel.co.uk).

3 How about the **Welsh Highland Railway Festival**? Every May this "rail ale" event takes place around the Goods Shed at Dinas railway station (near Caernarfon on the edge of Snowdonia National Park in the northwest of Wales), with around 100 beers and ciders to choose from. On the tracks outside, special steam trains run to other nearby towns where pubs also participate in the festival, meaning that you can grab a beer and jump on a train to the next pub. The combination of steam trains, Snowdonian scenery, lots of live music, and great local beers makes for a fun festival. Check out www.rail-ale.com for details.

4 **Hay-on-Wye** is a small town just on the Welsh side of the English border and it's famous for having many second-hand and antique bookstores. It's a nice place for a weekend break; you can spend the days wandering between bookstores and some of the excellent pubs in town, such as the Kilverts Inn (which has a good range of Welsh ales), The Old Black Lion, the Blue Boar, and the Three Tuns. In May every year is the Hay Festival, which celebrates writing and storytelling in all its forms (www.hay-on-wye.co.uk).

5 Not exactly beery, but it comes the morning before or after: eat a full Welsh breakfast. This includes the typical bacon and eggs, but also adds cockles and laverbread, a national delicacy made from seaweed. For a beer snack, find yourself a Welsh rarebit—maybe the world's tastiest cheese on toast. It's made by melting cheese and beer together, thickly spreading it on toast, and grilling until the cheese bubbles. It's perfect with a traditional malty Welsh ale.

If you like second-hand bookshops and beer, Hay-on-Wye is the place for you, with Kilverts being a must-visit pub in the center of town.

City Arms on match day boasts an incredible atmosphere.

A Great Cardiff Pub Crawl

Like all of Britain's capital cities, Cardiff is a place with traditional pubs and exciting modern bars. A good starting place would be **The Rummer Tavern** (14 Duke Street, Cardiff CF10 1AY), a 300-year-old, city-center pub that might be Cardiff's oldest drinking spot—it's also opposite the castle. Their house beer is Hancock's HB, a session ale that was originally made by Hancock's Brewery, formerly the largest in Wales, and since acquired by Brains. The Rummer also has up to six other mostly Welsh guest ales. **The Goat Major** (High Street, Cardiff, CF10 1PU) is another old pub near the castle that's run by Brains, so it's a good choice for trying their range of beers, plus they cook massive pies if you're hungry. **The City Arms** (10–12 Quay Street, Cardiff CF10 1EA), by the stadium, is another Brains pub, but this one specializes in a great range of different beers, both real ale and keg. One street away is **Tiny Rebel** (25 Westgate Street, Cardiff CF10 1DD), which has a large and excellent range of its own beers, as well as guest craft beers. For food, there are burgers, pizzas, and topped fries. The best thing about this pub crawl is that, regardless of the order in which you visit the pubs, the farthest you'll have to walk at one time is about 300 yards. Just remember the Welsh for cheers or good health: Iechyd da! (pronounced something like: "Yekky Dar").

An Edinburgh Pub Crawl

BEERS IN ONE OF THE WORLD'S FINEST DRINKING CITIES

Edinburgh is really great. The winding streets, the gothic cathedrals, the UNESCO old town, the mighty castle, the way you can walk around the center; plus, for beer, there's an impressive range of pubs, making it a city deserving of being on your go-to list.

Bow Bar (80 West Bow, Edinburgh EH1 2HH) is an essential stop. On one of the most perfect of Edinburgh streets, with a terrace level above, this pub is ornate and narrow, with old memorabilia hanging on the walls; there's a huge whisky list and one of the best-selected beer ranges in town—look for Fyne Ales and Fallen Brewing. While you're there, check out their cask founts, as they're the traditional, old-style, brass "tall fount" (pronounced "font"). They appear more like keg than cask and when the tap is opened the beer pours out; it was historically pushed out by air pressure generated by a water engine rather than pulled out by arm power in the usual British way (the water part has typically been replaced by an electric compressor today). You'll occasionally see a few of these founts when you're drinking around the city, so watch out for them.

The Athletic Arms is more commonly known as Diggers (1–3 Angle Park Terrace, Edinburgh EH11 2JX) due to its location between two cemeteries and for being the bar where the gravediggers came to drink. It's near Hearts' football stadium, so avoid on match days if you want a quiet beer and to look at the inviting old interior. It famously used to serve bucket-loads of McEwan's 80/- (80 Shilling, also known as "Wee Heavy"), but that's now been replaced by their own house 80/-, tag-lined "The House of Heavy," and made by Stewart Brewing. It's a traditional Scottish ale that's chestnut-brown and malt-forward, but not sweet; there's tea and toasty malts, subtlety, and endless drinkability. You have to drink an 80/- in Edinburgh.

Go to Cloisters Bar (26 Brougham Street, Edinburgh EH3 9JH) for a very good range of cask beers and a couple of interesting keg beers. On cask, check out Swannay from Orkney or the nearby Alechemy Brewing. The pub is in an old parsonage and is the essential stop for the best-kept real ale. Just up the road from Cloisters is The Hanging Bat, one of Edinburgh's top craft beer spots, where they have a long list of kegged beers, all served in two-third pint glasses, and a kitchen that cooks up some decent barbecue food. Another excellent craft beer stop is The Holyrood 9A (9A Holyrood Road, Edinburgh EH8 8AE), where they pour beers from hot Scot brewers such as Tempest Brewing Co. and Cromarty Brewing Co. Good burgers, too.

The Oxford Bar (8 Young Street, Edinburgh EH2 4JB) is the pub for literary fans (or fans of a good pub), because it's Inspector Rebus' local in Ian Rankin's series of books. You walk into a small serving area with a few cask ales, then you can head to the back bar for a simple cozy room that's ideal for a quiet day's drinking—perhaps that's why it's long been a favorite of writers. Have a Deuchars IPA (but don't start a discussion

---

LOCAL TIP: **Order "a Hauf an' a Hauf"**

This is a half pint of a beer and a "wee dram" of Scotch—either a chaser for your beer or a long drink to chase down the whisky's flames. It's thought that years ago the combination of beer and whisky both quenched your thirst and got you drunk quicker. Now it's a traditional bar order, with a malty Scottish 80/- with a smooth blended whisky the starting point, but you can improve upon that, for sure. Scan the tap list, look at the whiskies lined up behind the bar, and see how successful you can be at ordering a half and a half.

Located on Edinburgh's Royal Mile, with views of the castle just up the hill, Deacon Brodie's is perfectly placed for a bit of liquid refreshment while exploring the Old Town's historic streets.

about whether it's a proper IPA or not). This is the beer brewed just across the city and is a malty-sweet, grainy, smooth brew with a similar aroma and flavor to the malt sweetness that blows through Edinburgh's streets from the nearby distillery.

There are many others, too: **The Standing Order** (62–66 George Street, Edinburgh EH2 2LR) is one of the most impressive Wetherspoon pubs (see page 73) you'll find—it's a converted old bank and it's cavernous. They also have a very broad range of Scottish beers. **Deacon Brodie's Tavern** (435 Lawnmarket, Edinburgh EH1 2NT) is named after the real-life inspiration for Dr Jekyll and Mr Hyde—Brodie was hanged on Lawnmarket. It's an ornate space right in the old town. And **Blue Blazer** (2 Spittal Street, Edinburgh EH3 9DX) is a charming old pub with a good range of well-kept Scottish ales. Basically, Edinburgh is excellent for many things, especially drinking—you should go.

Traquair House

WHERE THEY STILL BREW WITH EQUIPMENT FROM THE 18TH CENTURY

Traquair House, which was used as a hunting lodge for kings and queens 900 years ago, is Scotland's oldest inhabited house. The house has been in the Stewart family since 1491 and Catherine Maxwell Stewart is the 21st Lady of Traquair, living in the house with her family and being very active in telling its story—particularly the brewing side of things.

As was common centuries ago, large private houses had small personal breweries. Brewing took place in the Traquair kitchen until a more substantial brewery was added to what is the "newest" part of the house, built in 1694. There are still receipts in the house's inventory for the original 200-gallon (7.7bbl) copper, dating from 1736, plus wooden fermenting vessels made from Russian Memel oak. It's a substantial size for a domestic brewery, but notes from the time explain how a strong dark beer and a small table beer were brewed for

consumption by the house and surrounding estate staff, which numbered around 30 to 40 people, with some of the staff also partly paid in beer.

In the early 19th century, brewing stopped. A combination of new beer taxation and the increasing scale of commercial breweries meant the private brewery was no longer viable and the old brewing wing on the side of the house became a junk room. But not just any junk room; there was so much stuff stacked in the old brewery that it remained undiscovered

Unlike many spurious marketing campaigns trumpeting a brewery's heritage, Traquair House Ale offers you a genuine example of history in a glass.

for 150 years—a couple of Lords down the line from the brewing days literally had no idea there was even a brewery in the house. It wasn't rediscovered until 1964 when the 20th Laird, Peter Maxwell Stewart (Catherine's father), found it while preparing to open the house to the public. And what he dug out from under the junk was remarkable: the old copper, the oak fermenters, the original mash tun, a flat cooling tray, and all the brewing equipment—it's surely the best-preserved brewery of its age anywhere in the world.

Peter could've cleaned it up and simply left it on display, but thanks to his entrepreneurial brother they decided not to do that: they decided to brew beer with it. They spoke to Sandy Hunter from Belhaven Brewery and together they brought the equipment back to life and developed a recipe for a traditional, strong Scottish ale, the kind that would've been drunk when the domestic brewery was active. And in 1965 the first batch of beer—brewed with the original 18th-century equipment—was released in bottles.

They continued to brew using the old mash tun and copper until the 1990s, when they added a new brewhouse next door, but they've always fermented their beers in the oak barrels, more recently also adding two additional Canadian oak vessels (there's no discernible difference in the taste of beer from the Russian and Canadian fermenters). And it remains a proper old-school brewery: Frank Smith, the brewer, told me they only have one push button that turns a pump on or off, while temperature control involves opening a window or turning the heater on. Wonderfully, they also continue to use the 18th-century copper for occasional special brews.

As for processes, the beers are brewed with soft natural spring water from the house's estate, plus British malts and East Kent Golding hops. The beer has its fermentation in the oak barrels (the smell in that room is incredible: raisins, leather, stewed plums, old wood), then moves into larger conditioning tanks where it'll stay for six to eight weeks. The beers are bottled and pasteurized off-site and then returned to the brewery (it's been done this way ever since the first brew in 1965).

Traquair House Ale is the classic beer, rather similar to the kind of beer brewed there 300 years ago, and regarded as the beer style-guide defining example of a Scottish Ale. It's red-brown and 7.2% ABV; there's a deep raisin quality, some toasted malt loaf, and vanilla, but it's not shy with bitterness. There's a definite house taste, an earthy-woody quality beneath all the sweeter malts.

Jacobite Ale is inspired by an old recipe and uses coriander seeds. It's 8.0% ABV and dark brown, there's caramel, cola, and a real depth of dark malts which mix with a spiciness, some licorice, the floral coriander, and dry oak to give something almost medicinal—like a bitter, non-sweet root beer, which is also akin to whisky.

Bear Ale is a 5.0% ABV, amber-brown Bitter with some tangy, toasty malts and the floral and earthy depth of East Kent Golding hops. The name refers to the Bear Gates at the house, which were built at the end of the long driveway in 1739. Following a visit from Bonnie Prince Charlie in 1745, the 5th Earl closed the gates and promised that they'd stay shut until the Stuarts returned to the throne. The "Temporary Drive" has been used ever since.

In 2015 Traquair House celebrated the 50th anniversary of the brewery—something only a few other breweries will achieve in this decade. It's a remarkable brewery to visit, especially to see those old oak fermenters; they are one of the finest and rarest sights in the beer world and produce a truly classic Scottish beer—a beer that tastes of history.

The Lowdown

WHAT: Traquair House

HOW: The house is open to visitors from 1 April until the end of October. You can tour the house, gardens, and maze, and visit the brewery. There's a gift shop in the old malt store above the brewery where you can taste the beers and buy bottles to take away—the shop also has lots of old information about the brewery. There are rooms available if you wish to stay overnight (www.traquair.co.uk).

WHERE: Traquair House, Innerleithen, Peeblesshire EH44 6PW

Visit BrewDog HQ and DogTap

FROM YOUNG PUNKS TO WORLD BEER SUPERSTARS

BrewDog is the greatest success story in British craft brewing. Friends James Watt and Martin Dickie started BrewDog in 2007, and in just over a decade have achieved remarkable things: they employ 700 people; they have breweries in Aberdeenshire and Columbus, Ohio; there's a distillery, lots of barrel-aging, a sour beer side project; they've made a TV series; through their Equity for Punks crowdsourcing, they've had tens of thousands of investors, together raising millions of pounds; they have over 40 bars around the world; they've even been awarded MBEs by the Queen. It's incredible.

You can visit their brewery and DogTap taproom in Ellon, about 17 miles (27km) from Aberdeen (there's a direct public bus). They run tours so that you can see where the beer is made in their brewhouses, plus the distillery, warehouses, packaging, and offices, before ending up in the bar. To look back on the icy warehouse in a remote fishing village where it all started in 2007 and then to see the brilliant bright new brewery is remarkable—no other British craft brewery is close to where BrewDog are in terms of what they've built. And like them or not—because a lot of people don't love BrewDog—it's impossible not to be impressed when you see this place.

When you're there, try their flagship beer, Punk IPA. It's inspired by US craft brewing and it was one of the first of its kind made in Britain. After a Punk, see what specials they are serving on tap,

as they always have a rotation of new brews. And if you stay in Aberdeen, then there's a really good BrewDog bar there where you can try even more of their beers—my favorites are Elvis Juice, a grapefruit-infused IPA, and Jet Black Heart, a luscious nitro Stout. To paraphrase a huge neon sign in their brewery, Watt and Dickie are loving hops and living the dream.

The owners of BrewDog are the living embodiment of this mantra.

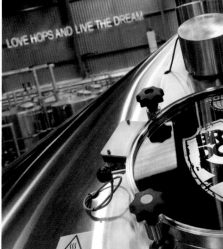

The Lowdown

WHAT: BrewDog DogTap and Brewery Tour

HOW: Tours take place on Monday to Wednesday (at 6pm), Thursday to Friday (at 4pm and 6pm), and Saturday to Sunday (at 12pm, 2pm, and 4pm). Book 48 hours ahead at www.brewdog.com.

WHERE: Balmacassie Industrial Estate, Ellon, Aberdeenshire AB41 8BX

Drink Harviestoun's Whisky Barrel-Aged Beers

THE PERFECT COMBINATION OF SCOTTISH BEER AND WHISKY

Harviestoun's Ola Dubh, pronounced "Ola-Doo" (which means "black oil" in Gaelic), was the first Scottish beer to link up with a Scottish whisky producer and create a range of whisky barrel-aged beers.

First released in 2008, Ola Dubh takes Harviestoun's recipe for their deliciously dark and velvety Old Engine Oil and beefs it up from 6.0% ABV to 10.5% ABV, then leaves it for a few months to mature in old whisky barrels from Highland Park, the highly regarded distillery on Orkney.

There are five expressions in the range, with the beer name referencing the age of the Highland Park whisky that was previously stored in the barrel: 12, 16, 18, 30, and 40. There are also occasional one-off special batches to look out for that come from different barrels.

It's no surprise that the Ola Dubh 30 and 40 are very rare. They are also some of the most complex and interesting barrel-aged beers you'll find. These are not thick, syrupy sweet brews; they are intense, dark, woody, spicy, edged with smoke, silky smooth, thought-provoking, engaging, drink-by-the-fireside beers. More commonly you'll find Ola Dubh 12, 16, and 18, which are all equally excellent and interesting, mixing that rich, chocolatey beer with the fine whiskies to give a warming, bourbon-like depth, coffee, peat smoke, oaky vanilla, and dark dried fruits, with each age revealing different complexities. It's the perfect Scottish combination and they come together to create an extraordinary drink—it's even better to have the beer with the corresponding whisky on the side to see just which characteristics are pulled from one to the other.

Harviestoun and Highland Park pioneered the use of Scottish whisky barrel-aging and they are among the best in the world at doing it.

Chasing Beer and Whisky

THE ULTIMATE SCOTTISH DRINKING TRIPS

It's common for beer-lovers to enjoy whisky as well, and Scotland gives us numerous opportunities to combine the two drinking pursuits, especially so on a couple of famous islands: Orkney and Islay.

Orkney has Highland Park and Scapa distilleries, plus two good breweries: Swannay and Orkney Brewery. Swannay brew excellent, modern pale and hoppy beers, fresh, vibrant, and smoothly rounded with malts, like their abundantly fruity Pale Ale. The Orkney beers are more traditional, with their famous Dark Island being a rich, hearty, malty ale and the Dark Island Reserve, a strong, Scotch whisky-matured beer.

Over on Islay, the different whisky distilleries are the main draw, but Islay Ales give you a break from the intensities of the heavily peated whiskies and refresh you with traditional British ales, many with lightly citrusy hop profiles. They also make Kilchoman Pale and Dark, both using malts from the Kilchoman Distillery to give a smoky, peaty, saline depth.

The Lowdown

WHAT: Guinness Storehouse

HOW: www.guinness-storehouse.com

WHERE: St James's Gate, Ushers, Dublin 8

Just the four taps of Guinness then.

Drink Guinness in Ireland

BECAUSE IT TASTES BETTER WHERE IT'S BREWED

Of course this is on the Beer Bucket List. It's a top-10 entry—or at least drinking in Dublin is essential and, if you're in Dublin, then you're going to drink at least one pint of Guinness.

Start at the Guinness Storehouse at St James's Gate, in the heart of the brewery, which is Ireland's most-visited tourist destination. There's a self-guided tour, which takes you up seven storys of the world's largest pint—the building is shaped like a beer glass. The tour itself is fine: some beer Disney, some old ads, a gift store; you'll learn some of the history, a bit about the brewing process, stuff like that. But it's the final destination that makes the tour worthwhile—the Gravity Bar at the top of the glass building, where you get a 360-degree view of Dublin and a fresh pint of Guinness.

While the view from the Gravity Bar is unsurpassed, and the beer is very good, the experience is soulless compared with the famous fun of a classic Irish pub, so descend, head back into town, and look for a few pubs where you'll get the proper Guinness experience.

The thing to know about Guinness is that it does taste better in Ireland than anywhere else. I thought this was nonsense until I went to Dublin and drank the beer fresh. And that's the key word: fresh. Guinness is a surprisingly delicate beer. Drink it in Ireland and it reveals unexpected fruity ester aromas, a lightness where most people think it's heavy, and a smooth, gentle, roasty bitterness. When it's not fresh, it can be fairly tasteless and bland, so the important thing is to find a pub that serves a lot of beer and serves it well.

Mulligan's (8 Poolbeg Street, Dublin 2; www.mulligans.ie) is a time capsule of Dublin's past, a dark pub built from old wood; it's intangibly wonderful to simply sit there with a beer or two and watch the world slowly pass by. **The Long Hall** (51 South Great George's Street, Dublin 2) is a beauty of an old Victorian pub—like drinking in an antique shop. **The Brazen Head** (20 Lower Bridge Street, Dublin 8; www.brazenhead.com) is Ireland's oldest pub (dating from 1198), which is worth visiting for that alone, but you'll stay for the beer and then the live music in the evening for that quintessential Dublin pub experience.

THE BEST OLD PUBS, BARS, AND BREWERIES

- The Beacon Hotel, West Midlands, England (see page 83)
- Traquair House, Peeblesshire, Scotland (see page 102)
- Mulligan's, Dublin, Ireland
- U Fleků, Prague, Czech Republic (see page 129)
- Hofbräuhaus, Munich, Germany (see page 113)
- Ølhallen, Tromsø, Norway (see page 156)
- McSorley's Old Ale House, Manhattan, New York (see page 18)
- The Royal Oak, Borough, London (see page 71)
- Café Vlissinghe, Bruges, Belgium (see page 148)
- In 't Aepjen, Amsterdam, The Netherlands (see page 154)

Cork City Beer Crawl

THE CRUCIBLE OF IRISH CRAFT BREWING

County Cork has three brewpubs: Franciscan Well, Rising Sons, and The Cotton Ball (a little out of the city center, but easily accessible); a brew-restaurant, Elbow Lane; plus specialty beer bars, The Friary and The Bierhaus. Cork also hosts the Easter Beer Festival, Ireland's longest-running craft beer fest held at Franciscan Well, which has since been joined by the Great Irish Beer Festival in September at Cork City Hall. Cork City is a compact, cosmopolitan, cultural, culinary, and cool place to visit and also a center of Irish craft beer. Note: I alliterated all of that without once saying the word "craic." Related: next time I'm in Cork City, I should head to Blarney Castle to kiss the famous stone, as it might help improve my currently lazy eloquence…

Note: With special thanks to **The Beer Nut** for help on this entry (I've essentially just copied and pasted what he wrote to me in an email and then added some filler). Read his excellent blog to learn everything you need to know about Irish beer (www.thebeernut.blogspot.co.uk).

Visit Galway Bay Brewery

DRINK SOME OF IRELAND'S BEST CRAFT BEERS

Head to the west of Ireland, to Galway Bay, for a paddle in the North Atlantic and a walk around the lovely little town, then go and drink some excellent local beers.

The Galway Bay Brewery began in the Oslo Bar down by the sea, a good walk from the center. Their beers are excellent, from the vibrantly hoppy Althea session ale to Buried At Sea, their smooth Milk Stout, to their beer geek-pleasing Of Foam and Fury Double IPA. Closer to town is The Salt House, which has another excellent selection of beers—up to 21 taps. If you can't make it to Galway Bay, the brewery also has a range of bars in the center of Dublin that you should look for, including The Brew Dock and The Black Sheep. More details here: www.galwaybaybrewery.com.

Alongside its core range, Galway Bay Brewery always have plenty of specials and seasonal brews available.

The Porterhouse, Dublin

DRINKING DUBLIN'S BEST STOUTS

Liam LaHart and Oliver Hughes made a bold decision in 1989: they would open a specialty beer bar in Bray, south of Dublin, and not serve Guinness. Instead they would import Belgian and German beers to sell. It was almost unthinkable and they later discovered that local bar owners had put bets on how long they'd stay in business; one gave them an optimistic two days.

As well as serving exceptional stouts, The Porterhouse also offers up some excellent live music.

Against the odds, things went well. In 1996, they opened a brewpub in Dublin's Temple Bar. It was the first brewpub in Ireland, and in the literal and figurative sense it was in the shadow of St James's Gate (see page 106). But far from avoiding dark beers, they showed their skills by brewing three of their own interpretations of Porter and Stout, each inspired by defunct Dublin brews: Plain, Oyster Stout (using real oysters), and Wrasslers 4X Stout.

The brewpub was a success and other bars followed: a cavernous pub in London's Covent Garden, another in Dublin, one in Cork, and then they took on the historic Fraunces Tavern in Manhattan.

All are worth the time and the effort to find them. I used to drink in the Covent Garden pub every time I was in London, always starting with one of the Porterhouse Stouts, then moving onto something unusual from the fridges. But the original Temple Bar brewpub (where they no longer brew, having moved that off-site) is the mecca of micro-brewed Stouts, so follow the path to their Plain Porter and enjoy it in the buzzing pub in the center of one of Europe's greatest drinking cities.

The Lowdown

WHAT: The Porterhouse

HOW: www.theporterhouse.ie

WHERE: The Porterhouse, 16–18 Parliament Street, Dublin 2

Chapter 3
Europe

Oktoberfest

THE WORLD'S GREATEST BEER EVENT

A deep roar is heard across the enormous tent, becoming louder as it gets nearer, the wave passing ever onward. People turn to the epicenter of the noise where a man, dressed in pine-green lederhosen, is standing on a bench with one arm raised heroically in the air holding his empty stein and the other arm wiping drips of beer from his beard. Within a few minutes of his sitting down, another cheer surges from across the other side of the tent.

This is Munich's Oktoberfest. Or at least it's one tiny moment of this massive festival—the greatest beer-drinking event in the world. From my seat, I can see thousands of people around me. Everyone is drinking amber lager, and everyone is smiling and laughing and talking with others. There's music, singing, pretzels, and roast chicken. I'm trying to take it all in, but it's just so big, so over the top, so unexpectedly amazing that I'm mostly just staring dumbly at what's going on around me. I'd held off coming here for years, not being especially drawn to it, but within minutes of arriving I'm loving it.

You've probably heard the story: the first ever event here, before it became the Oktoberfest we now know, took place on 12th October 1810 for the wedding of Crown Prince Ludwig and Princess Therese of Saxony-Hildburghausen. The party was so good, they repeated it the next year, with it evolving and growing annually. Beer was available at small stands from the beginning. The amusements arrived in later years. By 1896, the first large beer tent opened. Later they moved the festival forward to make use of September's warmer weather.

Today the festival is beyond astonishing. The 14 tents are like superstores, with the biggest capable of holding 12,000 people; the spaces between the tents are wide, busy boulevards; there's a fairground that's bigger than many stand-alone theme parks; there's also so much food, so much beer, and so many people—around six million people visit each year.

The "Big Six" Munich brewers—Augustiner, Hacker-Pschorr, Hofbräu, Löwenbräu, Paulaner, and Späten—each produce a special Oktoberfest lager for the event and all of these are a little different, though all the lagers are between 5.7% and 6.3% ABV. They are all good. My favorites are Hacker-Pschorr's, which is the darkest, the most bitter, the one with the deepest flavor, and Augustiner's, which is the smoothest, the creamiest, the one with the tastiest, toastiest malt—it is also notable because it's poured from 44-gallon (200-liter) wooden barrels. Each tent pours just one of the beers, so pick your tent based on what you want to drink. If you want a different beer, then go to a different tent.

Here's some extra stuff you need to know if you're visiting: the festival opens early in the morning, but it'll be full by lunchtime. The beer only comes in one-liter glasses and these cost around €11 each. Given the scale of the event, service is incredibly efficient and quick. When you enter a tent, it's your challenge to try and find somewhere to sit. When you do sit down, say hello to other people—it's a friendly festival. There are amusements and rollercoasters, so go on those before you drink too much. Eat lots of pretzels. And, ideally, don't stand on the bench and down your beer.

Oktoberfest isn't just a beer festival. It's the greatest drinking event in the world.

The Lowdown

WHAT: Oktoberfest

HOW: Takes place in mid-September for 16 days, opening at 10am on weekdays and 9am at weekends (www.oktoberfest.de).

WHERE: Theresienwiese, Munich, Germany

Augustiner Hell vom Fass

THE ESSENTIAL MUNICH LAGER

I could write thousands of words about drinking in Munich, but there are only five words that I personally think are fundamental: drink Augustiner Hell *vom fass* (or "on tap"). Even better: drink it *vom holzfass*—"from a wooden barrel."

Augustiner Hell is one of my favorite world lagers for how the malt is so powerful, yet so restrained, and for how the hops are deeply tucked within the beer, giving their bitterness and flavor without ever being overt—it's a lesson in balance and elegance, the kind of beer that can only be perfected after decades of dedicated brewing. It's also a quintessential taste of a real German Helles.

To be properly understood, you need to drink it on tap and near where it's brewed. When it comes from the wooden barrel—*vom holzfass*—there's a softness to the body, which makes it incredibly easy drinking and also enhances the fine German-hop aroma, easing the edges of bitterness and carbonation that a keg brings and giving it all a comforting roundness. After one gulp you'll already be contemplating your second glass.

There are several Augustiner pubs in Munich. The original **Augustiner Keller** (Arnulfstraße 52, 80335 Munich), which is a short walk from the Hauptbahnhof railway station, is a favorite in the summer, while the cavernous **Zum Augustiner** (Neuhauserstraße 27, 80331 Munich) in the center of town is a must-visit bar (look out for the Beer Hall side, as well as the different restaurant spaces).

Munich is one of the world's greatest beer cities. We all know that. And we all know that every beer-lover needs to go to Munich at least once in their lifetime to drink the different beers in the different beer halls and beer gardens, ticking off the "big six" Munich brewers. I want all of the other beers in Munich as well but, for me, Augustiner Hell is the one I want to drink first and the one I want to drink the most of.

Ask many beer geeks and they will tell you Augustiner make arguably the best Helles lager in the world.

Munich's Hofbräuhaus

THE MOST FAMOUS PUB IN THE WORLD?

This is probably the biggest pub you've ever seen. It's like a version of Oktoberfest that happens every day, with rows of benches lined with people sitting behind enormous glasses of lager and huge plates of meat. Or it's like the many, many German-themed pubs all around the world that try to recreate the Bavarian Beerhouse vibe—only in the Hofbräuhaus it's real.

Münchner justifiably proud of their brewing heritage, as demonstrated by the thousands of locals who gather to celebrate Munich beers at the Hofbräuhaus every week.

There's singing and laughter; it's always busy; and it's enormous (there's a capacity of around 5,000 people). You can drink their Helles or Dunkel; the latter is a great version of this type of lager, which most of the world thinks is rich and chocolatey with a roasted coffee bitterness, but it doesn't taste like that; it's like the easy-drinking Helles, just with a dusting of toast and a savory quality, almost as if the dark malt is only there to give the auburn-brown color. It's great with local sausages, but that's basically true of every German lager…

The Hofbräuhaus is infamous because of its place in Hitler's history (he held early Nazi meetings and later rallies there), but it's also famous for being a remarkable pub that serves excellent, traditional Munich lagers in a rarely rivaled atmosphere. None of those Beerhouse pretenders even comes close to this place.

The Lowdown

WHAT: Hofbräuhaus

HOW: www.hofbraeuhaus.de

WHERE: Platzl 9, 80331 Munich, Germany

Drink Genuine Zoiglbier

COMMUNAL BREWING IN THE OBERPFALZ

In the east of Bavaria, in the Oberpfalz or Upper Palatinate, which borders the Czech Republic, you'll find five small towns that are joined in one unique way: they each have a community brewhouse (*Kommunbrauhaus*), where a few citizens have brewing rights. Those citizens make beer and sell it in small bars (called *Zoiglstub'n*), which they open in or near their homes. The beer is Zoiglbier.

Zoigl continues a 600-year-old tradition whereby towns and citizens are given brewing rights and share a brewhouse, making beer for themselves or selling it to non-brewing citizens. Neuhaus was granted rights to brew in 1415, with six brewers remaining there today, while Eslarn, which has one brewer, is the most recent to get brewing rights—that happened back in 1522. There's also Falkenberg, which has two brewers, while Mitterteich has three and Windischeschenbach has seven brewing families. The brewers, who also typically have day jobs, pay *kesselgeld* or "kettle money" each time they use the brewhouse and then sell their beers (for around €2 for 18 oz/500ml). You can only get genuine Zoigl in the Zoiglstub'n run by the brewers, as they aren't sold anywhere else.

It's a unique story in the beer world: a small pocket of Germany where this system still exists and thrives. Also unique is how the beers are made: all the brewhouses are wood-fired, except in Mitterteich where they are heated by coal; the beer recipes have been passed down through the generations and use local barley and hops; once brewed, the liquid transfers to large, open cooling trays where the temperature drops overnight, before the brewers collect the liquid and take it back to

their homes to be fermented and conditioned until it's ready for serving. All the locals will have their *zoigltermine*, which is a calendar that says which Zoiglstub'n are open each weekend.

Traditional Zoigl is a bottom-fermented beer that's unfiltered and unpasteurized. Because of the processes used, and with each of the brewers having their own recipes, every Zoigl is different. However, there are similarities: it will be a hazy, copper-colored beer; it will have a toasty, full, and sometimes sweet malt flavor (a richness of malt typical of the lagers in this part of Germany); there will be a spicy, grassy hop quality, which might be gentle or very bitter; and they'll often have a rough edge from the fermentation, a hint of fruity-floral esters, or even buttery diacetyl. But Zoigl is far more than just the liquid: Zoigl is a community experience, one you can only get in the five Zoigl towns.

A night in the neighboring villages of Windischeschenbach and Neuhaus was one of the most fun drinking evenings of my life. Two Zoiglstub'n are open year-round in Windischeschenbach: **Oberpfälzer Hof** (Hauptstraße 1, 92670) and **Zum Weißen Schwanen** (Brunnenstraße 4, 56338), making this the best place to guarantee drinking Zoigl. Over in Neuhaus, visit **Schafferhof** (Burgstraße 6, 92670), where the beer is golden and smooth and the snacks are excellent. Back in Windisheschenbach we walked past the communal brewery, a yellow building in the center of town, before finishing in **Fiedlschneider** (Stadtplatz 15, 92670), a cozy bar packed with people. The beer was great, the service was friendly, the snacks were delicious, and we talked to people all around us. As others arrived and departed, they addressed the whole room, saying hello and goodbye to

The Lowdown

WHAT: Zoiglbier, a bottom-fermented beer unique to the Oberpfalz region of Bavaria

HOW: Nüremburg is the nearest airport to Oberpfalz, then look for the sign (see right.)

WHERE: Visit the towns of Eslarn, Falkenberg, Mitterteich, Neuhaus, and Windischeschenbach, Germany

Look for the Beer Sign

The tradition of opening your house to sell beer is said to have started when people accumulated excess that they wanted to use up. In the Oberpfalz or Upper Palatinate of Germany, they'd leave a bierzeigel or "beer sign," often a broom or brush, outside their homes to show that beer was available. In the local dialect zeigel becomes zoigl, and that's where the name comes from. Today's sign utilizes the traditional six-pointed brewers' star and only authorized Zoigl brewers and Zoiglstub'n can use it, so look for "Echter Zoigl vom Kommunbrauer"—and you know you're in the right place.

The sign translates as "genuine Zoigl from community brewers."

everyone. It's unlike anywhere else I've drunk beer before and that's what makes Zoigl such a wonderful experience. It is a community drink; it maintains centuries-old traditions; it's something to share with others; and the beers are unique in their varying tastes. Go and drink Zoigl at least once in your life.

All the information you need about Zoigl is on the official website: visit www.zoiglbier.de.

Munich's Starkbierfest

A MINI-OKTOBERFEST WITH A MUCH BIGGER HANGOVER

Rarely do you see people more drunk than "Oktoberfest Drunk." It's the Everest peak of drunkenness, one seemingly unattainable anywhere but in the tents at the Munich festival, but then you probably haven't seen what it's like to be "Starkbierfest Drunk."

Those Oktoberfest lagers are a watery 6% ABV compared to the 8% ABV Doppelbocks served at Munich's Starkbierfest—the Strong Beer Festival, which takes place from Ash Wednesday to Good Friday and is held mostly within the city's brauhauses. There's a monastic link to these brews and they originated with the monks who drank them during Lent to keep them going during fasting with some extra sweetness and calories. (Anyone who is counting should know that a stein of these "liquid bread" beers might contain over 600 calories in a mug.) Paulaner's Salvator is the famous original of these beers, so that's a good starting point. Just beware that these strong beers really are strong and a couple of liters can knock down even the biggest drinker.

The Lowdown

WHAT: Starkbierfest

HOW: Ash Wednesday to Good Friday.

WHERE: Beer halls across Munich, Germany

Forchheim's Annafest

THE WORLD'S LARGEST BEER GARDEN

To make great lagers, you need cold temperatures. Years ago in Forchheim, a town in Upper Franconia, almost exactly between Bamberg and Nüremberg, brewers dug cellars into the nearby soft sandstone hills to mature their beer, meaning they'd brew in the town and transfer the beer to age in the cellars, before taking it back to town to drink. But one day someone realized that the beer was cold in the cellars, but lost its refreshing coolness on arriving in town, which didn't make much sense. So they decided to go to the hills and drink in the shaded gardens around the cellars. They probably didn't expect that centuries later people would still be drinking there in what is now called "the world's largest beer garden."

Today the Kellerwald has 24 *kellers*, or "cellars," within 820ft (250m) of each other. Most of the cellars date back to the 18th century, but the oldest is from 1609. The underground spaces still exist, but it's the areas above ground that attract people to drink there. A handful of beer gardens and bars are open all year round, serving local beers (though there are far fewer open in the winter). However, every year, for a 10–11 day period centered on July 26th, they all open for Forchheim's **Annafest**, with 600,000 people visiting. (Good fact: there are 32,000 seats at Annafest, which is also the same number as the population of Forchheim.)

Annafest is a huge folk festival where every bar serves an Annafestbier—a strong, pale lager similar(ish) to Oktoberfestbier. There's music, food, and lots of fun, all in this unique environment on a hill above Forchheim surrounded by trees and above a network of beer cellars. Think of it as a small Oktoberfest and definitely one of the world's best drinking festivals.

But don't just go to Forchheim for Annafest… Forchheim has four breweries: Greif, Hebendanz, Eichhorn, and Neder. They all have restaurants or bars, although the opening hours can be a little unusual (sometimes closing from 2pm, even on a weekend). The Kellerwald is always open, especially in the summer, but it's best to check opening times first. Another fun fact: in Forchheim, they are able to say that they go up to the cellars to drink beer, as they're cut into the hills above the town—though this also means, of course, that they have to walk uphill to get there…

Some Franconian Beer Knowledge…

- This is a part of the world where breweries often serve beer in krugs or steinkrugs (meaning "stone mugs"). But if you can't see how much beer is left, then how do the bar staff know if you need another one or not?

- If you have a krug with a metal lid, then leaving the lid open means that you want another beer; if you leave the lid closed, then the barman will know you're still drinking.

- If you don't have a lid, then when you want another beer you need to lay your empty krug on its side. If you want a small beer—or schnitt, which is basically the half you have when you're leaving—then you need to try and balance the mug on its handle.

- And if you're ready to leave, then place your beer mat on top of your mug.

As well as being famous for beer, Forchheim is filled with historical gems and several buildings date back to the 14th century and beyond.

The breweries make a range of beers, but they often only have one on tap. At Greif that's a bright, golden Helles, while in Neder it's an Export, which is pale and rich with malt and spicy hops. They all typically have a fuller malt flavor than the beers of Munich, something more bready, or more amber in color, and then also more bitter— something generally characteristic of Franconian beer.

Why Annafest? The name comes from Saint Anna, Jesus's grandmother. The Church of St Anna is near Forchheim and on July 26th, the day of St Anna, people would make a pilgrimage to the church, stopping for beer in Forchheim on the way. The first version of Annafest was held in 1840. You can read more about Annafest here: www.annafest-forchheim.de.

Schlenkerla Tavern, Bamberg

SMOKING BREWS IN BEER'S MOST HANDSOME TOWN

Bamberg is an essential beer city to visit. It's undoubtedly one of the biggest draws for beer-lovers visiting Germany, a small place famous for its handsome old town hall, the UNESCO-listed center, the seven surrounding hills (each crowned with a church), the peaceful river, and the cathedral. There are also many liquid attractions, including nine breweries (at least, see opposite), plus the famous Rauchbiers, or smoked beers.

Centuries ago, barley was malted with a lick of flame, turning it a dark color and giving it a singed, smoky flavor. As maltsters found ways to produce paler malts and eliminate the smoke, that flavor largely disappeared from beers, but a couple of Bamberg brewers still make their malts using this old method to produce smoky lagers. Bamberg is seen as the home and heart of Rauchbier brewing.

The **Schlenkerla Tavern** is where you'll want to go to drink smoked beer. The tavern is run by Heller-Bräu Trum, but everyone knows the brewery, the beer, and the tavern by the name of Schlenkerla. Stepping inside is like walking into a bonfire: wood, flames, smoke, bacon. All around is wood, as well: dark wooden beams, wooden arches, wooden beer barrels, roasting and smoked meats.

Start with the brewery's flagship Märzen. It's a deep, dark purple-brown beer with a fat foam on top. The first impression from the aroma will inevitably be the smoke: think smoked ham and wood embers. The body is rich and smooth with deep smoky flavors, where it's both sweet and has a perception of savoriness. It's astonishing

and powerful and, while it might not be to everyone's taste, you should order a second just to be sure. And try it with food, as it's one of the world's greatest beer styles for food, adding an umami punch, especially to meaty dishes like sausages and steak.

Also in Bamberg is **Brauerei Spezial** (Obere Königstraße 10, 96052 Bamberg), the city's other Rauchbier brewer and another like Schlenkerla that has its own maltings. Spezial's smoked Märzen is lighter than Schlenkerla's in color and smoke; it's softly toasty, still dry and savory, with the smoke being sweeter and more immediately inviting. I prefer the Spezial Rauchbier over Schlenkerla's—the Spezial version is easier to drink and more subtle. They also have some unsmoked lagers on tap.

By the end of your second glass of Rauchbier you probably won't notice the smokiness in the beer anymore. Instead, you'll have a feeling that the whole world is now smoky, that everything smells like the heady fragrance of roasting meat and billowing smoke. Very few beer experiences are so evocative and very few beer towns are so nice to visit.

The Lowdown

WHAT: Schlenkerla Tavern

HOW: Nüremburg is the nearest airport to Bamberg, which is less than 50 minutes by train from Nüremburg's main station. Or it's a two-hour train journey from Munich. The tavern opening hours are 9.30am–11.30pm, with hot food served from midday (www.schlenkerla.de).

WHERE: Dominikanerstraße 6, 96049 Bamberg, Germany

Outside the Schlenkerla Tavern.

Bamberg's iconic *Altes Rathaus*.

Bamberg: the Ultimate Beer City

Bamberg has nine breweries in its small town center (or between eight and 11 breweries, depending on who you do and don't count). While it might be famous for its Rauchbier, a wider variety of beers are also brewed there. Two of the world's best-known maltsters are in Bamberg: Bamberger Mälzerei and Weyermann's. The city is within easy access of the hop-growing region of Germany. Kasper Schulz is a 10th-generation family business, which originated as a coppersmiths and now produces some of the world's top brewhouses. Bamberg really is a beer city.

For me, it's the malt that sets Bamberg's beers apart more than anything else—and this is something you'll find in many Franconian beers. Overlooking the Rauchbiers, the general pale lagers in the region are more amber in color than those from Munich; they have a rounder, richer malt depth and flavor, a fullness compared to Helles's light simplicity—Mahr's Brau's Ungespundet is a great example of this; it's a beer that's full with toasty, sweeter malts, satisfyingly rich, yet still refreshing. The hops are all there, too, and indeed some of Bamberg's beers stand out for their hop character, including Keesman's Herren Pils, which is extraordinarily bitter, but otherwise malt is at the heart of these beers.

Visit the World's Oldest Brewery

AND DRINK CLASSIC GERMAN WHEAT BEER

In Freising, 25 miles (40km) north of Munich, there has been a monastery on the hill of Holy St Stephen since the year 725. While beer was probably made there before 1040, this was the year Weihenstephaner officially received the rights to brew beer commercially, allowing them to claim that they are the world's oldest continually operating brewery.

It hasn't always been easy for them: the brewery was completely burned down four times; it was destroyed or depopulated by three plagues, several famines, wars, and even a great earthquake, plus the secularization of the monastery in 1803 also caused problems, but through every catastrophe they rebuilt and moved forward and continued to make beer—although the fact that they've ceased brewing numerous times does allow other almost-as-old brewers to suggest that Weihenstephaner hasn't necessarily been brewed *continually*.

The world's foremost brewing school is based at the Technical University of Munich and shares Weihenstephaner's campus, meaning that many of the world's qualified brewmasters learnt their skills from this brewery. Today you can visit the charming campus, stroll around the leafy grounds, and see the large, yellow brewery on top of the hill. Plus, you can go to the restaurant and drink some beers alongside some hearty German food.

Brewing may have taken place there for a long time, but Weihenstephaner is definitely a modern brewery and the world's foremost brewer of Hefeweizen—German wheat beer. Their standard Hefe Weissbier is the classic of its type: pale gold, handsomely hazy, with a thick whip of white foam on top, where its distinctive yeast gives you banana, vanilla, and a creamy texture; and it all finishes refreshing and light for the beer's 5.4% ABV. Ideally, you should arrive early and have the beer with some weisswurst ("white sausage"), served with a pretzel and mustard.

Go to (what is probably, or arguably) the world's oldest brewery and drink one of the world's most famous beer styles.

The Lowdown

WHAT: Weihenstephaner Brewery

HOW: Open daily from 10am
www.weihenstephaner.de

WHERE: Alte Akademie 2, 85354 Freising, Germany

Are There Other Contenders for the Title of World's Oldest Brewery?

50 miles (80km) north of Freising is Weltenberg Abbey, in Kelheim, a postcard-pretty monastery on the bend of the River Danube. (By the way, if you're in Kelheim, then this is also home to Schneider-Weiss—like Weihenstephaner, this is another of the world's great Hefeweizen brewers.) There's been a Benedictine monastery at Kelheim since 620 and they have brewed beer commercially and continuously there since 1050 (probably making them the oldest monastic brewer in the world). They have a restaurant and beer garden where you should drink their Asam Bock, a rich amber lager with soft, mouth-filling malts, a sweet bready depth, and a long, dry finish.

Drink Craft Beer in Berlin

BEER THINGS TO DO IN GERMANY'S CAPITAL CITY

Berlin does not have the postcard Oktoberfest oompah of Bavaria. Instead, you go to Berlin for the best in modern German beer and food, and also to visit a fun, liberal city where craft beer has changed the drinking environment to create Germany's most progressive and varied beer destination. Try out the following bars and brewpubs in this great city.

It's hard to beat the experience of enjoying beer outside during the Berlin summer.

Visit **Markthalle** IX (Eisenbahnstraße 42–43, 10997 Berlin) for exceptional HeidenPeters beers with delicious street food. The beers change often, but you can rely on some great hop-forward brews—just check the limited opening hours before you go. Nearby is **Hopfenreich**, one of the best craft beer bars in town, and you're also close to **Burgermeister**, a very good burger joint in a converted public restroom beneath the elevated Berlin U-bahn tracks.

Go to **Stone Brewing World Bistro & Gardens** (Im Marienpark 23, 12107 Berlin). It's a vast, barely believable brewing and drinking space in the south of the city, and includes some gorgeous gardens. San Diego's Stone Brewing (see page 49) make all of their famous Californian beers here, plus a few local specials. You'll also find good guest beer and an American-accented menu with a few German inflections. They offer tours daily, but check the times before you go.

Drink at the city's many brewpubs, where you can sip traditional Helles, Dunkel, Hefe, or Pils, or find the latest liquid beer trends. I've always loved **Eschenbräu** (Triftstraße 67, 13353 Berlin) for their straight-up lagers; nearby is **Vagabund** who brew big hoppy beers on a small-scale kit—their taproom is fun and has good guest beers on tap; **Straßenbräu** (Neue Bahnhofstraße 30, 10245 Berlin), in Friedrichshain, has a large range of beers in its busy, bare-bricks-and-blackboards taproom; and look out for **BrewBaker's** (Sickingenstraße 9–13, 10553 Berlin) and their range of Berliner Weisses (though they don't have a taproom).

Gloriously—and especially on a sunny day because Berlin is unbeatable on a sunny day—you can buy bottles of world-class lager from corner stores for €1 and drink them on the streets. There's something liberating about that, especially if you're heading to a park to sit and chill in the warm weather (because day-drinking is also fine in Berlin).

Drinking the Regional Beers of Germany

IT'S A LAGER-LOVER'S DREAM

A consistent desire while writing this book was to drink the various beer styles in their hometowns. To do this is to gain a greater understanding of how the classic versions of these beers taste, to learn how people enjoy them locally, to see their influence locally, and then to try and understand their place in the rest of the world. With northern Europe being the old world of brewing, it's there that most of these traditional beers can be found.

Germany is especially interesting to travel around, as there are great regional differences in the beers, depending on where you drink: in the north, the lagers are crisp, light, bitter, lean, and dry; in Upper Franconia, the amber lagers are rich in malt and round in the middle; around Munich, the Helles lagers are smooth and toasty, elegant and gluggable; while the Dunkel lagers are smooth with darker malts, but certainly not dark or coffee-like in flavor, especially when compared with the drier, roasted Schwarzbiers of central north Germany.

Then there are the idiosyncrasies: Bamberg's smoked beers, the sour wheat beers of Leipzig and Berlin, the occasional Franconian red or brown lager, and the community-brewed Zoiglbiers of the Oberpfalz (see page 114). Then there's Kölsch and Altbier, from Cologne and Düsseldorf, respectively, in the North Rhine-Westphalia, in the west of Germany. To travel around the whole of Germany and to drink locally is to taste a wide variety of traditional beers.

A small selection of the range of beers on the German brewing scene.

Altbier in Düsseldorf and Kölsch in Cologne

LOCAL BEER STYLES AND A UNIQUE LOCAL RIVALRY

Düsseldorf has its brown Altbiers. They are toasty with dark malts and most are very bitter and dry. The name refers to the old style of ales long-brewed in this part of the world and the town's resolution to stick to their traditional beer style, as pale lager spread around Germany.

Just 25 miles (40km) away in the cathedral city of Cologne, you'll find Kölsch, gleaming gold, light, refreshing, and delicately hoppy; while these may look like lagers, they are brewed as ales. As with Altbier, Kölsch was a local backlash against pale lager's dominance, where they stuck with their local top-fermented style.

Drink in Düsseldorf and small glasses of brown Altbier are almost exclusively what you'll see; go to Cologne and it'll just be golden Kölsch. Nowhere else in the beer world does one unique type of beer dominate such a small, parochial area in the same way as these two beers in these two neighboring cities. The love-hate relationship between the two cities is built on their beers (but goes way deeper), so don't even think about trying to order an Altbier in Cologne, or vice versa.

Part of the fun of these beers is how they're served: they come in small 7fl-oz (200-ml) glasses, handed to you by köbes who carry the full glasses on trays, whipping away the empties as soon as you take your last sip. And both cities do this, meaning they're actually ironically similar for two places that want to make out they're very different.

Drinking Altbier in Düsseldorf and Kölsch in Cologne are two unmissable stops on a world-beer tour. The styles have become popular around the world—especially the clean, crisp Kölsch—but to drink them in their hometowns, where the beers are objects of delicious local pride, is to gain a wonderful insight into both the beers and the places. Plus, the cities are very nice to visit and easily explored on foot, meaning

Früh is an ever-present on the streets of Cologne.

you can drink in a lot of different breweries and bars.

There is a lot more to the story of Kölsch versus Altbier, but, if you do decide to visit, then my top beer in each place is the snappy, aromatic, and bitter Kölsch in Päffgen, which is served from wooden barrels, while in Düsseldorf I love how the refreshing bitterness of Schlüssel's Altbier balances the toasty, toffee, and earthy malts.

LOCAL TIP: **Where to Drink**

In Düsseldorf you will find great Altbier at **Brauerei Schumacher**, **Uerige** beer hall, and **Zum Schlüssel** brauhaus. The latter is on Bolkerstraße, known locally as the "largest bar top in the world." In Cologne, be sure to pay a visit to **Früh am Dom**, **Päffgen** brauhaus, and **Brausteller**, one of Germany's smallest and most unusual breweries.

Drink Baltic Porter in Poland

AND CELEBRATE BALTIC PORTER DAY

Porter is among the most storied drinks and once the world's greatest beer. It has its home in London, but its popularity reached around the world, with stronger export versions sailing everywhere, including the Caribbean, India, and through the Baltic seas—it's the Baltic journeys that we're interested in here.

These chilly countries presumably enjoyed the warming richness of strong Porter, which also further benefited from a long, slow, cold maturation at sea, mellowing into a finer beer. Initially imported, it was eventually brewed domestically, with the British Dark Ale being transformed by Germanic brewing traditions into a dark, strong lager, with the bottom-fermenting yeast loving the extended cold conditioning and allowing it to mature majestically. It was a staple beer in these countries, primarily—and now patriotically so—in Poland.

For a long time it was only the big brewers that made Baltic Porters in Poland, producing one alongside their more standard pale lagers, but now craft brewers are making them as well, improving them, evolving them, and championing them, and it's these smaller brewers who are making Baltic Porter world-famous again.

Every January, bars around Poland—and further afield—take part in Baltic Porter Day,

which is a celebration of the style. The event first took place in 2016 and grew significantly in 2017. It was the brainchild of Marcin Chmielarz. "Baltic Porter is something that's ours," he told me in Jabeerwocky, a world-class beer bar in Warsaw. His dream is for every Polish brewer to make a Baltic Porter and further enhance this as Poland's national beer.

Most Polish Baltic Porters are lagers, but not exclusively so—and, in fact, Marcin doesn't think they have to be lagers. For him, what matters is the processing and flavor profile, where a long, cold maturation mellows out the beer, leaving something powerful but still with a clean-finishing elegance.

Marcin's aim with Baltic Porter Day is to "make people see the importance of this beer as a Polish style." And it's a great celebration. I went to Warsaw and drank many excellent Baltic Porters, each of them varied and different, some sweeter, some more bitter, some vinous, some smoky, some bready, but all smooth and satisfyingly rich to drink and all with a deft and surprising lightness at the end, which makes them so drinkable—that's where the lagering shows itself best.

Poland is the best place to try the best versions of Baltic Porter and January is the best time to go if you want to try as many as possible.

When the cold weather comes, there's no better place to enjoy Baltic Porter than in Warsaw's Jabeerwocky.

Three Baltic Porters to Try

Kormoran's Imperium Prunum is extraordinary. It's an Imperial Baltic Porter brewed with suska sechlońska, which are smoked dried plums, and has a Protected Geographical Indication (PGI) from a small village in the south of Poland—it has a sort of comforting, familiar taste for many Polish people. The beer has a big smoke and plummy aroma. It's rich and sweet at first, like eating a cherry praline by a roaring fire; it's deliciously complex, then it finishes unbelievably light for an 11.0% ABV beer, a product of its extra-long maturation. It's vinous and one of the most wine-like beers I've had, being similar in texture to a mouth-filling Malbec. Its rareness and high online rating also add to its appeal.

Browar Podgórz's 652m n.p.m. is more common than Imperium Prunum. It has a lighter 8.0% ABV, but is no less worthy of attention. In fact, it's probably more worthy,

as this is a perfect, straight-up example of Baltic Porter—lots of caramel, milk chocolate, mocha, dried and dark fruits, skipping the roasted coffee-like bitterness you typically find in Imperial Stouts. It drinks very light for its strength, with a creaminess that I like a lot. For me this is the template for a Baltic Porter and is exemplary for its easy-drinking lightness—that really is a key quality of this style.

Żywiec Porter (pronounced something like zhiv-ee-ets) is worth trying since it's excellent, but also because it's one of the original and longest-lasting Baltic Porters, being first brewed in 1881. It's a hefty 9.5% ABV but, again, the long, cold maturation leaves you with an elegant, light, and somehow refreshing beer that's robust in flavor, with light coffee and smooth chocolate. It's a good starting point for seeing the directions the Polish craft brewers will take this style.

Great Bars To Drink in Warsaw

Warsaw surprised me with the variety and quality of its beers and bars—add it to your list of European beer cities that are worth visiting. The city is great because it's fairly small and cheap, and also because there's not a huge amount of touristy stuff to see, so you really can just focus on drinking excellent beer (as with most places, there's a concentration on IPAs, but still lots of variety) and eating lots of hearty Polish food.

- **Jabeerwocky** (Nowogrodzka 12, 00–511 Warsaw) has 17 well-picked taps, mostly Polish, with a big, bright beer board giving plenty of information about what's on tap—you can order three sizes of pour and they do flights if you want to try a few. Staff are very good, too.

- **Kufle i Kaplse** (Nowogrodzka 25, 00–511 Warsaw), just down the street from Jabeerwocky, is a bare-brick kind of industrial space with sofas and soft furnishings out the back on a raised level. LArge front windows make it bright in the day, while the sofas and old lamps make it cozy at night. Lots of Polish beers on tap, a cool space, and a good atmosphere.

- In the old town, by the Barbakan, is **Same Krafty Multitap** (Nowomiejska 10, 00–001 Warsaw) and opposite is **Same Krafty Vis-a-Vis**. The Multitap has a central bar out the back and a small space in front where people eat pizzas and choose from the many taps of mostly Polish beers. Vis-a-Vis is more of a straight-up beer bar. The list of Polish beers ranges from perky Pale Ales to potent Porters. Go to both, as the beer lists are different.

Drink Pilsner Urquell, the Original Golden Lager

AND DRINK IT UNFILTERED IN THE BREWERY CELLARS IN PILSEN

Pilsner Urquell is the world's original golden lager, first brewed in 1842 in the Czech city of Pilsen, 56 miles (90km) west of Prague. It's perhaps the greatest and most important beer ever brewed, and to visit the brewery and drink the unfiltered beer straight from huge wooden barrels in the underground cellars is undoubtedly one of the Top 10 most essential world beer experiences—and I'd probably put it at number one.

The story begins in 1838. There were 250 people with rights to brew in Pilsen, using a communal brewhouse and then drinking their beer or selling it (like Zoiglbier—see page 114). But much of the beer was undrinkable and the local tavern owners were sick of bad beer and worried about the growing imports of cheaper, tastier Bavarian dark lagers. Then one day, 36 barrels of disgusting dark ale were dumped into the city's drains.

It was one of the most significant moments in beer's 10,000-year history because this expedited discussions to build one large brewery for the town, to be owned by the people of Pilsen, and one which could make excellent beer that was also affordable—it was an early shift from small-scale communal brewing to industrial brewing.

The people of Pilsen hired a young architect, Martin Stelzer, who traveled to Bavaria to learn about their breweries, while a Bavarian called Josef Groll got the job of brewmaster. What makes the story really interesting are the processes and decisions made by Stelzer, Groll, and the Pilsen citizens, plus the unique geographical quirks, which all combined to create the world's first golden lager.

They built the brewery on soft sandstone, so were able to dig deep cellars beneath the brewhouse where the beer could be stored in large wooden barrels at cold temperatures (to make great lager, you need these cold temperatures); they had a natural and very soft water source, which was virtually mineral-free and perfect for brewing lager; they received

a good batch of lager yeast from Bavaria, probably thanks to Groll; they were able to get local Czech hops which were deeply aromatic; and, fundamentally, they used a new malting process, something pioneered in Britain and which was slowly being used in Germany and Austria, to produce pale malts instead of dark ones.

Put more simply: soft water, pale malts, fragrant hops, clean lager yeast, cold cellars, and knowledge of Bavarian lager-brewing techniques. All of these factors had to come together to create the world's first golden lager and that happened on October 5th 1842 when Josef Groll brewed the first batch of beer at the new Citizens' Brewery in Pilsen. It was ready to drink on November 11th 1842 and was an immediate success in the town.

We take bright golden lagers for granted today because the style has been aped around the world, but over 175 years ago this was an industry-defining moment that quickly spread change throughout Europe and then America. By the end of the 19th century, pale and amber lagers were known worldwide.

What's great is how the brewery has preserved its heritage, continuing to brew as closely as possible to the way Groll did, meaning the original Pilsner is still brewed in the original way. For example, they still use copper kettles when most other breweries use steel; those kettles are wood-fired, creating a hot spot that gives a caramelized quality to the malts, which is amplified by the brew going through a triple decoction, taking a portion of

If you have to chose just one experience to try from this book, make it this one.

the wort and grain out of the mash tun and rapidly boiling it before returning it to the rest of the mash. They still use Czech Saaz hops, where the beer's 39 units of bitterness require a very large amount of these subtle, fragrant hops to be added. They still have a similar timescale from when the beer is brewed to when the beer is ready to drink (about five weeks). The brewery still employs a team of coopers to produce and repair the wooden barrels. And, while most of the Pilsner might now be matured in steel instead of wood, they have maintained that traditional wood-fired element of the beer's history and this is the part that's the truly unmissable world-beer experience.

Today when you visit the brewery and go on the tour, you end up in the old brewery cellars—at their peak there were 5½ miles (9km) of cellars cut under the city, where everything after brewing and before drinking took place. To preserve the history, the brewery still ferments and matures beer in large wooden barrels down there, and to stand in the cold, damp cellars, to be deep underground surrounded by history and old wooden barrels filled with beer, is to get a very rare insight into what beer would have been like in the 19th century. The unfiltered Pilsner Urquell in the

brewery cellars is lightly hazy; it has a thick, white foam that holds all those wonderful Saaz hop aromas; the body is smooth, rich, yet very bitter and refreshing. This is the closest we'll get to drinking what Josef Groll presented to the people of Pilsen in 1842.

It's the setting and the story that make Pilsner Urquell brewery so special: thousands of people have worked underground there, while millions more have drunk the original golden lager they produced—the brew that changed beer forever. It's a special beer, a hallowed brewing location, and the ultimate Beer Bucket List tick.

The Lowdown

WHAT: Pilsner Urquell Brewery

HOW: Guided 90-minute tours throughout the day. Pilsen is a 90-minute train ride from Prague's central station. If you want more of the unfiltered beer, then Na Parkánu, in Pilsen, serves it year-round (www.prazdrojvisit.cz).

WHERE: U Prazdroje 7, 304 97 Pilsen, Czech Republic

Drink Polotmavý

CZECH SEMI-DARK LAGER

No other country makes pale lagers like the Czechs and you need to go and drink a variety to really understand what pale Czech lager is really like—the round malts, some caramelization, the bitter-sweet balance between hop and malt, the fragrance of Saaz hops.

These lagers are not at all like the famous German Helles or Pils (though there are some similarities between Czech pale lager and the malty lagers of Upper Franconia). Yet while pale lagers are what the Czechs are most famous for, I think there's another style you should drink there: Polotmavý. This "semi-dark lager" is uniquely Czech. It's amber-ish in color; there's toffee and toasty malts, a hint of roasted nuttiness, then more of those superb Saaz hops with their floral, spicy, lemon-pith, and grassy aromas. My favorite is produced by the Klášterní Pivovar Strahov brewery in Prague. It's gloriously smooth with malt, then sharp with hops, and has that essential Czech see-saw balance of bitter-sweetness.

The Lowdown

WHAT: Klášterní Pivovar Strahov Brewery

HOW: www.klasterni-pivovar.cz

WHERE: Strahovské nádvoří 301/10, 118 00 Prague 1, Czech Republic

Four Great Czech Lagers to Look For

The Czech Republic is one of my favorite places to drink and I always want to find great lagers there. To me, they are the most interesting and exciting beers; they're beers to sit down and drink by the half liter (16-oz glass), preferably a few in a row, because you can't get their greatness in a sip and it takes several glasses to properly understand what makes them so good.

- **Únětické** have a filtered 10° and 12° lager, plus an unfiltered 10.7°and all versions are good. I prefer the 10° beer for its classic flavor of golden Czech lager and the lighter, leaner, crisper body.

- **Břevnovský Benedict Světlý Ležák** has a dense white head, as well as grassy, spicy Saaz hop aromas and bitterness, plus some sweeter malts to balance those hops.

- **Beer Factory Světlý Ležák** is a classic Pilsner-style beer brewed in Pilsen by an ex-Pilsner brewmaster. People say it's like Pilsner Urquell used to be years ago. I say that it's delicious and a must-visit stop in that great brewing city.

- **Dalešické 11°** has a lighter body than the others, but still a nice creaminess with that typical thick foam. The hops give a lovely, lemony, spicy quality.

Pivo, meaning beer, is the only Czech word you need to know.

Visit U Fleků, Prague's 500-year-old Brewery

AND DRINK ONE OF THE WORLD'S GREATEST DARK BEERS

The chunky mug of almost-black beer, complete with custard-thick foam, is thumped onto the table in front of you as the server scratches pencil ticks on your beermat (helping both you and he keep count of how many you've had). This is the only beer they make at U Fleků — a Prague pub that's been brewing beer since 1499—but the beer is so good that you'll quickly forget that other beers even exist.

The beer is called Flekovský Ležák 13°, but you don't need to worry about that. At U Fleků, just say "pivo" (or "beer") and this is what you'll get. Expect brown bread, cocoa, dried fruit, and cola. It's supremely balanced, being both sweet enough to really please you with its round mouthfeel, then dry and bitter enough to sate and make you want more. It's a quintessentially Czech dark lager that's very different from Munich Dunkels, and has a taste you'll rarely find anywhere else.

The restaurant is remarkable and enormous. There are drinking spaces throughout, big dining rooms, a large and leafy garden, and smaller rooms hidden away. There's traditional Czech food, the kind that fills your stomach (dumplings are basically beer sponges); there are waiters carrying trays of the black beer and shots of local spirits (don't drink the shots); and there'll be a musician somewhere, probably with an accordion. If you're really lucky, you'll be able to smell the beer brewing, a gloriously bready, heady aroma of dark malt and fragrant Czech hops.

You can only drink this beer in this pub and they serve around 2,000 glasses of it a day. It's one of the world's great dark beers and a brilliant Czech drinking experience.

The Lowdown

WHAT: U Fleků

HOW: www.en.ufleku.cz

WHERE: Křemencova 1651/11, 110 00 Prague 1, Czech Republic

They may serve only one beer at U Fleků, but when it's one of the world's great dark beers the lack of choice is understandable.

The Beer Spa

WHERE YOU LITERALLY SIT IN A BATH OF WARM BEER

I was dubious at first, especially when I was handed a towel and abruptly instructed by the attendant to "Go there, take off clothes, wait."

Unsure of whether to wear swim shorts or not, I took a chance and left them in my bag along with the rest of my clothes. Then I waited. And it was exactly then that I questioned my actions. I love beer. I travel to try as much of it as I can, to experience different cultures, to see the world through the prism of my favorite drink, but did I want to sit in a bath of beer?

An hour later and I had the answer: a resounding "yes." Yes, I do want to sit in a warm bath of dark lager—with added hop flowers, brewing yeast, and crushed herbs. They even gave me a house-brewed, unfiltered lager to drink while I was in the bath.

There are health benefits to this: your heart rate gently rises to increase circulation; the pores of the skin are opened and you'll sweat out "unhealthy substances;" the hops and herbs, plus a light carbonation, are exfoliating; the beer gives B vitamins; and the beer you drink is "good for your digestive system." Maybe this sounds like nonsense—it probably is nonsense—but it's great fun. After 20 minutes you get out and they tell you not to shower (don't worry, you won't be sticky), to allow the purifying effects of the liquid to soak into your soon-to-be super-soft skin. Then they leave you to relax in a dark, quiet room for a short time, letting you gently drift into a beery sleep.

There are numerous beer spas around the Czech Republic. I experienced one at Chodovar, a brewery with a spa, restaurant, and hotel in the very west of the country. Closer to Prague is the Bernard Beer Spa, which comes with unlimited beer while you bathe. More details at www.pivnilaznebernard.cz/en.

The Lowdown

WHAT: Chodovar Beer Spa

HOW: Chodovar is 100 miles (160km) west of Prague—the route takes you via Pilsen, home to a beer spa and hotel at Purkmistr Brewery. You can share a bath with a friend if that's your thing (www.chodovar.cz).

WHERE: Pivovarská 107, 348 13 Chodová Planá, Czech Republic

Four Czech Craft Beers To Look For

Czech brewers understand balance better than any others. They've grown up with their excellent pale lagers and their balance between malt and hop, and they've translated that essential Czech quality into modern craft beer styles such as Pale Ale and IPA. The four breweries listed here all make excellent beers across broad styles.

- Matuška are the stars of Czech craft brewing and their **Apollo Galaxy** is a perfect example of bold malts meeting bold, juicy, fruity hops, and it all working wonderfully well.

- **Raven's Cream Porter** is brewed in Pilsen and often on tap at the excellent Francis beer bar off the town square. It's silky, luscious, and smooth, and one of the best beers of its kind you'll find brewed anywhere in the world.

- **Pivovar Zhůřák beers** are brewed by an American, 15½ miles (25km) south of Pilsen. All the styles are covered, with the Stouts and IPAs being especially good. This is another great brewer to find at the Francis beer bar in Pilsen.

- **Falkon Idiot IPA** is piney, grassy, tangy, citrusy, and tropical, with a soft, smooth golden body that illuminates all of the US hops used.

Drink Vienna Lager in Vienna

IT'S HARDER THAN YOU THINK...

We can thank Anton Dreher for Vienna Lager. It was a road-trip visiting European breweries with Munich's Gabriel Sedlmayr (see page 162) that showed both guys different malting and brewing techniques and enabled them to produce paler malts than they had previously used. Each of them named those malts after their home cities and each brewed rich amber beers—which were a change from the typical dark lagers.

Dreher's beer was a success and the taste for paler lagers quickly spread. We can link this to the birth of golden lager in Pilsen, to the beers that emigré brewers were making in America in the 19th century—and which craft brewers still make today—and, a little more unexpectedly, to a taste for those amber lagers in Mexico.

Today if we say "Vienna Lager" to a beer drinker or brewer, they have a certain expectation of an amber-ish color, a toasty and nutty body, and a clean, dry finish, probably with an ABV in the 5.0% range.

A glass of Vienna lager being poured. If you find a bar selling this style, make sure you stick around as it might be the only chance you get to try the increasingly rare lager being served in its home town.

But go to Vienna and it's almost impossible to find a "Vienna Lager." Through the flows of beer history, styles and tastes have changed, following fashions and cultural shifts. For Vienna Lager it transposed to Märzen (with some links to Oktoberfest, though probably via German brewers and not Austrian ones), a style that is, in essence, very similar. And you can find Märzen in Vienna—it's a core beer for many breweries—and, in fact, these have more likely become Vienna's beer, or Vienna Lager (it's all just semantics, really).

For the best we can put forward as Vienna Lager, there's Ottakringer's Wiener Original, which uses Vienna malt and Saaz hops, and is based on a recipe that's over 100 years old. Or there's Schwechater's Weiner Lager, a new brew from the originators of this style. It's toasty and deeply bitter, with a lovely chewy malt body.

As for the Märzens, which you should try, look to the Salm Bräu brewery for one of the best examples of what is a more typical Vienna-style lager. It has a full and smooth richness from the colored malts, that toasty nuttiness, a powerful flavor (thanks to being over 5.0% ABV), and the distinctive depth and complexity of noble hops.

What the craft beer world thinks of as Vienna Lager is unlikely to be what the beers of old would've tasted like—it's a modern interpretation of the style, forged by beers like Brooklyn Lager and Great Lakes Eliot Ness. To drink a Vienna or Märzen in its home city is to find a lager that's elegant, yet still has a great, expressive flavor from the malts, which is what ultimately makes these beers special. Just don't go to Vienna expecting to see lots of beer called Vienna Lager.

Augustinerbräu Kloster Mülln, Salzburg

EXPERIENCE AUSTRIA'S BIGGEST BEER HALL, SERVING BEER AS IT WOULD HAVE BEEN TWO CENTURIES AGO

I found my new favorite beer hall. It's on the edge of Salzburg, pretty much dug into the large hill that runs from the fortress banking the city to the monastery which houses the brewery.

It's a traditional style of beer hall, exactly the kind of thing you imagine when you read old reports of Bavarian beer houses from the 19th century. In the middle of the huge venue are large cabinets of gray stone beer mugs—half liter or one liter, take your pick. Next to these is a fountain of water where you can rinse your mug. Even though the mugs are already clean, everyone still gives them a rinse, just like they would've done 150 years ago when you picked up a dirty mug from the table to get it filled. Next, you come to a cashier. You can order beer or a bottle of soft drink, that's all. You pay, get a ticket or receipt, and hand that piece of paper to the bloke stood next to a big wooden barrel, who will fill your mug for you. They only have one beer most of the time and it comes out of a 200-liter barrel, where it'll froth over the top of your mug and make the floor around you sticky. It has a unique charm.

The beer is wonderful. A 4.6% ABV Austrian Märzen that's a hazy amber lager with smooth and toasty malts, it's one of the most gulpable beers you'll ever find. I stopped by the brewery to have just the one half-liter mug and left an hour later having had two liters of beer. I then went back the next day.

When you've got your beer, you can find a seat in one of the many dark and traditional beer halls or head into the large beer garden sheltered from sun or rain by tall chestnut trees. If you're hungry, there's no table service here, instead you go back inside to an arcade of food stalls: a butcher, a cheese seller, a baker, a man spiral-cutting radishes. These are all independent to the brewery, so you buy your beer and food separately.

Augustinerbräu in Salzburg is the closest you'll now find to what the beer halls and gardens of the past were like 200 years ago in Bavaria or this area of the world. It's wonderful to see and experience and it truly is one of the greatest beer halls in the world.

Patrons rinse their stone beer mugs before heading to the bar to drink lager served from a traditional wooden barrel.

The Lowdown

WHAT: Augustiner Brewery Beer Hall

HOW: Open from 3pm–11pm Monday to Friday, 2.30pm–11pm on weekends (www.augustinerbier.at)

WHERE: Lindhofstraße 7, 5020 Salzburg, Austria

Drink Tipopils at Birrificio Italiano

THE HOME OF ITALIAN PILSNER

For my book, *The Best Beer in the World*, I went around the globe in search of the greatest beers and stories, but in my head I was saving one place until last, and that was Birrificio Italiano, in Lurago Marinone, north of Milan. Agostino Arioli started the brewery in 1996, making it one of the oldest craft breweries in Italy, and with his first beer he created Italy's first local beer style: the Italian Pilsner. Inspired by clean, dry, and bitter German Pilsners, such as Jever, the twist is that they are heavily dry-hopped. The resulting beer is Tipopils, a "kind of Pils," and you need to drink it.

The best place to drink Tipopils is at the brewery's pub, where the beers were made before a new facility was built nearby. You'll get a tall, thin glass of gleaming golden beer with a thick, white foam on top, a foam that holds all the amazing hop aromas, such as citrus pith, grass, and blossom. The body is lean, just a touch of malt comes through, but it's strong enough to hold onto all the hop flavor, allowing the beer to finish bitter and refreshing.

One of the best beers in the world.

Tipopils is an incredible beer and just one of the many amazing beers that Birrificio Italiano brew: Delia is an extra-hoppy, but lighter, Italian Pils; Bibock is a marvelously malty bock that's still bitter and aromatic; there are excellent IPAs; and a range of sour and fruited beers. The bar also serves good food to go with the beer.

It's an essential beer pilgrimage to try this classic Italian style of beer in the original Italian brewery. The reason I saved this brewery to the end of my world beer search was because I thought it might be the best beer. I wasn't disappointed.

Every year in May, the brewery also hosts Pils Pride, which is a celebration of Italian Pilsners. I've never been, so that's definitely still on my Beer Bucket List.

A BUCKET LIST OF WORLD LAGER

- Birrificio Italiano Tipopils, Lurago Marinone, Italy
- Augustiner Hell, Munich, Germany (see page 112)
- Mahr's Bräu Pils, Bamberg, Germany (see page 119)
- Pilsner Urquell, Pilsen, Czech Republic (see page 126)
- Klášterní Pivovar Strahov Jantar Polotmavý, Prague, Czech Republic (see page 128)
- Firestone Walker Pivo, Paso Robles, USA (see page 57)
- Bierstadt Lagerhaus Helles, Denver, USA (see page 44)
- Emerson's Pilsner, Dunedin, New Zealand (see page 191)

The Lowdown

WHAT: Birrificio Italiano pub/restaurant

HOW: www.birrificio.it

WHERE: Via Castello, 51, 22070 Lurago Marinone (CO), Italy

Rome Craft Beer Drinking

GO TO VIA DI BENEDETTA AND YOU'LL BE HAPPY

It'd be easy to write a few hundred words on Rome as a Bucket List city. You've got the sights, the history, the food. We all know that and we should all have been or want to go to this remarkable place. It's also a great city for beer, with many great bars, but if you were only to go to two places, then head to Via di Benedetta, in Trastevere, because there, opposite each other, you'll find Ma Che Siete Venuti a Fà (at number 25) and Bir & Fud (number 23).

Ma Che Siete Venuti a Fà (which means something like "what the hell are you doing here?") is otherwise known as "the football pub" because of the football memorabilia and scarves on the walls. It's a small bar with a big reputation for the best beers, where you're always going to find exceptional Italian beers on tap, plus a lot from Belgium and Germany. On hot nights people spill onto the cool, shaded street outside, and from there you can eye up where you'll be going for dinner, because, as the name basically tells you, at Bir & Fud you'll get your beer and your food. They have excellent pizza and a lot of craft beer—and we all love pizza and beer.

The Lowdown

WHAT: Italian craft beer bars/restaurants

HOW: Ma Che Siete Venuti a Fà (www.footballpub.com) and Bir & Fud (www.birandfud.it)

WHERE: Via di Benedetta, Trastevere, Rome, Italy

In a city packed with beautiful neighborhoods, Trastevere is up there with the best, but it stands alone when it comes to the quality of its beer bars.

Visit Baladin in Piozzo

ENTER THE WORLD OF THE VANGUARD OF ITALIAN CRAFT BREWING

The world of Baladin officially started in 1986 in Piozzo, Italy, when Teo Musso opened Le Baladin (it's an old French word meaning "storyteller") in a converted old inn. It had 200 different beers and is regarded as one of the catalysts in the Italian craft beer movement.

In 1996 a more significant thing happened: Teo opened a brewery and Italy's first brewpub. Having worked in some Belgian breweries and with help (both physical and philosophical) from Jean-Luis Dits from La Brasserie à Vapeur, Teo built the brewery himself from old milk vats, producing a blond and amber beer for draft in the bar—an abbey-ish beer called Super followed the year after, packaged in bespoke wine-like bottles (an extravagance for a new brewery).

Teo's philosophy was to introduce Italians to a new way of thinking about beer and to approach it with food—Italy was very much a wine-drinking country. In fact, the opening of the brewery was a way of sticking a middle finger up at wine. Teo persevered through the early years to become the voice and face of Italian craft beer. He's since gone on to build a small Baladin empire, which includes the original bar, a restaurant, and a hotel; a barrel-aging space (in the old brewery, which was previously a large chicken coop); numerous Open Baladin bars around Italy; plus a link to the Eataly chain. There's also a larger production brewery now (the milk vats were emptied long ago), which is an "agricultural brewery" that works closely with growers to get local ingredients, as well as a new farmhouse space that Teo calls Open Gardens. This will be a large space with markets, a "beer park," and a 17th-century farmhouse,

which is being renovated to work as it would have originally done over 300 years ago. And of course there are the beers, too: over 30 of them, ranging from a mix of spicy, dry beers to richer, malt-forward beers and some funky, fruity, barrel-aged brews.

A visit to Baladin in Piozzo is like being whirled into a varied and exciting world, as different as the circus-themed Le Baladin, the five-room hotel with Turkish baths, and the high-quality beer cuisine at Casa Baladin, where you can have a six-course dinner with a glass of beer with each course. Then there are the Open Gardens and the brewery, a space unlike any other brewery—one that is again changing what beer is, and what it can be, in Italy. Teo Musso is Italy's greatest beer renegade and innovator, and continues to be progressive in Baladin's own pioneering, single-minded way.

Find out more about the Baladin empire at www.baladin.it.

All of the ventures in Teo Musso's empire are underpinned by a creative vision that's unique in the beer world.

Chasing Bière de Garde in Lille

FRANCE'S OLD FARMHOUSE BEER STYLE

At the end of summer, across Northern France and into Belgium, the grain fields had been harvested, the wild hops were at their plumpest, the farmworkers had finished their long working days, temperatures were beginning to drop, and the ideal time came for brewing what we now, rather starry-eyed, call "farmhouse beers."

A few months earlier, in the peak July heat, the men were too busy in the fields, the weather was too hot for clean fermentations, and there was no fresh grain. The hops weren't ready for picking yet and so, through a combination of necessity, harvest, and weather, seasonal brewing became established and the etymology of Belgian "Saison" comes from this.

In France and Belgium they brewed in early autumn and matured their beer over the winter—Bière de Garde means "beer for storing." Both beers would have been relatively low in alcohol and there would've been a large dose of hops to prevent them going bad. Fermentation would've been from a mix of wild yeast and bacteria, meaning that the beers would have inevitably had a funky, tart edge to them, mixing with a dry finish and aiding their satiability. When spring and summer came, the beers were refreshing and restorative drinks for the farmworkers, with the added benefit of being more nutritious than water.

What went from being a necessary beer brewed on farms has evolved greatly over time, taking on new identities and being romanticized by their backstories (I doubt there was anything romantic about Saisons 200 years ago—it was rough yet refreshing, something to quench a worker's thirst). In the shift from farm brewing to commercial brewing, these beers have changed. Today Saisons are around 6.0% ABV, malt-forward, well-attenuated (dry), and bitter, and they display qualities such as fruitiness or spice from the yeast. This type of beer dates back to the 1940s and 1950s (see Brasserie Dupont on page 143 for more on this). Likewise with the French versions, which bulked up at a similar time as Saisons and developed into a richer, more malty, stronger beer compared with the originals. Bières de Garde mellow and mature over time, aging not into the dryness of Saison, but into a fullness of malt. Many have a rough, rustic edge, a not-quite-balanced mix of malt, hop, and yeast.

Although never a hugely popular or far-reaching style in France, a few brewers have persisted with these local

If you think France lacks a depth of beer culture in comparison to other nations, a visit to Lille will help to change your preconceptions.

beers, brewing with French barley, giving three versions of varying color (Blond, Ambrée, and Brune), and using French, German, or Belgian hops and a variety of yeast strains. Now Bière de Garde remains as France's gift to the beer world, with names like St Sylvestre, Castelain, Duyck, and La Choulette traditional examples.

St Sylvestre's 3 Monts has a full sweetness of pale malts, a fruity, pineapple-like aroma, some subtle spice, and a general richness of flavor that you only find in this style of beer (it's strong like a Tripel, but much fuller and without the yeast-driven aromatics). Brasserie Duyck's Jenlain Ambrée is caramel-colored; there's some toasty and nutty malts, a general orchard fruitiness, plus a roundness in the body that's cut with some dryness and, if the bottles are matured, then a musty quality—it's one of the original stronger Bières de Garde and a good example of the amber version.

Lille is a good place to explore this style of beer, due to its proximity to Belgium and the farming area. Many restaurants around Lille offer a few French beers to go with the local food. At **Estaminet 't Rijsel** (25 Rue de Gand, 59800 Lille), which has some dishes cooked in beer, they have Ch'ti beers on tap, plus a good local bottle selection. Lille's must-visit bar is **La Capsule** (25 Rue des Trois Mollettes, 59800 Lille). It's the main craft beer bar, with around 28 taps and, in many ways, it's a textbook craft beer bar: bare brick walls, simple back bar, blackboard beer list, young staff and drinkers, cool music. What makes it special is the range of French beers on tap, including lots of IPAs (of course) and also a few Bières de Garde. La Bavaisienne Ambrée is chestnut-colored; it has malt richness, but retains a taut lightness; there's nutty, toasty, roasty malt, some dusty hop-sack aroma, and a deep bitterness—it feels rustic, not quite in complete balance or control, but it somehow seems more authentic or true for those reasons. Brasserie Lepers' L'Angelous gives lots of yeast fruitiness, which is enhanced by the spices used in the beer, and that comes above a round, golden, doughy malt body, plus a hop-sack aroma and peppery dryness.

Like most traditional beer styles, Bières de Garde have evolved almost unrecognizably over their lifetime. Where they were once brewed as light, refreshing, dry beers, made in the fall when conditions combined perfectly and then stored through the winter to be drunk the following spring and summer, today they are stronger, rich in malt, and yet still retain a signature of the old from their rusticity and aged character. Go to Lille because it's a fun city to visit to try to understand what Bière de Garde is really like and then drink a wide range of great French craft beers in the world-class La Capsule.

Four Essential Paris Beer Bars

Even Paris has great beer now and these places are worth a visit.

- **La Fine Mousse** (6 Avenue Jean Aicard, 75011 Paris) is the top hop-stop. They have 20 taps of mostly modern French beer in a smart, cool bar. They also have a restaurant opposite the bar with exceptional food and great beer suggestions to go with it. The bar opens from 5pm and the restaurant from 7pm. Consider these the go-to places to take a snapshot gauge of what's going on in French craft brewing.

- **Brewberry** (11 Rue du Pot de Fer, 75005 Paris) started as a bottle store and then opened a bar opposite. There are 24 taps, many of these interesting imports. Open from 5pm midweek and 4pm at weekends.

- **Le Supercoin** (3 Rue Baudelique, 75018 Paris) is a fun, colorful little bar in the north of town with a tight draft selection and a large French bottle list. Open from 5pm.

- **L'Express de Lyon** (1 Rue de Lyon, 75012 Paris) is an old-school café near the Gare de Lyon and, while it might look quite ordinary from the outside, it has 15 taps, mostly French and Belgian, plus some geeky treats from farther away. Open from 8am.

Drink Orval Vert at the Monastery

ONE OF THE WORLD'S MOST REVERED BEERS

There are around a dozen Trappist breweries in the world and drinking a beer from each of them should definitely be on your Beer Bucket List. Even better is to visit all the monasteries that are open and drink the beers where they're made. However, the monasteries are not exactly like your local brewpub. I want them to be dark, churchy places, reverential and quiet, but they are bright cafés that could belong to any national park—it just doesn't match my expected vision. But they are still essential stops on the world beer map.

In Belgium, you can visit Achel, Chimay, Orval, Westmalle (this is a separate restaurant, but at the end of the monastery's driveway) and Westvleteren (see page 139)—the only one not open is Rochefort. All but Westvleteren have draft beer, plus they all sell their bottled beers and some simple food. They are good places to visit, but just don't necessarily expect a heavenly beer experience. The one exception to this is Orval.

Orval has the best-looking monastery, and there's a nice tour through the grounds and a small museum, which you should walk around if you visit. Their café is called À l'Ange Gardien. It's bright and a little sterile, like the other Trappist cafés, but they offer Orval Vert ("Orval Green") on draft and this is the only place in the world where you can drink this beer.

The regular bottles of Orval are around 6.2% ABV. They are amber in color, deeply bitter and aromatic from being dry-hopped, and then each bottle is also seeded with the wild yeast *brettanomyces*, which gives the beer a secondary fermentation in the bottle. This dries out the beer and gives off some funky, tangy, earthy aromas, which change over time. It is a unique beer but one that is a favorite of many beer lovers, with individuals having a preference for how young or old they like it (they offer both old and young bottles at the café).

Orval Vert is a 4.5% ABV draft beer but without the addition of *brettanomyces*, meaning you've got a bitter Amber Ale, something like an old English IPA, bitter and powerful, yet intriguing with its floral hops and fruity-estery yeast aromas, and all with a softer, fuller texture than the bottled versions. If you like Orval, then you need to drink this beer and you should order it with some of the cheeses they also produce at the abbey.

There's one other Orval beer that's even harder to taste: Petite Orval. This is a low-alcohol version of the regular Orval, essentially watered-down, and it's what the monks drink. This isn't commercially available and only people who stay at the monastery are able to try this beer. It's one of the rarest beers in the world—a definite bucket list beer.

The Lowdown

WHAT: L'Abbaye d'Orval

HOW: www.orval.be

WHERE: Route d'Orval, No. 1, B-6823 Villers-devant-Orval, Belgium

Drinking Orval is a heavenly beer experience.

Drink Westvleteren 12

THE BEST BEER IN THE WORLD?

In 2005 the collected reviews on Ratebeer.com announced a strong, dark beer simply called "12," brewed by Trappist monks at The Abbey of Saint Sixtus in Westvleteren, to be the best beer in the world. Over a decade later and it's still at the top of the list. But is it really the best?

Westvleteren 12 is a Belgian Quadrupel. It's a deep, dark brown; it has a remarkable depth of dark fruits, plums, raisins, figs, rum-soaked cherries, sweet tea, almonds, tea bread, doughy cake, and some fragrant spices. The body is soft beneath the initial burst of carbonation and its joy lies in the initial pleasing sweetness and the smooth depth of flavor—few other beers can rival it. It's also a beer made by monks and it's very rare and hard to get hold of—if you want to buy a case, then you need to call the brewery/monastery during allotted times and then arrive and pick them up during another allotted time frame. This all adds to its allure.

The monastery has a café, **In de Vrede**, and a store on site that sells six-packs, but you never know what beer it'll be when you get there. You can also sit and drink the three beers the monastic brewers produce: Blond, 8, and 12. The Blond is one of the best Belgian blonds brewed anywhere (it's fruity, there's yeast esters, toasty malt, vanilla, peppery hops; and it's supremely drinkable—it's a world-class brew), and the 8 is an excellent Dubbel—

richly malty and dense with dried fruits—but the Blond and the 8 both sit in the enormous shadow of the 12.

The café is the place to go for the Westvleteren beers, but it's a curious experience. These great beers are served unceremoniously, just poured quickly into your glass and placed in front of you. The café is large, bright, and open, whereas I want to drink the beer in small, dark bars. Plus, while you can order some of the world's most exceptional beers, the food options include some of the world's most average toasted sandwiches (although you should order the monastery's cheese when you have the Blond, as that's a perfect food pairing). On my most recent visit, the 12 was the best I'd ever tasted it, making it worthy of its elevated status. But the Blond was also at that level. You should go to In de Vrede, work your way through the beers, and by your third or fourth or fifth bottle, you'll be very happy but probably no closer to knowing whether Westvleteren 12 is the world's best beer…

The Lowdown

WHAT: In de Vrede

HOW: Check the opening times before you go as they vary through the year (www.indevrede.be).

WHERE: Donkerstraat 13, 8640 Vleteren, Belgium

LOCAL TIP: **Go East**

If you're in Westvleteren, head east to Oostvleteren and Struise brewery (Kasteelstraat 50, 8640 Oostvleteren; www.struise.com). They make a huge mix of beers but are best known for strong, rich Imperial Stouts, like Black Albert, and Pannepot, which is a bit like a Belgian Quadrupel. The brewery Het Oud Schooltje, or "In the Schoolhouse," opens to the public every Saturday from 2–6pm. Time your visits to East and West Vleteren accordingly.

Visit Three Classic Belgian Breweries

TO BETTER UNDERSTAND THREE CLASSIC BELGIAN BEERS

You can't properly understand a beer until you've got very drunk on it. That means spending some serious time with the beer, getting to know it well, to know how it changes as you go from a full glass to an empty one, and from your third glass to your fourth.

Likewise, you can't fully understand a beer—even a beer you class a favorite—until you see where it's made and learn what makes that place special, to learn some of its secrets. For example, I never knew where the sweetness in the middle of a Saison Dupont comes from until I walked into the brewhouse and saw a flame driving right to the bottom of a copper tank, creating a hot spot and some caramelized flavors—seeing that fire, it now made sense.

So when I started writing this book, I knew I had to visit three Beer Bucket List breweries that make beers I love (and beers which I've been very drunk on). Here is what I discovered on my visits to Rodenbach, Duvel-Moortgat, and Brasserie Dupont.

You can't come to Rodenbach without taking a picture very similar to this one.

Rodenbach Brewery

For the wine of the beer world

If you visit a lot of breweries, then you get used to seeing rows of silver tanks that look like upturned torpedoes. Rarely are these especially interesting to look at, making the cellar section of any brewery fairly samey (and why people tend to take more photos of hoses than conditioning tanks…), which is precisely why some of the most interesting brewery visits include those with huge barrel-aging capabilities or unusual cellars, such as Pilsner Urquell, Cantillon, Wicked Weed's Funkatorium—and Rodenbach.

At Rodenbach they have 294 wooden foudres, ranging from 2,640 gallons (12,000 liters) to a staggering 14,300 gallons (65,000 liters)—I've lived in places smaller than their biggest foudres. There's one vat from 1836 and the oldest still in use is around 120 years old; the "youngest" is about 60 years old. And what happens in these barrels is something magical.

Rodenbach is a mixed-fermentation, red-brown beer and one of the few brands that has kept this old style of beer alive. The beer is sour, but it's always been a sour product. It's also a blended beer, mixing old and young beers together, something that takes place to create a perfectly balanced beer, combining sweetness, acidity, and tannin—think of these as a triangle of taste with balance meeting right in the middle. And key to the balance is the pH level, which stays relatively consistent at the point of maximum drinkability and digestibility (about 3.5 pH, which is in the same range as wine, and with non-sour beer being around 4.2 pH). In fact, one of the origins of beer blending is thought to come down to mixing the beer to achieve this optimal pH level.

The brewing process uses colored malts and some corn, and undergoes a decoction mash. They use local Belgian hops, but they're under the taste level and mainly used for foam and the beer's general stability. The yeast is a mix of cultures, including some wild yeast and bacteria, and it goes through a warm fermentation. Once that's finished, one of two things happens: it's either used young for blending (and doesn't see any wood) or it goes into those huge wooden foudres, where it can sit for up to four years. It'll evolve in different directions, with each vessel having its own character, some turning more acidic, others acetic, some fruitier, and others funkier. A bottle of Rodenbach is a combination of that fresh beer from the tank and the aged beer from the foudres.

The standard Rodenbach beer is 75 percent young beer and 25 percent aged beer, meaning you get a sweeter, fruitier beer with just a little sourness and some pleasing caramel, cherry, and apple flavors—it has the playful fruitiness of youth, but lacks the complexity of age. The Grand Cru is a more interesting beer with a mix of one-third young to two-thirds old beer, and it has a great sweet-sour balance, nice woody tannins, lots of fruitiness, an apple-like acidity, and some balsamic qualities. They also bottle Vintage, which comes from just one foudre (with perhaps a small amount of young beer to perfect the balance), and you might get to taste the Foederbier straight from the barrel. This can vary hugely from barrel to barrel, but has a coarser quality in general, in my opinion needing the younger beer's sweetness to create a complete beer.

Rodenbach is the wine of the beer world; its acidity is closer to a Burgundy than a Brown Ale, and it's an excellent beer to go with food. The taste is an idiosyncrasy, something that's been preserved by the brewery and which we can still see and experience today. The cellars lined with hundreds of big wooden barrels are one of those rare sights in the beer world that is capable of leaving you speechless—no big silver tank has ever had quite the same impact.

The Lowdown

WHAT: Rodenbach Brewery

HOW: Tours and visits are by appointment. You can find details on the Rodenbach website (www.rodenbach.be).

WHERE: Spanjestraat 133, 8800 Roeselare, Belgium

Duvel-Moortgat

For devilishly delicious Golden Ale

In 1958, a recipe was developed for a new beer at the Moortgat Brewery in Breendonk, north of Brussels. The strong Golden Ale was "a real devil of a beer" and so took on the name Duvel, meaning "devil" in Brabantian. Today it's one of Belgium's most famous and most-loved beers.

A vintage sign for Duvel.

Duvel-Moortgat is a family-owned brewery and the third largest in Belgium—and it's still in the same village where the brewery started in 1871. They are growing rapidly in their current location and buying other breweries, such as Firestone-Walker, Boulevard, and Ommegang in the US, plus La Chouffe, Vedett, and De Konink in Belgium. They have a lot of different brands under the family's stewardship.

The brewery runs interesting and detailed tours, telling you the history of the brewery and focusing primarily on Duvel. Around 25,000 people do this tour every year and you get to see the large brewhouse and walk around the huge tank farm, with some of the tanks being as big as five-story houses and capable of holding one million bottles' worth of beer. You know that bit in the Rodenbach entry where I said silver tanks aren't very interesting? Well, Duvel is the exception. A giant tank containing one million bottles is quite something—if you personally drank one full case a week, it'd take you 800 years to drink the tank dry.

The brewing of Duvel deserves attention because it's a 90-day process. On day one the beer is brewed. It has a week-long primary fermentation, then three weeks in lagering tanks. From here it's bottled, then has two weeks in warm maturation, where it develops its bright carbonation, and then six weeks in cold maturation to further aid that fine fizz. When it's sold, it's ready to drink and tastes better fresh. What makes Duvel stand out is its mix of lightness and strength: for an 8.5%-ABV beer, it's very dry and lean, giving it a non-fatiguing drinkability (its use of sugar during brewing aids that terminal attenuation). There are lots of hops in Duvel—it gets its 32 IBU from aroma hops (Styrian Golding and Saaz)—lacing the beer with a deep hop flavor and complexity and lifting it with a spicy fruitiness that complements the aromatic banana, pear, and pepper driven out by the yeast. And all with the brisk carbonation keeping it refreshing.

At the end of the tour you get to the Duvel Depot, which is light and modern, yet feels classic—much like the beer itself. It's smart, clean, and decorated with old brewery memorabilia, plus lots of taps of the Moortgat Family beers. The bar is open after tours and has additional hours, but it's best to check the website to make sure it's open. In early 2017, the brewery put Duvel on draft for the first time—it took two years to develop a way to serve this highly carbonated beer on tap. Hopefully this will always be available, as it's exceptionally good. And if you're at the Duvel Depot, then also look for Duvel Triple Hop, a 9.5% ABV, bulked-up version of the beer with lots of Citra hops added at the end—it's got the kind of effortless, delicious drinkability that Double IPAs can only dream of.

I think Duvel is one of the best beers in the world. It's certainly one of my favorites and one that's always in my fridge. To see where it's made, to learn about the processes that go into brewing it, just makes me love the beer even more, where each new bottle I open still leaves me in awe of its combination of power and dexterity and lightness. There seems to be a continuous newness about this beer because, no matter how many bottles I drink, I always notice something new and interesting about it.

The Lowdown

WHAT: Duvel-Moortgat Brewery

HOW: Tours run Monday–Saturday. There are three tour options, including one with cheese-tasting. Book at www.duvel.com.

WHERE: Breendonk-Dorp 58, 2870 Puurs, Belgium

Brasserie Dupont

For the Saison specialists

Saison Dupont is the textbook-defining beer of its style. It's a near-untouchable beer, one that no other brewer dares to replicate, and a beer that many drinkers, including myself, call a favorite. Brasserie Dupont is based in farm buildings that date from 1759, to which a brewery was added in 1844. Originally, like the other farmhouse brewers in this region, they only brewed in winter using whatever ingredients were to hand. The beers were matured in wood and were low in alcohol, dry, and tart or funky; they were refreshing for the farm workers, but didn't leave them falling over in the fields. Modern Dupont beers are inspired by those old brews and still have an aromatic bitterness, a dryness, and a striking yeast depth, though they are now brewed to be stronger, with the recipes shifting in the 1940s and 1950s.

The brewery and processes are a fascinating mix of modern and traditional. Their brewhouse still has a fired copper from the 1920s, which creates a hot spot and a caramelization that you can taste in the beers. Their yeast is also crucial; it's from the 1950s and has a phenolic and fruity quality and has to be looked after properly. They have unusual shallow square fermenters that are only filled to a depth of a few feet, meaning there's less pressure forced down on the beer—this increases fruitiness. The yeast also impacts secondary fermentation: the beer is bottled and then left in a warm room for six weeks, where the 26fl-oz (750-ml) bottles lie on their sides, creating more coverage for the yeast as it can spread across the length of the beer and not just accumulate at the base (the large bottles are the ones you want to buy).

Dupont's Saison is the beer I want to learn more about. In 1990 they only brewed it twice a year, but now it's hugely popular, thanks to the attention thrust upon it by US brewers. It's been brewed to the current recipe since the 1940s, when Saison was suffering from a lack of popularity. That new recipe upped the ABV to 6.5% and it's been there ever since. (If you want to try their version of an old-style Saison, try Biolégère—a 3.5% ABV beer that's dry, bitter, and endlessly refreshing.)

Saison Dupont is golden in the glass. It has a deep bitterness, a grapefruit pithiness, and a rich malt flavor that comes out initially, but then it dries right out. There's a deep hop flavor and the spicy yeast drives through the middle with its phenols and fruitiness. It's a complex and beguiling beer, a mix of bitter, sweet, spicy, and dry, and those qualities make it one of the world's greatest and most versatile food beers.

Locally the brewery is best known for Moinette, essentially a stronger version of the Saison using the same ingredients and process, only to a higher gravity—this was also introduced during the period when Saisons weren't popular. It's also worth knowing that the beers improve with time in the bottle and leaving them will lead to a drier beer with more yeasty aromatics—a year from sale is ideal.

Saison is different today to how it was when it was a true farmhouse beer, something light and refreshing. New Saisons look to Brasserie Dupont as the quintessential example and, given that the beer is no longer needed as a seasonal product, the shift simply reflects the ever-changing beer world. You really should go to Brasserie Dupont. The tour is great and the brewery, still within the original farm buildings, is fascinating to look around. And the beer is among the best you'll find anywhere.

Pouring the gold standard saison.

The Lowdown

WHAT: Brasserie Dupont

HOW: Tours take place on the first Saturday of the month and are run in French, Dutch, or English. The €15 cost covers the tour, three tasters, and a six-pack to take away. The onsite store (open Monday–Saturday, 9am–6pm) sells beer and merchandise (www.brasserie-dupont.com).

WHERE: Rue Basse, 5, 7904 Tourpes, Belgium

In de Verzekering Tegen de Grote Dorst

THE GREATEST LAMBIC BAR IN THE WORLD

If you like Belgian Lambic, Gueuze, and their fruited friends Kriek and Framboise, In de Verzekering Tegen de Grote Dorst, or "The Insurance Against Great Thirst," is the essential beer bar for you because it has the world's greatest selection of sour beers.

What makes the Grote Dorst a little more special, or elusive, or peerless, is that it's only open every Sunday from 10am–8pm. It's an inconspicuous concrete cube from the outside, but step inside and it comes alive with a lift of conversation and excitement. It's a small café-style bar with wooden beams above your head and worn patterned tiles beneath your feet. Behind the curved wooden bar you'll see what looks like twinkling diamonds—the huge selection of branded glassware. There's seating for 40-odd people and little standing space, so arrive early because, once you see the menu, you'll want to stay all day.

To begin, there are about seven draft Lambics—this is the flat, unblended, youngish stuff. Play yourself into the day of drinking with one of these. The people serving will disappear behind a door, presumably into a magic cellar of dusty, delicious old beers (I wish I'd asked to see it now), returning with your glass or bottle. As for the bottles, the list is enormous: there's Gueuze and fruited Lambic/Gueuze (conveniently they color-code the fruit beers on the menu) in a mix of 13fl-oz (37.5-cl) and 26fl-oz (75-cl) bottles. Then there's an extensive selection of vintage bottles—you'll find many beers over a decade old, some from the 1990s or earlier, with bottles arriving on tables with the labels faded and disintegrating. There was also, seemingly, an unlimited supply of Westvleteren (see page 139), with some drinkers fancying something non-sour as a change-up. It'll be overwhelming because you'll want to drink everything. And there's excellent cheese, too, if this place wasn't already perfect.

The bar is about 12 miles (20km) west of Brussels, but it's easy to get to: from Brussels Gare de l'Ouest, jump on the 128 bus and ride it for about 30 minutes, then it's a five-minute walk. On that stroll you still won't believe what's coming because you're just passing houses and trees, and it's very quiet. When you see the big church tower you know you're almost there. But you still won't believe what you'll see when you go inside, because on a Sunday morning in this sleepy town, there will be dozens of people sitting inside sharing amazing bottles of beer.

This is a once-in-a-lifetime beer experience. Go in a group so you can share big bottles. Take as much money as you can (it's cash only and you will want to buy bottles that cost upward of €30). Arrive at 10am, maybe earlier, drink incredible and rare Lambics, picking vintage bottles you'll never see again, and know that you're in one of the world's greatest, most uniquely brilliant beer bars. They will ensure that your great thirst is sated—though you'll still want to go back for more.

THE WORLD'S BEST BEER BARS

- In de Verzekering Tegen de Grote Dorst
- Moeder Lambic, Brussels (see page 150)
- 't Brugs Beertje, Bruges (see page 148)
- Akkurat, Stockholm (see page 159)
- Mikkeller, Copenhagen (see page 81)
- Falling Rock Taphouse, Denver (see page 44)
- Blackback Pub, Waterbury, Vermont (see page 15)
- BiaCraft, Ho Chi Minh City (see page 196)

A display of empty lambic bottles at In de Verzekering Tegen de Grote Dorst.

The Lowdown

WHAT: The world's best lambic bar

HOW: Open on Sundays only, 10am–8pm (www.dorst.be).

WHERE: Frans Baetensstraat 45, 1750 Lennik, Belgium

Drink Lambic in the Payottenland

FOR SENSATIONAL AND SPONTANEOUSLY FERMENTED BEERS

Lambic, Gueuze, and other idiosyncratic sour beers inspire some of the most devoted drinkers, and these quirky beer styles inspire some of the most unusual beer events, pulling beer geeks in from around the world.

Lambic is brewed to the south and west of Brussels in the Payottenland region. All Lambic is essentially brewed in the same way: a mix of wheat and barley, then a small amount of aged hops are added for their antibacterial qualities, not for flavor or bitterness. At the end of the brew day, the liquid is left overnight in cooling trays, which attract different yeast and bacteria from the air and walls around them. This beer "spontaneously ferments" and then matures for up to three or four years in wooden barrels or big foudres. Fruit can be added to the barrels as well to create Kriek (cherries) or Framboise (raspberries) or other fruited brews that include strawberry, peach, or blackcurrant. All these flavors are commonly found across Belgium.

While the processes are similar, each brewery has a different microculture of yeast and bacteria, plus different barrels to house those yeasts (with each barrel also maturing the beer differently). This means that each brewery produces something a bit different, which is then rounded out by the process of blending beers from a range of barrels.

Lambic is the base product. It comes from one barrel or one batch; it's uncarbonated; it's a mix of sweetness and acidity and some funky yeast aromas—it's more reminiscent of farmhouse cider than anything in the beer family. It's also not common to see Lambic. Gueuze is the main product of a Lambic brewery and this is a blend of different ages of beer, meaning a mix of sweet young Lambic and funky, acidic old Lambic to produce a balanced and consistent final beer. When the beers are blended together in a sealed, corked bottle, the beer continues to ferment and produces a lively, Champagne-like carbonation. In the Payottenland there are a number of brewers, plus a few non-brewing blenders who buy the base Lambic from the brewers and then mature it themselves in their own barrels, with their own house-yeast character, before blending.

You want to drink Lambic, ideally poured from the barrel into a ceramic jug, then into a Lambic glass. Typically only found in the Payottenland, plus a few good bars, it's a taste of traditional beers still brewed in the same way today.

The Difference Between Brewers and Blenders

Lambic brewers do everything, from making a base beer to blending and bottling, while blenders buy wort from brewers and age it in their own barrels before blending it to produce new beers. Look out for these brewers, blenders, and beers:

Brewers		Blenders
• 3 Fonteinen	• Cantillon	• Bokkereyder
• Belle Vue	• De Troch	• De Cam
• Boon	• Girardin	• Gueuzerie Tilquin
• Brasserie Mort Subite	• Lindemans	• Oud Beersel
	• Timmermans	

Three Lambics to look for:

- Boon's Lambic is wonderfully refreshing and balanced; it has a low acidity, a full texture, a subtle cider depth, and a grape-like freshness.

- Oud Beersel's Lambic, or even better their Oud Lambic, is apple-like, fruity, and tangy; it has the perfect triangle of balance, where sweetness, acidity, and tannic dryness all meet in the middle.

- Cantillon's Lambic is lemony, tangy, tannic from the wood, a little peppery, and very easy drinking for its pleasing sweetness.

All these brewers also produce exceptional Gueuzes; they are vibrantly yet lightly acidic; they are lemony and apple-y, refreshing and lively, and invigorating with their bright carbonation.

Visit Cantillon Brewery

IT'S A TOP-10 BUCKET LIST TICK

The practical stuff first: Cantillon is a short walk from Brussels Midi Station. You can go just to sit and have some beers in their small bar area or you can take a self-guided tour, which ends with a glass of Lambic and a taster of another beer (and then carry on drinking).

Drinking at Cantillon is one of the best beer experiences on the planet.

The Lowdown

WHAT: Cantillon Brewery

HOW: Cantillon is open from 10am–5pm every day except Wednesday and Sunday (and public holidays, so check the website, just in case; www.cantillon.be). A self-guided tour costs €7. You can buy bottles at the bar to drink in or take away.

WHERE: Rue Gheude 56, 1070 Brussels

Now for the romantic stuff: **Cantillon Brewery** is an inner-city farmhouse and harks back hundreds of years. They make some of the world's most revered beers. Those beers are spontaneously fermented, so they're sour. Once brewed, they're aged in rows and rows of old wooden barrels for up to three or four years—to walk among these barrels is wonderful, like a cathedral of wood (the smell is so good, too). The brewery is peerless and the beers are amazing—deep with balanced acidity and complexity. It's somewhere beer geeks dream about going to and it always lives up to the expectation.

The rarer experience is to go to one of their twice-yearly open brew days. At one of these you can spend the day in and around the brewery and follow the full brewing process—it's remarkable to see the old brewkit working. Rarer still is Quintessence, which happens every other year. It's a celebration of beer and food in the brewery, where you'll get to taste around 25 rare world beers, each paired with a small snack. It's a ticketed event with entry staggered throughout the day.

Two More Sour Beer Experiences

• **The Toer de Geuze** Every other year—on the odd numbers—most of the Belgian Lambic brewers and blenders (plus a couple of bars) open their doors for visitors for the Toer de Geuze, a celebration of spontaneous fermentation. Buses carry drinkers between all the participating venues. It's a rare chance to see inside some of these famous breweries (www.toerdegeuze.be).

• **Weekend of Spontaneous Fermentation** With over 100 Lambics, including some rare and old bottles, The Weekend of Spontaneous Fermentation is a must visit for sour lovers. It takes place over a weekend in May and is an unusual but lovely beer festival; a calm place where people are buying and sharing rare bottles of old, sour beer.

Bruges' Best Beer Experiences

SPEND THE WEEKEND IN A WONDERFUL BEER CITY

One of the finest, old, beer-drinking cities, there's much to love about a long weekend spent strolling the cobbled streets of Bruges.

The city's most famous beer bar is 't Brugs Beertje (Kemelstraat 5, 8000 Bruges). Meaning "Bruges's Little Bear," this bar has been the go-to for beer lovers for over 30 years. It's a charming and busy little bar with around 300 beers to choose from. You might go for the beer, but you'll stay for the atmosphere.

With De Garre, the first challenge is finding it. The second is finding a space to sit. The third is leaving without falling over because the house Tripel is a formidable beer. Although they have over 100 beers, you'll want to order their house beer first. It comes in a unique thick-stemmed glass; it's deep gold with a fat white foam; it's rich with malt, yeast, and hops; and it's 11.0% ABV. It's definitely a must-drink beer in the city, made better by the setting and the way in which it's served to you, which includes that great glass and a bowl of cheese cubes. The address—simple, it's De Garre 1— is unhelpfully vague. Basically walk off the Grote Markt, down Briedelstraat, then look to the right for a tiny alleyway—it's down there.

Café Vlissinghe (Blekersstraat 2, 8000 Bruges) is Bruges's oldest pub—it celebrated its 500th birthday in 2015—and it's in the

nice, quiet part of town to the north, near the canals and away from the crowds. In winter there's a stove to heat the place and there's a shaded garden in summer. The beer menu isn't extensive, but it's good; the food is home-cooked, with salads, sandwiches, and spaghetti, and it's all made excellent by the convivial surroundings of this old bar. It's simple and simply great.

Le Trappiste (Kuipersstraat 33, 8000 Bruges) is a busy, atmospheric underground bar with characterful cloistered walls and a large beer list, including some rare and wonderful things on tap, plus some hop-forward beer and a lot of bottles. It's dark, cozy, and hidden away, with flickering candlelight so you can read the menu. The dark alcoves make you want to hide down there for hours.

For such a well-known beer city, there are only two breweries in the center—and one of these only properly opened at the end of 2015. Both should be on your list to visit. The oldest is The Halve Maan, meaning "The Half Moon" (Walplein 26, 8000 Bruges). They brew Brugse Zot (too many of these and you'll also turn into a "Bruges Fool"), the Straffe Hendrik Tripel, and Quadruple. The brewery tour takes you around the cramped old location, up onto the roof for a great view of the city, and then down into the old decommissioned brewery. At the end of the tour you'll get an unfiltered blond Brugse Zot. The Halve Maan is also notable for having built a 2-mile (3-km) beer pipe under the city, which runs from the brewery to a separate conditioning and packaging building.

The new brewery in town is Bourgogne des Flandres (Kartuizerinnenstraat 6, 8000 Bruges). This is one of the slickest tours and set-ups you'll find, clearly designed with visitors in mind; it's engaging and interactive, with some

De Garre's charm lies in its great atmosphere and even better beer.

Medieval Bruges offers beer-and-food lovers the perfect weekend getaway.

nice touches such as a glass-floor over the conditioning tanks and their open fermenters. The beer is produced in an unusual way to give something like a traditional Flemish Red or Brown: they brew Den Bruinen Os ("The Brown Ox") as a strong, sweetish dark beer, which is then blended (roughly 50/50) with young Lambic that they get from Timmermans Brewery. This creates a pleasingly fruity,

sweet-sour cherry, apple, and plum-like beer. It's especially good with the huge croques that they serve in the brewery restaurant. If you can, and it's sunny, sit by the canal out the back.

For more information, and a general guide to the city, its beers, bars, restaurants, and sights, go to **www.visitflanders.be**.

Three Essential Belgian Bar Experiences

YOU MUST TRY IN ANTWERP AND BRUSSELS

Two cities, lots of beer—here are a couple of Belgian cities and some bars that you should really add to your Beer Bucket List. Trust me, you won't be disappointed.

Café Kulminator in Antwerp for the Best-aged Beers (Vleminckveld 32, 2000 Antwerp): This quirky, cozy, jumbled-up, old brown café in Antwerp is best known for its unrivaled cellar of vintage beers. The bar is initially overwhelming. There's mismatched beer memorabilia and general stuff everywhere, plus occasionally some cats, but these all add to the quirky charm of the bar, which is run by a husband-and-wife team. Once you're settled in and scanning the beer list, you'll soon be boggle-eyed at what's available because it's the most intriguing, beguiling, wow-inducing beer list—it's a unique experience to be able to pick from so many old beer treasures. The only questions will be where do you begin and when do you end.

Delirium Café in Brussels for the Most Beers (Impasse de la Fidélité 4, 1000 Brussels): This mainly seems to be a tourist attraction now, but it's a tourist attraction with 2,000 different beers. Every time I go, it seems to get bigger and vaster, but no less busy. It's also become a block party in its backstreet location where you can pick between a range of bars, such as the Hoppy Loft for craft beers, the Monasterium for Trappist and Abbey brews, or just the main massive Tap House. As well as the overwhelmingly big bottle list, the draft selection is exceptional—so good that you probably won't even want a bottle. You can also buy two-liter glasses of certain beers, including Delirium Tremens, the strong-sweet-spicy golden beer that the bar is named after, but you probably shouldn't do that…

The entrance to the Delirium Café.

Moeder Lambic Fontainas in Brussels for the Best Beer Bar (Place Fontainas 8, 1000 Brussels): Situated between the Midi Station and the Grand Place, this is one of the world's greatest bars—and one of my favorite drinking places. It's the huge selection of beers that pulls me in. This is mostly a modern selection from the best Belgian brewers, though, of course, they still have the classics. There'll be a few Lambics, plus plenty of rare beers that you won't find anywhere else. Plan to stay for a long time.

LOCAL TIP: A Warning about Belgian Opening Times

Opening times are variable. Only a few places consistently open every day from lunchtime to bedtime. It's common for bars to close at least one or two days a week. In January a lot of places don't open at all or have reduced hours. Some places close in the summer. Some don't open until the evening; some only open in the afternoon; some shut for a few hours between lunch and dinner. It's always best to check ahead to see when bars are open (but don't necessarily believe what you read).

This sign will help clear up any confusion about opening times.

Belgium's Best Beer Cooking

BECAUSE YOU SHOULD EAT MORE BEER

Belgium does beer cooking—*cuisine à la bière*—better than any other beer nation. Go to the best places and everything on the menu includes beer as an ingredient—a slow-cooked stew, a quick sauce to go with a steak, game braised in sour beer, Witbier steamed with mussels, Blondes baked into bread, or dark ales stirred through a sweet dessert. Here are some of the best places to visit.

't Hommelhof (Watouplein 17, 8978 Poperinge) is a fine-dining beer restaurant in Watou, set across the town square from Van Eecke Brewery. Here the food is elegant and high-end, thoughtful and flavorsome, and definitely an elevated, special experience for beer and food. They have a couple of tasting menus, which I recommend, and they do beer-matching for the dishes. They serve Van Eecke's Hommelbier, a boldly hoppy, grassy, peppery Belgian Pale Ale, and that's the ideal beer to start with. Chef-owner Stefaan Couttenye has also written a book on cooking with Belgian beers. Essential.

In Bruges, Bierbrasserie Cambrinus (Philipstockstraat 19, 8000 Bruges) is a famous food stop that serves all the classic beer dishes, such as carbonnade and Trappist cheese croquettes, plus some of their own recipes, including chicken and mushrooms in Oud Bruin and crème brûlée with Dubbel.

De Heeren van Liedekercke (Kasteelstraat 33, 9470 Denderleeuw) is one of the top-rated beer restaurants in the world. The beer-cuisine menu isn't as extensive as others, but the dishes are exemplary and the beer list is excellent, including aged vintages of many beers. Each dish also comes with a suggested beer pairing, such as their famous house Bolognese with Malheur's dark ales.

De Drie Fonteinen, the Lambic brewer, has an excellent restaurant in Beersel, just south of Brussels, which specializes in cooking with their beers, including the traditional dish of rabbit à la gueuze, plus mussels, chicken, and beef cooked in different ways using different beers. It's all very good. They also have their own beers available on tap and in bottle (Herman Teirlinckplein 3, 1650 Beersel, Brussels).

In the center of Brussels, there's Restobières (Rue des Renards 9, 1000 Brussels), which uses beer in every dish and should be an essential stop for anyone interested in beer cooking. They do the classics, but also have a lot of their own dishes, including some excellent desserts (like passion fruit mousse with Avec Les Bon Voeux). It's a cozy place with old kitchen utensils all around and a very good beer list. And in a country famous for its frites, Restobières makes some of the best you'll find, with a superb homemade mustardy mayo on the side.

Also in Brussels is Nüetnigenough (Rue du Lombard 25, 1000 Brussels), another rightly well-regarded restaurant that has dishes such as white sausage in Orval and duck breast in Framboise. They have Brasserie Dupont's Pilsner and Saison on tap, plus a couple of rotating guest beers.

Restobières offers the best beer and food in a city filled with great beer and food.

Frites and bière, a perfect combination—especially at Restobières.

Five Perfect Belgian Beer and Food Combinations

- **Croque monsieur with hoppy Belgian Blonde:** A toasted ham and cheese sandwich is a great lunch with the dry hoppiness of a Belgian Blonde, such as Brasserie De la Senne's Taras Boulba (this is a perfect beer for me: dry, bitter, and aromatic with Saaz hops), being the most refreshing choice.

- **Moules frites with Witbier:** A classic match. The lively, spicy freshness of a Witbier works so well with the onion, garlic, and celery the mussels will have been cooked in. It's great with the frites and mayo, too.

- **Carbonnade with Dubbel or Quadrupel:** Often cooked with sour beer or dark, strong ale, I like the malty richness in a Dubbel or Quadrupel to give some sweetness to balance the savoriness of the stew.

- **Sausage and stoemp with Saison or Tripel:** Stoemp is potatoes mashed with alliums and other vegetables, normally topped with sausages and often a beer sauce. Have a spicy, dry Saison or Tripel to lift the veg flavor and cut through the meat's fat.

- **Belgian chocolate mousse with Kriek:** A staple dessert and with the fruity tartness in a proper Kriek you'll enhance the chocolate's natural fruitiness and then cut the richness with acidity.

Amsterdam's Brown Cafés

WONDERFUL, TRADITIONAL OLD BEER BARS

Many go to Amsterdam for the red or the green, but the smart beer traveler should be going for the brown.

Amsterdam's brown cafés are traditional old bars, often very small, and dark with wood and a lack of sunlight; they are as cozy as a room filled with wooden furniture can be, with quirky collections of knick-knacks all around and nicotine-stained walls from decades of passive smoking. They're homely, relaxed, honest, and good fun. They'll serve bar snacks (such as *bitterballen* and cubes of cheese), jenever spirit, and a couple of local lagers like Grolsch or Heineken. You can sneer at those beers if you like, but when they're super fresh, as they are in many brown cafés, they are excellent: snappy with a dry bitterness, clean, and refreshing, especially so as they're served in small glasses. This is a uniquely Dutch beer experience.

Café 't Smalle (Egelantiersgracht 12, 1015 RL) is on the canal-side, which is a tempting place to sit, until you see how handsome it is inside: big chandelier, bar stools, brilliant back bar, candlelight, and a lot of charm.

Café De Doktor (Rozenboomsteeg 4, 1012 PR) is tiny (one of the smallest bars in Amsterdam); it's dark, it's packed with antiques and clocks and bottles and birdcages—and it's wonderful. You feel you could hide in there drinking crisp, cold lager for days. It was opened in 1798 and still remains in the same family.

In 't Aepjen (Zeedijk 1, 1012 AN) has a ridiculous story and history. First, it's one of only two wooden buildings in Amsterdam and it dates from the 1540s. But that's not the ridiculous part: the name translates as "In the Monkey's." This refers to how sailors docking in Amsterdam from exotic places would get so drunk that they couldn't pay their bill. So they would use monkeys as currency instead, leaving the place over-running with animals. Today there's still monkey memorabilia all around this small, handsome old bar on the edge of the red-light district.

Café 't Smalle, with its position by the canal is at its best in the sunshine.

Antwerp's Brown Cafés

Want a similar brown café experience in Belgium? You'll find these bars throughout the northern cities, but Antwerp has many small, dark, cozy bars with the same style as Amsterdam's cafés. They'll have simple food and a few good beers on tap, including the city's iconic and much-loved De Koninck, which you can order just by saying the name of its glass: a *bolleke* (pronounced boll-ok-er). Look out for **Boer van Tienen** (Mechelseplein 6, 2000 Antwerp), **Oud Arsenaal** (Maria Pijpelincxstraat 4, 2000 Antwerp), and **Café Den Engel** (Grote Markt 3, 2000 Antwerp).

Arctic Circle Beers in Tromsø

BEER AND LIFE BUCKET LISTS COMBINE

The beer bucket list and life bucket list cross over neatly in Tromsø, a city 200 miles (320km) north of the Arctic Circle. It was once "The Gateway to the Arctic" and a place where explorers, expeditions, and animal hunts started and finished. I went there on my own hunt: to see orcas swimming in the wild and to watch the Northern Lights that dance in the sky most evenings during the long winter.

Obviously, when I travel somewhere new, I always look up the local breweries and beers, and Tromsø offered a lot more than I expected, including Mack Bryggeri, formerly the northernmost brewery in the world and one of Norway's oldest brewers, as well as a few small craft brewers.

Seeing orcas and the Northern Lights were beyond my expectations. As were the beers. The most exciting brewery is Graff Brygghus, which specializes in German and US styles, with brewer Marius Graff spending some time in breweries in Portland, Oregon, before returning to his hometown to brew with business partner Martin Amundsen—the Graff beers are exceptionally good. Also in town are Polden and Bryggeri 13, with a range of pale and hoppy and dark and malty beers between them—you can find these throughout the town's bottle stores.

Mack Bryggeri is worthy of attention for its great story and predominance in northern Norway. The Mack family (pronounced closer to Muck) were merchants and bakers from near Hanover, in Germany. Baking took Georg Mack to Norway in the 1830s, where he worked in Bergen before heading north, settling in Tromsø and having kids, including Ludwig Mack. Lugwig followed his father and learnt to bake, spending a few years in Germany before returning to his father's bakery.

At that time Tromsø was a wasteland of wasted fisherman, drunk on hard liquor. Ludwig had tasted German beer and knew its culture, so he decided to combine water, grain, and yeast in a new way. In 1877, Mack, then 35 years old, opened his eponymous brewery and started selling his first beer, Bayer—a dark, Bavarian-style lager—the following year. It wasn't an easy beginning, and being a remote and small fishing town the prosperity of Tromsø long paralleled the successes or failures of the fishermen. But it did survive and did manage to grow, becoming synonymous with northern Norway, and it's still a family-run brewery today. As well as the beer, they added capacity to produce soft drinks and bottled water, plus in 2000 they installed a smart craft brewery. In 2012, the large production brewery had outgrown its original location, squeezed within the tight infrastructure of a small city, and so they built a new production brewery 44 miles (71km) away, leaving the microbrewery in Tromsø. That's also still run by the same family.

The best place to drink the beer is Ølhallen, the Beer Hall, a 67-tap pub connected to the brewery—it's also the oldest pub in Tromsø. Like the brewery, the pub was opened to stop unruly public drinking and create a pleasant and comfortable place to enjoy a beer (though it was strictly a man's place to begin with: the female restroom was only built in 1973). Today a huge polar bear stands over the bar, to provide a reminder of how this place would've been filled with fishermen and hunters. Ølhallen has all the Mack beers, including the hop-forward craft beers brewed a few yards from the bar, and it also has many beers from Norwegian microbreweries. It's a great pub serving many great beers. You should start with

The Lowdown

WHAT: Mack Brewery and Ølhallen bar

HOW: Brewery tours run daily, finishing at the Ølhallen bar (www.olhallen.no).

WHERE: Storgata 4, 9008 Tromsø, Norway

Tromsø sparkles in the twilight.

a Mack Bayer, their excellent dark lager. Locals like to order a "Blanding," which is a Bayer topped up with Mack's Pilsner—this balances the malt sweetness with the Pilsner's hop bitterness.

Tromsø is a great city to visit. You'll discover amazing nature, lots of mountains nearby, a nice old town, plus top food and beer. I love it when the life bucket list meets the beer bucket list. Want to go on a Beer Safari around Tromsø? Then check out this informative tour on www.budgettours.no/beersafari.

LOCAL TIP: **Norway is Expensive**

A half-liter of local lager in a bar might cost NOK50–80 (US$6–10), while a craft beer can range from NOK90–160 (US$11–20). Also, the government regulates the sale of alcohol for anything over 4.7% ABV. Any store can sell beer up to 4.7% ABV—meaning that the majority of Norwegian beers are 4.7% and under. If you want anything stronger, including wine and spirits, then you can only buy these from the Vinmonopolet stores. Note that these have restricted opening hours, but also tend to have excellent selections of beer and no crossover with what's sold in regular stores.

The World's Northernmost Brewery

JUST WATCH OUT FOR POLAR BEARS...

Tromsø's Mack Bryggeri was the world's northernmost brewery for decades until 2015 when Svalbard opened—after having changed a law with the Norwegian Parliament to allow brewing to take place on this Arctic island.

Svalbard Bryggeri is definitely one to add to the Beer Bucket List, but it's one for the more dedicated drinker: it'll take a couple of flights to get there, you'll be on a remote Arctic island, and there are lots of polar bears on Svalbard—more bears than people. (A warning for cat lovers: cats are not allowed on the island because they threaten the Arctic bird population.) If you do make it, they offer brewery tours and the beer is great, with a Pilsner, Pale Ale, IPA, Weissbier, and Stout as the core range—the Stout in particular is rich, smooth, and warming against the cold. The beers also use glacier water in the brewing process, which is (literally) very cool.

The Lowdown

WHAT: Svalbard Bryggeri

HOW: www.svalbardbryggeri.com

WHERE: Sjøområdet, 9170 Longyearbyen, Norway

Nordic Farmhouse Ale

FOR THE SERIOUS BEER LOVER

"Farmhouse" means little on the label of an urban craft brewery, but if you're hundreds of miles from a town, surrounded by fields, in a shed adding juniper branches to a pot over an open fire, then "farmhouse" has more significance.

Not that I've stood in that farmhouse. I wish I had. Sadly, I'm yet to experience genuine Nordic farmhouse brewing. Sure, some commercial examples exist, with Finnish Sahti being made by a few brewers, but I don't want that. The trouble is, to try true farmhouse ale is hard. First, you need to go to remotest Norway or Finland. Then you need to find someone to invite you into their house while they brew, and then you need to hope they offer you something to drink— you see, unlike Lithuanian farmhouse ales (see page 164), which are found in bars, the Nordic tradition still reserves drinking for at home. This fascinates me, as does the way farmhouse ales are brewed. Finnish Sahti begins with juniper and water being heated together over a wood fire, typically in a sauna. That hot, juniper-infused water is slowly poured over the malts for the mash; it's later strained through more juniper and then a baker's yeast is added. When it's ready, you get a lightly refreshing tartness, some sweetness, plus the herbal fragrance of juniper.

Norweigan Maltøl is an umbrella term for a variety of regional beer types. Crucial to many of these beers is the use of "kveik," or ancestral yeast strain. Some beers are dark, smoky, and made with commercial beer yeast; others are pale, fruity, cloudy, raw (not boiled), and made with juniper and kveik; then there are red-brown beers, which are fruity, sweetish, have a juniper flavor, use kveik, and are boiled. They vary widely in terms of processing, appearance, and taste, and these are just three of numerous varieties.

Both Sahti and Maltøl rely on ancient methods; they are brewed using passed-down knowledge and techniques, and made with the senses rather than science. To learn more, visit Lars Marius Garshol's excellent website: www.garshol.priv.no (where much of the above information comes from). For the most dedicated drinkers, there are a couple of beer festivals. The best one is the Kornøl Festival in Hornindal, in October—just don't expect anything like modern craft beer festivals...

Visit Stockholm for Super Swedish Beer

AND GO TO THE STOCKHOLM BEER & WHISKY FESTIVAL

Sweden is accelerating forward faster than most other beer-loving countries, taking inspiration from American and other Scandinavian brewers, and then creatively pushing brewing in different directions. This means that you'll find some unusual, interesting, and excellent beers in the full range of beer styles—it's also definitely one of the geekiest of beer destinations. Stockholm is the go-to Swedish beer place. Listed below are three bars, but there's a dozen more you'll want to check out if you have the time (and the money—it's not a cheap city).

Akkurat (Hornsgatan 18, 118 20 Stockholm) is widely regarded as one of the best beer bars and restaurants in Sweden, Scandinavia, and the rest of the world—they certainly have one of the very best beer lists in Europe. There's always a large mix of Swedish beers and only the best ones are selected. There are top Belgian beers, including Cantillon and Brasserie Dupont, plus many other excellent imports. And there's a lot of whisky. The food is tasty too, so you should eat there.

Oliver Twist (Repslagargatan 6, 118 46 Stockholm), which is a three-minute walk from Akkurat, feels like an American brewpub with flags and tin brewery signs all around, plus the kind of long beer list you'd expect Stateside. That list includes some great American beers, some from Britain, and also a lot of the best Swedish brews. The food is also good.

Omnipollo is a leading brewer that makes some classic craft styles, plus some of the most unusual beers around, including a series of dessert-inspired beers. They have a busy bar, Omnipollos Hatt (Hökens Gata 1A, 116 46 Stockholm), which sells their own beers, as well as the beers of their collaborators. Tasty pizzas help against the effects of the high-alcohol brews.

If you can, time your visit to coincide with the excellent Stockholm Beer & Whisky Festival, which takes place over two

The traditonal architecture of Stockholm is in contrast to the modern forward-thinking beers created by breweries such as Omnipollo.

consecutive weekends in September and October. You'll find many of the country and some of the world's top brewers there, plus spirit producers, at an event that encourages sipping small pours rather than gulping pints (for more details, check out www.stockholmbeer.se). It's definitely a nerdy beer event, but it's also a lot of fun and a good chance to discover what's happening in the world of beer.

Mikkeller's Copenhagen

DRINK AND EAT LIKE A DANISH GOD

Do you want a line-up of sour beers or would you prefer IPAs? Do you want barbecue, tacos, ramen, or Danish open-faced sandwiches, smørrebrød? Do you want to drink in a warehouse surrounded by wooden beer barrels, in a cool brewpub, or in a smart, chic bar? Whatever you want, you can find it with Mikkeller's Copenhagen because this worldly brewer, which has opened bars as far afield as Taiwan, San Diego, and the Faroe Islands, has taken over its home city with a range of incredible beer bars, restaurants, and a brewery.

Mikkeller, the original gypsy brewer, has elevated the beer-drinking experience, creating an exciting and diverse range of spaces in Copenhagen. Their first flagship bar—**Mikkeller Bar**—has a textbook, contemporary, Nordic design: uncluttered bare wood, simple and still homely, with easy-to-read beer boards and small glasses designed more for tasting than volume boozing. **Mikkeller & Friends** (Stefansgade 35, 2200) extends the concept of the original bar and adds more taps of incredible beer. They also have industrial spaces such as their **Mikkeller Barrel Room** (Refshalevej 169A, 1432), for aging their beers and with some rare beers on tap, as well as their **Warpigs brewpub** (Flaesketorvet 25, 1711) and barbecue joint, which is a joint collaboration with US rock-star brewers Three Floyds. At **Koelschip**, a bar near Mikkeller & Friends, they specialize in Belgian and Belgian-style beer, primarily Lambics, spontaneously fermented beers, and sours. They also have **Ramen To Bíiru** (Griffenfeldsgade 28, 2200) for noodles and beer (drink their house yuzu beer—it rocks), **Øl & Brød** (Viktoriagade 6, 1620) for beer and bread, and **La Neta** (Nørrebrogade 29, 2200) for tacos. There's even the **Bottle Shop** (Torvehallerne 21, Hal 1, E4, 1360) if you want to take some beer home with you, while **Mikropolis** (Vendersgade 22, 1363), which is a cocktails and craft beer bar, is ideal if you want to sip something different (check out www.mikkeller.dk for more info).

Altogether these destinations have made Copenhagen one of the great cities in which to drink beer. Mikkeller has also been able to change the perception of what beer is, what a beer bar is like, and the ways in which beer and food can work together—and they're doing it in cities beyond their home, activating change, especially in South East Asia. No small feat for brewers that don't technically have their own main brewery in their home city.

Copenhagen Beer Celebration is effectively craft beer's equivalent of the All-Star Game.

Be sure to try the Lazurite IPA.

Mikkeller Beer Celebration

Mikkeller is probably the best-connected brewery in the world and, every May in Copenhagen, they use those connections to throw one of the best and nerdiest (in a good way) beer festivals in the world: the Mikkeller Beer Celebration.

It's the kind of event that has beer geeks gawping and gasping and gossiping for months in advance. Somehow the line-up of breweries gets more impressive every year, with those breweries attending taking more and more incredible beers with them.

There are four four-hour sessions over a weekend. Tickets get you entry, one glass, and unlimited tasters of the beers on tap—but bear in mind that tickets invariably sell out very quickly.

Carlsberg Brewery, Copenhagen

BREWING YEAST'S SCIENTIFIC HOME

In 1847 J.C. Jacobsen established his new brewery on what was then the outskirts of Copenhagen. He'd spent some time in Bavaria and his goal was to brew Bavarian-style beer in his hometown, using bottom-fermenting lager yeast that he sourced from Gabriel Sedlmayr's Spaten Brewery in Munich.

The beer was a success and the brewery grew and expanded from there. However, something was holding back Jacobsen's beer because, while he had excellent clean water, he didn't have clean yeast. In 1875, the brewery built a laboratory so that they could study their ingredients better and, in 1883, Dr Emil Christian Hansen, who knew that most bad beer was down to bad yeast, made a major breakthrough in his studies: he developed a method of isolating and propagating pure yeast, which took the name *Saccharomyces carlsbergensis* (although now it's better known as *Saccharomyces pastorianus*, after Louis Pasteur). Before this point brewing yeast would've been made up of a mix of different yeast strains and bacteria, but, with this

discovery, yeast could be "clean" and pure. This was a revolution in world brewing and, rather than keeping it a secret, the brewery told others about it, thus enabling better brewing for everyone.

In 2013 the brewery found three very old bottles of Carlsberg and opened one to examine it. They took the yeast from that bottle and in 2016 got the Carlsberg Laboratory to brew a beer using this original Carlsberg yeast, following the original brewing process and recipe as closely as they could. "The Re-Brew Project" was a coppery-amber beer with some residual sweetness in the middle and a dry bitterness, in keeping with the Munich Dunkel style that the beer would have been like at that time.

Sharing Brewing Secrets

In the late 1830s, there were brewers who were willing to share their knowledge with others in the hope of improving the overall quality of beer. The grandfathers of this knowledge are Gabriel Sedlmayr, of Munich's Spaten Brewery, and Anton Dreher, from his brewery in Vienna. They took a study leave to travel through northern Europe and into Britain, visiting as many breweries as possible. They would've seen huge Porter vats and barrels of Pale Ale destined for India; they learnt about different yeasts (famously stealing samples by using a walking stick with a valve in the base).

British malting techniques, which gave paler malts, were among the most significant things they learnt about. Sedlmayr and Dreher took this knowledge back to their hometowns and produced Munich malt and Vienna malt respectively, turning these into new paler beers in 1841. We know that the German brewing brethren were smart about good-quality yeast and fermentation, passing on that knowledge to others, including Jacobsen at Carlsberg, who then, in turn, passed on his new discoveries to other brewers. We can assume that Pilsner Urquell's first brewmaster Josef Groll (see page 126) also learnt something about malt from these guys and probably about bottom-fermenting lager yeast too.

Today you can visit the Carlsberg Brewery in Copenhagen and the self-guided tour is definitely worthwhile—it ends in a large, smart bar where you can drink some beer, including those from their varied and interesting Jacobsen range.

Dr Emil Christian Hansen's discovery enabled beer to leap forward in quality and consistency.

It was a very important moment in the history of brewing and indeed the Carlsberg Laboratory continues to be an industry-leading pioneer in brewing research.

Don't overlook the big breweries—often they are the most interesting places to learn about and visit. If you're in Copenhagen, go to Carlsberg.

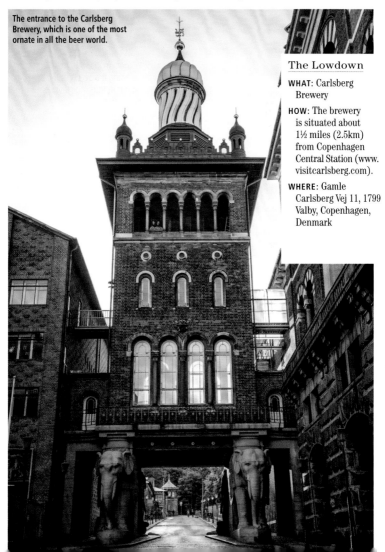

The entrance to the Carlsberg Brewery, which is one of the most ornate in all the beer world.

The Lowdown

WHAT: Carlsberg Brewery

HOW: The brewery is situated about 1½ miles (2.5km) from Copenhagen Central Station (www. visitcarlsberg.com).

WHERE: Gamle Carlsberg Vej 11, 1799 Valby, Copenhagen, Denmark

Kvass in Russia

TURNING BREAD INTO BEER

An unlikely resurgence in Russia's bread-based, low-alcohol beer, Kvass, has seen the drink rapidly go from old-fashioned to new and fashionable.

Kvass served from the tank.

Kvass is made using stale bread, plus fruit and spices, and is around 0.5%–2.0% ABV, making it more of a lightly fermented soft drink. There are major commercial brands of kvass brewed in Russia, varying geographically depending on whether the area prefers a sour or sweeter flavor. Restaurants have also started making their own kvass, brewing it to suit the different foods served, and this small-scale production is changing the appreciation of one of Russia's famous homebrews—and that's the part I'm most interested in, because it rejuvenates an old drink and makes it relevant and new. In summer, trucks, which look like small fermentation tanks with big wheels, stop on street corners and dispense the drink directly. And summer is when most kvass is consumed, as it's refreshing and cheap in the warmer weather. I couldn't make it to Russia to drink kvass while researching this book, so it's a personal Bucket List tick that I still want to achieve.

Drink Lithuanian Farmhouse Ales

AND TASTE BEERS LIKE YOU'VE NEVER HAD BEFORE

At a time when drinkers were always looking for the newest styles, they realized they'd completely missed some very old styles of beer, with the Baltic beauty of Lithuania revealing a deep local beer culture and a whole range of beer styles that are unique to the country—no beers anywhere else in the world taste like these.

Farmhouse brewing has long traditions across Europe, but in most places it died out or turned into a commercial endeavor. Not so in Lithuania where it survived, in part thanks to the Soviet occupation, which saw the authorities take over commercial breweries, demanding that they made just six fixed recipes and also determining the total output of a brewery. Homebrewers, or farmbrewers, didn't have such limitations, and with grain growing all around and enough local hops at their disposal, they continued to brew their beer, their way. Which is to say: not like any other beers brewed anywhere in the world.

When the Soviet hold was broken, the big brewers were slightly freed but, more importantly, the small, local brewers were able to become more commercial. Many of the brewers had learnt from their mothers or fathers, who learnt from their parents, and so on; recipes are unwritten and the processes are unscientific. This is how beer used to be made and it's still made that way today. Some brewers still make their own malt; some still grow their own hops or pick wild ones (sometimes with the hops made into a tea before being added, especially in the case of raw, or unboiled, beer); a lot of them use wooden brewing vessels and open fermentation tanks. But it's the yeast that's the really unique thing: something passed like a family treasure through the generations. It's this yeast that separates Lithuanian farmhouse beers from all other beers and it has no equivalent or similar strains in any other beer.

Lithuanian beers to look for

Kaimiškas, meaning "from the countryside," is a general grouping of farmhouse beers made in a traditional way, meaning with homemade malts, wild hops, and the brewer's ancestral yeast strain. The beer could be **Šviesusis** or **Tamsusis**, which is pale or dark; it may or may not be boiled during the brewing process, which is significant and adds to the beer's instability and unique flavor. Fermentation can also happen at very high temperatures (around 86°F/30°C), which in turn kicks out unusual qualities. **Jovaru Alus**, which is unboiled and brewed by the "queen of Lithuanian farmhouse brewers," is a great example of this type of beer: both sweet and bitter, with chewy, nutty malts in the middle and some faraway fruitiness and spice mixing with fermentation flavors.

These beers may look like Kellerbier, Saison, or a hazy Best Bitter, but they don't taste like them. They are often full and sweet in the middle, yet they dry right out at the end; bitterness is very low and you won't find hop aroma; there's an earthiness, something farm-y or cellar-like, likely coming from a combination of the malt, yeast, and brewing process used. Brewing faults such as diacetyl, phenols, and esters (think banana, strawberry, apple, smoke) are not considered bad in these beers, they are part of the flavor profiles; the beers are always unfiltered and unpasteurized, and their tastes vary from batch to batch.

Keptinis is an unusual type of Kaimiškas, which begins as baked barley bread. Baking adds caramelized qualities and extra sweetness when the bread is steeped in brewing water on its way to becoming beer. It's rare to find, but this old beer type has not been lost to modern beer culture. Look for the one made by Čižo Alus, a cult figure in Lithuanian brewing. This beer is sweet, spicy, doughy, and filled with banana and other esters, but still dry at the end, showing the gymnastics these yeasts are capable of. You may also see **Gira**, which is made with rye bread and other fermentables such as starchy vegetables, fruit, and honey (similar to Russian Kvass, see left). It's very low in alcohol (so sometimes not considered a beer) and may or may not be spiced—the ones I've tried had a funky, cola-like taste.

And where to drink them

Vilnius is the most accessible city in which to drink these beers, with a variety of bars serving them—often in very unique locations and with unique atmospheres. The drinking experience matches the unusual beers.

There are a few **Šnekutis** bars and they are must-visits in Vilnius. They all serve a variety of farmhouse beers on tap and in bottle, plus rustic, home-cooked food, and it's worth visiting all of them if you can as the beer choice differs (the Užupio location is essentially a wooden shack and it's brilliant). Try Šv. Stepono, g.8, Vilnius 01138 and the Užupio bar, Polocko g.7A, Vilnius 01204.

Bambalynė (Stiklių g.7, Vilnius 01131) is a basement bar with a lot of different local beers to choose from, both on tap and in bottle. **Alaus Namai** (A. Goštauto g.8, Vilnius 01108) is a short walk from the center of town. This is basically a Soviet bunker that plays rock music and it's wonderfully unique—you should be able to drink Čižo Alus there. There's also **Špunka** (Užupio g.9–1, Vilnius 01203), which has some Lithuanian craft beers on tap. This is a short walk from Šnekutis Užupio, making it worth stopping (if only to recalibrate your taste buds with something more familiar). There are some good craft beers in Lithuania—look for Sakiškių alus and Dundulis alus.

If the descriptions seem vague, this is because these beers aren't easy to understand and they change each time you drink them. But Lithuania's idiosyncratic beer culture is one of the most interesting in the world for how this type of brewing has survived and may now even begin to thrive as a result of a new appreciation by beer drinkers. A visit to Vilnius to try different Lithuanian farmhouse beers is a must-do for serious beer drinkers.

If you want to know more about these beers, then the go-to source is Lars Marius Garshol, who is largely responsible for the current interest in Lithuanian brewing. Lars has written a "rough guide" to the country's beers, which is available to download for free from his excellent website (www.garshol.priv.no).

Chapter 4
Australia and
New Zealand

Beer in Australia's Margaret River Wine Country

FOR THE WORLD'S HIGH-END TASTING ROOMS

It would seem that you need a lake and a few acres of land (plus a fat cheque book) in Margaret River, Western Australia, to even bother opening a brewery, because there are some spectacular locations to drink at, each among the largest, highest-end, most open-aired brewery set-ups I've seen. It's the MTV Cribs of beer and it's astonishing.

If you're driving down to Margaret River from Perth, then **Eagle Bay Brewing Co**. (236 Eagle Bay Road, Naturaliste, Western Australia 6281) is the first place you'll get to. The brewery has a view across its own lake that reaches over forests to the sea and is surrounded by all the blue sky your eyes can possibly look at. There are chairs and tables on the huge, sloping lawns, while inside there's a bright, smart restaurant space, with all the seats facing toward the view—it's unlike any brewery I've been to before (something I repeat to myself a few times over the day). There are a lot of kids at the weekends, but these venues are set up to give the kids somewhere to play while the adults eat and drink. The beers are good, especially the Kölsch, though I was mostly too busy running around the gardens to drink (I got more focused as the day wore on, I promise).

From Eagle Bay you can head south, bouncing east and west via plenty of breweries—the only trouble is that you really need to drive to these places, though some brewery tour companies in the area will drive you around. The next stop down the line is **Bootleg Brewery** (Puzey Road, Wilyabrup, Western Australia 6280), the original brewer in this part of the world. They also have a lake and are surrounded by trees—they are, in fact, almost in the trees. There's a kids' play area, and it's all very serene (aside from the screaming children). My tip: if kids and beer aren't for you, then go mid-week. It's a huge location, though not as high-end as others, feeling more like a massive permanent outdoor gazebo. I didn't actually love any of their beers, but it's still an amazing place to stop at.

Black Brewing Co. (3517 Caves Road, Wilyabrup, Western Australia 6280) is the most flabbergasting brewery I've ever been to. Outside, it's like a lavish villa, with marble walls, water features, and fountains; there's even a majestic statue of a horse. It's unbelievable—seriously, just image-search it on Google and you'll see. The view out the back is over a lake that shimmers a money-can't-buy turquoise. There are grape vines behind you. The kitchen cooks Thai food, and the heady spices waft through the warm air. And it's huge. It's also genuinely wonderful to drink somewhere like this—you have to kick yourself to remember that this is a brewery and you haven't just landed in the judges' houses part of **X Factor** by accident. Black's beers stand up to the surroundings: XPA, in particular, is tropical with guava, pineapple, melon, and soft stone fruits—it's also a good match for the Thai food.

Cheeky Monkey Brewery & Cidery (4259 Caves Road, Wilyabrup, Western Australia 6280) also has a lake and, of course, and it's a very nice one. This is a chilled-out, relaxed space that spreads into the garden. Like the other places, Cheeky Monkey is versatile: there's a garden space and play area; there's smarter dining and a bar inside, and a good kitchen. There are more good beers, too, especially the West Coast IPA, which is orangey, grapefruit-pithy fresh and dry with a melony freshness.

I now think I've cracked why Margaret River has so many breweries like this in such a small area. It's quite simple, really: the sun is always out and they have lots of room. You couldn't have a location so open and outdoorsy on an industrial estate in the US

Midwest or England's West Midlands. But this is Australia and it's massive, plus not many people live out in the west, so there's loads of space. Plus, there's an outdoorsy, beer-garden lifestyle there that just fits. Mix all this with the fanciness of the region's wineries, which creates a "standard" for the drinking spaces, and it all comes together to elevate the drinking location, while somehow retaining a "brewery-in-the-backyard" atmosphere.

My final stop was **Colonial Brewing Co.** (56 Osmington Road, Margaret River, Western Australia 6285). Their lake is particularly massive—as is their tasting room and the grounds, where kids can run around, while adults work their way through tasting trays and pizzas, before they come together to play catch, cricket, or swingball. It's the ultimate beer garden and the ultimate playground for both big and little kids. Colonial have a punchy little 3.5% ABV beer called Small Ale and there's a lemonade-like Wheat beer that's gloriously refreshing.

And there were still others that I didn't get to: The Beer Farm, Cowaramup Brewing Company, and Bush Shack Brewery. They all looked enormous as well, obviously. And I bet they've all got at least one lake each.

Margaret River is where Western Australia's vineyards are located and, if you were to write a parody piece about beer being the new wine, you might describe breweries exactly as they are there—especially Black Brewing, which is so far from being a grungy, gungy, garage-band-pumping brewpub. Yet it's wonderful for being so grand and gorgeous.

These breweries and taprooms were so different that I felt I was discovering them and discovering something new in beer— something that I didn't know existed. And that was an exciting feeling. Going from one to the next, I was constantly surprised and wowed by what I saw. The Margaret River breweries are unlike anywhere I've drunk before and far removed from the cold, gray industrial estates I'm used to traipsing around. And, while on cold, gray, wet days those industrial-estate

The taproom at Cheeky Monkey Brewery and Cidery. Order one of their terrific IPAs and head outside to the beer garden to enjoy the warm Australian sunshine.

breweries have their own allure and solace, on warm Aussie days, it's amazing to be at the world's most high-end breweries, in the world's greatest, largest, showiest beer gardens, surrounded by green trees, blue skies, turquoise lakes, and the golden sun, as well as a rainbow of different beers.

The Settler's Tavern, Margaret River

If you're in Margs, then stay in the main town and head to The Settler's Tavern (114 Bussell Highway, Margaret River, Western Australia 6285) for dinner. There are 12 taps of beer, a couple of local ciders, 25-plus wines by the glass, and over 400 bottles—they've won awards for their wine list, but the beer list is strong, too. The food portions are huge, served quickly, and it's very tasty. They also brew their own beers under the Margaret River Ale Co. After a day of visiting breweries or vineyards, it's the ideal end-point.

Go to Little Creatures Brewery

FOR THE ORIGINAL AUSSIE CRAFT BEER

It happened again. My expectations were high—almost as high as my thirst on a hot day in Fremantle, on the coast outside Perth—and those lofty hopes were topped by something far greater than I imagined.

The Little Creatures Brewery is comprised of three side-by-side sheds, overlooking the harbor in Fremantle. They were built in the 1980s as boat sheds for the America's Cup and two of them were later used—this is delightfully Aussie—as a crocodile farm. Some beer-loving mates moved a brewery into the two croc sheds in 1999 and released their first beer in 2000. A few years later, they took over the shed next door and knocked it into a new, bigger space, into which they added a new, bigger brewhouse.

Before you even get to the bar, you'll be amazed to find yourself in a theater of beer. You can't miss that you're in a brewery—there are pipes above your head, tanks on every side, and pints all around you. You can visit hundreds of breweries where the tanks are visible, but there are very few places in which the drinker is at the center—it's a show-in-the-round, only you sit in the middle with the action playing around you.

There's a central bar in The Great Hall with walkways all around—the same walkways that people once stood on to look at the crocodiles. There's an open kitchen with the glow and heat of a pizza oven and the never-ending job of rolling out and proving dough balls (thousands of these are made each week by a team of 75 chefs—it's one of the biggest à la carte restaurants in the southern hemisphere. Fun frites-based fact: 80 tonnes of potatoes

are hand-cut each year to be turned into their excellent frites.

You've got fermentation, conditioning, and serving tanks to one side (they sell around 500,000 liters of beer a year). The other side leads you through to the brewhouse—where you can walk around and see everything—and to the Brewhouse Bar. There's seating everywhere—including overlooking the fishing-boat harbor (this is the same view the brewers enjoy every day from the brewhouse)—on the mezzanine walkway, with a view over everything, or outside in the sun. I bought a pint and just walked around a few times, astonished by the place and in awe at being able to drink surrounded by the brewery. The beer I was drinking was their first beer, their flagship beer, and the beer that has built this space: Little Creatures Pale Ale. Brewed with whole leaf hops, it's Cascade-focused with some Chinook, plus a mix of other varieties from America, Australia, and New Zealand. The whole leaf hops give a gentle grapefruit and floral quality that's characteristic of Cascade, while Chinook plays wingman by bringing pine and pith and the Aussie and Kiwi hops add a little fresh stone fruit. The base brew is round in malts, a little fudgy, with a pleasing softness. When this beer was first brewed in 2000 it was polarizing for its high hop flavor and bitterness, a beer unlike any other on the continent. While it may no longer astonish with hoppiness, it's certainly the most important Aussie beer and still revered as the original craft beer, a beer that transcends the country's state-based beer preferences—VB in Victoria, XXXX in Queensland—to be regarded as belonging to all of Australia.

Little Creatures Pale Ale is an "everybody beer," an all-inclusive beer, a beer for all occasions; it's a gateway beer, a go-to fridge beer, a favorite beer, one that's balanced and fruity and gentle, yet impactful. It's the Sierra

The Lowdown

WHAT: Little Creatures Brewery

HOW: Tours run daily (12–3pm, on the hour), starting at the Brewhouse Bar. The bar is open every day from 10am (from 9am on weekends) until late (www.littlecreatures.com.au).

WHERE: 40 Mews Road, Fremantle, Western Australia 6160

Little Creatures successfully manages to pull off the trick of offering a comfortable, cool taproom space that seemlessly blends into a working brewery.

Nevada Pale Ale of Australia. This is the beer that started craft brewing, continues to be a benchmark of quality, and that drinkers return to because it's so good. And it's good without having to show off. It's not necessarily meant to make you say "wow;" it's meant to make you say, "I'll have another Creatures."

A few years ago the brewery realized that shipping beer from Fremantle on the far west coast to the distant east coast of Australia—some 2,500 miles (4,000km)—just didn't make sense. So they built another brewery, twice the size of the original one, in Geelong, just outside Melbourne. This is also a great place to visit. The beautiful brewhouse is immaculate. There's a large drinking space inside, leading to an outside courtyard, which is chilled out and bright. You're not surrounded by tanks, but it's a great place to visit if you're in Melbourne.

I expected the Fremantle brewery to be impressive, but it went far beyond my expectations. You have to start with a Pale Ale, because it's the beer that introduced American hops to Australians, then try some of their other beers. And definitely order food, as you'll want to hang around for a while. It's one of the Top 10 best brewery spaces in the world to drink in and an essential place to visit.

Visit Feral's Swan Valley Brewpub

THE AUSSIE BACKYARD ON THE EDGE OF THE BUSH

Feral Brewing's brewpub, around 20 miles (30km) outside Perth, could be ripped from the dog-eared pages of the *How To Build A Brilliant Brewpub* guidebook: there are lots of taps, including core beers and brewpub specials; the tanks are behind the bar; there's a blackboard beer list, with growlers and bottles to go; there are T-shirts for sale; and there's top-quality bar food—some of the best you'll find in brewpubs anywhere.

Outside there are lush gardens within the 11 acres (4.5 hectares); there's loads of space for kids and adults to run around; there's an outdoor bar, with a food truck that cooks burgers on the barbie at weekends; and there are grapes, fruits, veg, and herbs growing in the gardens. The brewpub is spread out in the red-dust ruggedness of the bush, where it feels loved and lived in, a little busted at the sides, but dented with good times and good memories. It's a great Australian backyard, with one of Australia's great breweries in the middle.

The liquid significance of Feral begins with Hop Hog, a strong-ish, American-styled Pale Ale. It was first brewed in 2008—nine years after the brewery was founded—and was inspired by brewer and owner Brendan Varis's trip to San Diego, where he drank Ballast Point's Sculpin IPA. It wasn't just the way the beer tasted; it was that if you had an immaculately balanced beer, then it could be an everyday drink, even if it was hoppy and strong by Aussie standards. When Hop Hog was released, it was the hoppiest beer in Australia; it remained the hoppiest, regularly available beer in Oz for many years, having the same huge hop impact of beers like Sculpin, only reining in the alcohol to 5.8% ABV. If Little Creatures showed Aussies what US hops could taste like, then Feral taught them to love big, hoppy brews.Hop Hog is an outstanding Pale Ale. Clean, bright, and fresh, with oily oranges lacing the beer with a richness of hop flavor; there's a dryness that highlights some pithy hops and some subtle savoriness—it's a proper West Coast US brew made near the west coast of Australia.

Following the success of Hop Hog and their other beers, in 2012 Feral added a production facility midway between the Swan Valley and Perth. There they brew and package their core range of beers, leaving the brewpub for the

The Lowdown

WHAT: Feral Brewing Co.

HOW: Open Sunday to Thursday, 11am–5pm, and Friday to Saturday, 11am–late (www.feralbrewing.com.au).

WHERE: 152 Haddrill Road, Baskerville, Perth, Western Australia 6065

Is Feral's Hop Hog Australia's most influential craft beer? It's definitely one of the tastiest.

Good Aussie and Kiwi Pub Grub and Beer Matches

- Fish and chips is a staple, along with burgers, in Australia and New Zealand. Often the fish is beer-battered, typically in something pale and hoppy, which leads you to the best match: a zesty, punchy Pale Ale.

- Chicken Parma is an Aussie pub classic. It's a flattened, breaded chicken breast topped with some sliced ham, tomato marinara sauce, and cheese, and it's always served with chips and salad. Go all-Aussie with the pairing and pick a local Australian-hopped Pale Ale.

- Calamari, often Asian-influenced with five spice and salt and pepper, is a snack on most menus. The fragrant spiciness is great with a hoppy NZ Pilsner. You'll also often see huge green-lipped mussels on Kiwi menus. Pilsner and Wheat Beer are the top beer picks for these meaty mussels.

- Kumara is a Kiwi sweet potato, a little more textured and creamier than regular sweet potatoes, and makes amazing chips. A smooth Stout is the best buddy of a kumara chip—though, as with all chips, they work with all beers. Always take the "upgrade to kumara chips" option in New Zealand.

- Lamb is big in New Zealand, and chops or steaks are found on many menus. I always like Saison with lamb, with the dry, peppery spices being a nice match for the meat's richness.

small batches and fun stuff. At the brewpub you'll find everything, from Bavarian-esque lagers to IPAs to fruited sours to big Imperial Stouts. Their other hoppy brews include War Hog, a bold, bitter, bright, and beautifully clean IPA with a load of powerful citrusy hops, and B.F.H, a barrel-fermented Hog, creamy from the oak, which lends a smoothness to the brashness of the citrusy hops. On the sour side they utilize barrels from their setting surrounded by vineyards and their best-known brew is Watermelon Warhead, a sub-3.0% ABV sour beer, aged in wine barrels and using the juice from visually imperfect watermelons grown by a perfectionist local farmer. It's tart, tangy, and complex from the barrel and limitlessly refreshing from those watermelons.

Feral were one of the first Australian craft breweries and they remain one of the best. Their Swan Valley brewpub is a perfect encapsulation of Aussie brewing, all with the atmosphere of a great Australian backyard. It's an ultimate destination brewpub—something Western Australia has a lot of with Little Creatures (see page 170) and the high-end Margaret River brewers (see page 167). Go to the brewpub and drink their exceptional Hop Hog—the beer that made Australia love hops.

THE BEST BUCKET LIST SPOTS FOR BEER AND FOOD

- Cruz Blanca, Chicago, USA (see page 30)
- Stone Brewing Taproom, Escondido, USA (see page 49)
- Feral Brewing Taproom, Swan Valley, Australia
- Restobières, Brussels, Belgium (see page 152)
- Casa Baladin, Piozzo, Italy (see page 132)
- Bundobust, Leeds and Manchester, UK (see page 90)

Drink Stone & Wood Pacific Ale

THE ULTIMATE ALL-AUSSIE BREW

On January 26, 1989, Australian national radio station, Triple J, held a countdown of the previous year's Hottest 100 Songs as voted for by listeners. It's happened every year since (apart from 1992) and is the cultural gem of a generation of Australians.

The emerging Australian craft beer community, clearly fans of the famous radio show, launched their own Hottest 100 for beer, with the results of the drinker-voted list also being revealed on January 26, which is Australia Day. Since 2010, Stone & Wood's Pacific Ale has been in the top three, winning the competition three times, where it typically leapfrogs onto the podium with Feral's Hop Hog.

Stone & Wood was started in 2008 by three mates, Brad Rogers, Jamie Cook, and Ross Jurisich. They built their brewery a few miles from the beach in Byron Bay. Their first beer was Pacific Ale and it's remained their bestseller ever since.

Pacific Ale is now an iconic beer that created a new style of Australian ale—most other brewers call their versions "Summer Ale," but we all know they're copying Pacific Ale. It uses all-Aussie ingredients, including barley and wheat, and Galaxy hops from Tasmania. It was a leader in fruit-forward aromatics, thanks to those glorious Galaxy hops, which give passion fruit, pawpaw, mango, and tropical fruit, which are the signature accents of this beer and of the style. It has a subtle sweetness, which plumps up those fruity hops, and is aided by a satisfying weight from the yeast and by being unfiltered. It has a brightness, a lightness, a beauty all of its own.

When walking around Byron Bay you will instantly spot a glass of Pacific Ale. It has a fluffy white cloud of foam above a hazy yellow beer, which looks almost neon in the glass, as

Byron Bay, right on the Pacific Ocean, is the home to Stone and Wood, and the Pacific Ale will always be linked to this epic beachside setting.

if the sun is reflecting off the beer. And when you're there, drinking by the sea, you can see how evocatively and perfectly Pacific Ale fits this place and suits the Australian summer.

The best place to drink Pacific Ale in Byron Bay is at **The Beach Hotel** (1 Bay Street, Byron Bay, New South Wales 2481) a large open bar opposite the sea. This is where the beer was designed to be drunk and even the most land-lubbed and city-slick drinkers will grasp this imagery: you're in the summer surf, you're sweaty and salty, and hot and hanging for a cold one. You walk off the sand and straight to the bar, and there's a glass of brightly hazy Pacific Ale waiting for you. It's fresh and fruity, oh so fruity, and dry and refreshing. It's hard to imagine another beer being quite so able to quench a summer thirst like this one.

You can visit the **Byron Bay Brewery** (1 Skinners Shoot Road, Byron Bay, New South Wales 2481), which is open every day from 12pm until around 5pm. In 2016, they added a larger production facility out of town; you can't visit that, but Byron Bay is cooler anyway. It has a cellar-door style, so you go along and have a tasting tray that includes the core beers, plus some small-batch specials. Other beers include

Cloud Catcher, which is basically a bigger version of Pacific Ale and uses Galaxy and Ella hops; there's Green Coast, a very good, soft-bodied lager, with a light freshness of hops, and Jasper Ale, an Altbier-ish copper ale. Once you've had your tasting tray, then head back to town to the other essential place to drink—The Rails (officially called The Railway Friendly Bar, but no-one calls it that)—which has played free live music every night for over 30 years.

Stone & Wood's Pacific Ale is an important beer for its use of all-Australian ingredients, for being the first fully fruit-forward Aussie beer, deliberately hazy in a country of sparkling, bright pale ales, and for being the beer that

The Lowdown

WHAT: Stone & Wood Brewing Company

HOW: Open for tasting sessions and tours every day of the week (although there are no tours on Tuesdays). Check the website before visiting, as the address may differ by the time this book is published (www.stoneandwood.com.au).

WHERE: 4 Boronia Place, Byron Bay, New South Wales 2481, Australia

A pint of Pacific Ale served in the taproom is a welcome refresher after a day at the beach.

has created a new style of Australian Summer Ale. It's one of my favorite beers, something I often drink in London (which, the Internet tells me, is over 10,300 miles/16,600km away from the brewery), and a beer that was right at the top of my Beer Bucket List must-visit destinations. While it's always good in London, it's even better in Byron Bay, where there's an intangible link between the beer and the place, an evocative and emotional placement, and something that now shines warm in my memory and allows me to sit at home in the rain and think of the sun, summer, and surf of Byron Bay.

It's a beer that's definitely in my top three Hottest 100 list of Aussie beers. Also on the podium would be Blackman's Mervyn and Feral's Hop Hog.

GABS & Melbourne Good Beer Week

THE BEST BEER FESTIVAL IN THE SOUTHERN HEMISPHERE

To gauge just how good the beer and brewing are in Australia and New Zealand, go to the Great Australasian Beer Spectacular (or GABS). It used to just take place in Melbourne, but has since expanded to Sydney and Auckland—the Aussie versions take place on consecutive weekends at the end of May, while the Kiwi one is a few weeks later in the middle of June.

You'll find over 600 beers at the Australian GABS (and 300 in Auckland). One of the fun things about this festival is the number of special beers brewed especially for the event—you can expect over 180 new and unique brews in Australia (80 in New Zealand)—which have never been tasted before and often have odd inspirations. There's also cider, street food, live entertainment, meet the brewers, and more. The quality of beer in these places is very high and all the best brewers attend.

The Melbourne GABS tops the end of Melbourne Good Beer Week, which is the very best beer week in the world and it runs from early to mid-May, with the dates varying each year. What makes it so good is the volume, variety, and quality of events, which number over 300 during the festival, and the fact that it brings in breweries from across Australasia, Asia, and farther away, including America and Europe. It's not just a range of beer geek events; you'll find everything, including dinners with some of the world's best chefs, fashion shows, master-classes, beer versus whisky and wine, exclusive tap takeovers, and so much more. Reading the programs for the festivals, I wanted to go to almost everything. No other beer week comes close.

The Lowdown

WHAT: Great Australasian Beer Spectacular (GABS)

HOW: Visit www.gabsfestival.com and www.goodbeerweek.com.au for details.

WHERE: Melbourne and Sydney, Australia, and Auckland, New Zealand

---

LOCAL TIP: **Learn the Lingo, Mate**

Pint, schooner, pot, middy… The sizes and names of beer glasses vary all around Australia. First of all, if you order a large beer then it's usually 14oz (425ml). In Southern Australia, Western Australia, and Tasmania that's called a pint—but you can also get a 20-oz (570-ml) pint. In Victoria, Northern Territory, Queensland, and New South Wales a large beer is called a schooner. If you're in South Australia and only want a small beer (10oz/285ml), then that's called a schooner. In New South Wales and Western Australia a small beer is called a middy, but in Victoria and Queensland it's called a pot. In Tasmania a small glass might be a ten (or a six, seven, or eight if you want them even smaller), while in the Northern Territory it'll be a handle or just a beer. Confused? Just ask for a jug, that size is universal (40oz/1140ml). Got it?

Melbourne Good Beer Week now attracts around 95,000 attendees to 300 beer-related events in around 200 venues across Melbourne and wider Victoria.

Australian Hotel Pub Crawls

Ever heard of the "six o'clock swill"? Well, under old Australian licensing laws, pubs could only serve beer from 10am until 6pm, which was inconvenient for most workers with a 9-to-5 day job. So, at 5pm, they'd jump from their desks, run to the nearest pub, and gulp down as much as possible in the one hour of drinking time available to them. The six o'clock swill had obvious negative effects and eventually the laws changed to allow pubs to stay open until later, which in turn had the impact of creating the possibility of pub crawls. If you're reading this, then there's a good probability that you like a pub crawl.

While it's true that there aren't many (or any) unique world pub crawls, there are definitely some great ones to go on, including visiting historic London pubs, bouncing between tapas bars in Madrid, sampling Munich's brauhauses, or trying out the ruin bars in Budapest. However, big Australian cities have many old hotels that are now pubs and these have become uniquely Australian drinking places.

These hotel pubs—typically now just pubs—were once multi-purpose places: a bar to drink in, a restaurant to eat at, somewhere to sleep, to meet, to do business, to send and receive mail, plus some also served as a general store. Often in grand old buildings with elaborate balconies and lots of space, they have since been repurposed and taken over by plenty of great beer.

Both Sydney and Melbourne have numerous great examples of these pubs spread around the cities. And they're proper pubs. They sell chips and bar food and there's sport on TV and the beer is ice cold. In Sydney, **The Australian Heritage Hotel** (100 Cumberland Street; australianheritagehotel.com) in The Rocks is an important old pub and in a prime locations, while the nearby **Lord Nelson Brewery Hotel** (19 Kent Street; www. lordnelsonbrewery.com) specializes in British-styled beers and is the oldest continually licensed hotel in the city.

In Melbourne, there's **The Great Northern Hotel** (644 Rathdowne Street, Carlton North

3054; www.gnh.net.au) with a great garden and even greater tap list. **The Royston** (12 River Street; www.roystonhotel.com.au) is a dark, horseshoe-shaped bar opposite Mountain Goat Brewery. Have a parma and a pint.

Drink on the Manly Ferry

If you're in Sydney, then a ferry over to Manly makes a nice day out, with the views of Sydney Harbour alone being worth the ticket money. In Manly, when you're done at the beach, drink at **4 Pines Brewery** (29/43–45 East Esplanade, Manly, New South Wales 2095), where the Indian Summer Ale is especially good, before jumping on a ferry home. Fantastically, this ferry serves beers (mostly mainstream stuff, but they have a decent James Squires Pale Ale too) and also allows you to bring your own, so either grab some to-go brews at 4 Pines or pack a bag in preparation, so you can drink a cold one while enjoying the ride.

The Australian Heritage Hotel. For visitors to the city it's conveniently located near the major tourist attractions of the Sydney Opera House and the Sydney Harbour Bridge.

The Mussel Inn

THE PUB WORTHY OF NATIONAL ICON STATUS

In the middle of nowhere, somewhere in the faraway north-west of New Zealand's South Island, around a two-hour drive west of Nelson, switch-backing perilously up then down Takaka Hill, passing almost nothing except trees, you'll eventually, finally, hopefully spot a barrel-shaped sign that says The Mussel Inn—and you will have arrived at one of the most wonderful, charming, and unique brewery-pubs in the world.

In the 1980s, Andrew and Jane Dixon were building houses out of wood for a living. Having built them for other people, they decided it was time to build their own home on land they owned in Onekaka. Andrew was also home-brewing beers, but prior to craft beer there were no cafés or bars in which customers could drink anything interesting, so, in 1992, they built The Mussel Inn in front of their house in order to serve great non-mainstream beers. Three years later, thanks to the success of the pub and positive responses to the homebrew, they added a small brewery. Today this is a locals' pub that happens to attract many tourists; the locals help to make this pub what it is, some physically by building bits of it, others by helping to create its arms-open atmosphere.

The pub is essentially a one-room wooden hut—but it's the greatest one-room wooden hut I've ever drunk in. It's made from local macrocarpa wood. There's an atmospheric and acoustics-friendly pitched room and a fireplace on one side; at weekends there's a stage set up for live music; the bar is small and simple, with six beer taps and one for cider. Outside there are covered verandas and seating, while the rest of the beer garden is open and in the greenery—in fact, the gardens grow around, into, and with the pub.

The Dixons grow hops; there's an orchard, feijoas, and lemons, plus a vegetable patch that supplies the kitchen. They are exceptionally eco-conscious at The Mussel Inn. They recycle glass bottles and any that can't be re-used are turned into sand by a bottle-crusher and distributed around their land; any potential waste water from the brewing process irrigates the orchard; they shred cardboard boxes and put the shreddings in their "humanure" composting toilets; and they've also bought a machine to blow-mold plastic bottles, rather than having them blown in Auckland and freighted to the pub.

They brew all their own beers, ciders, and soft drinks, and all the food is homemade—it's also very good (try the quiche to maximize the garden-grown veggies you eat). The brewery is most famous for Captain Cooker Manuka Beer. When Captain James Cook arrived on these distant islands, he brewed

BEST NON-US TAPROOMS AND BREWERY BARS AROUND THE WORLD

- The Marble Arch, Manchester, UK (see page 94)
- Mahr's Brau, Bamberg, Germany (see page 119)
- Augustiner-Brau, Munich, Germany (see page 112)
- Stone Brewing, Berlin, Germany (see page 121)
- BrewDog DogTap, Ellon, Scotland (see page 104)
- Mikkeller Bar, Copenhagen, Denmark (see page 160)
- Dieu du Ciel!, Montreal, Canada (see page 64)
- Little Creatures, Fremantle, Australia (see page 170)
- The Mussel Inn, Onekaka, New Zealand
- Pasteur Street Brewing, Ho Chi Minh City (see page 196)

With its remote location, not many beer lovers make it to The Mussel Inn, but those who do will be treated to a beer experience they'll remember for the rest of their lives.

The Lowdown

WHAT: The Mussel Inn

HOW: Open seven days a week (11am–late), but closed mid-July to mid-September (www.musselinn.co.nz).

WHERE: 1259 State Highway 60, Onekaka, Golden Bay 7182, New Zealand

a beer with manuka honey to help fight off scurvy in his crew; he also released wild pigs into the country, which became known as Captain Cookers—hence the beer's name and the pig on the beer's logo. At the time Andrew started brewing, there were a couple of popular brown beers made by New Zealand's larger breweries and drinkers would come in and ask for them. Andrew decided to give them something visually similar but very different in taste. The resulting Captain Cooker is ostensibly based on its namesake's recipe and brewed with fresh manuka tips (it's been analyzed by boffins and they've said the beer is far higher in antioxidants than regular beers).

Captain Cooker is a singular beer. It's peppery, spicy, deeply herbal, dry, and almost savory, which the toast and cocoa of darker malts round out with some sweetness. It's bitter, botanic, and idiosyncratic, and reveals more and more of itself as you go from glass to glass, though you'll never quite manage to figure it out properly. You'll also never forget it. The Mussel Inn's other brews include the English-tasting Pale Whale IPA and also Dark Horse, which has a deep, dry Stout bitterness. Golden Goose Lager is pleasingly simple, plus there are other ever-changing brews and a refrigerator filled with bottles, including some

sour beers. Their Apple Roughy cider (made using their own apples) is zingy, tangy, and crunchy like a Granny Smith apple, plus their Feijoa "Cider" is brewed with the guava-like fruit that they grow themselves. It's melony, limey, tropical, and grape-like—it's really good. For drivers, there's homemade lemonade and ginger beer.

The remote location, the people, the beer, the food, the live music, the gardens, the wooden buildings, and the eco-consciousness all combine in a remarkable way. The marvel of The Mussel Inn is that you get the feeling of going from the *middle of nowhere* to being *now here* and there's a warm sense that you've arrived somewhere special, built by the hands of a few and the hearts of many, many more. It is a national and cultural icon of New Zealand. A legendary place. If ever a brewery deserved a UNESCO listing, then The Mussel Inn should receive it. I think it's a Top 10 must-visit world beer destination.

The Moutere Inn

NEW ZEALAND'S OLDEST PUB

This might not be a must-visit destination in isolation, but, if you're in the Nelson area, this short, pleasant detour allows you to drink at New Zealand's oldest pub: The Moutere Inn.

There was a drive in the 1840s to bring European migrants to this part of New Zealand and this brought a significant number of Germans, who built a town with all the essentials: a church, school, store, post office, and an inn. Cordt Bensemann was the German migrant responsible for the inn. After a few years living in the region with his family, he moved to what is now Upper Moutere, where he first built a house and then started work on the main wing of the inn, which was completed in 1853. He added an additional wing in 1857 and moved his family into this part of the building—they lived there for 36 years. The inn was clearly well built, as it still remains today with only limited structural change. It's this enduring building that allows The Moutere Inn to claim to be the oldest pub in New Zealand—other "oldest pubs" have been burnt down or destroyed and rebuilt, but not this place.

The Moutere Inn is not just one of New Zealand's oldest pubs, it's only 30 years younger than its oldest surviving building.

Today the pub is run by beer-lovers and that's immediately evident when you walk in and see the range of New Zealand craft beers on tap. They also have a couple of their own beers that are contract-brewed for the pub, including 1516, a very nice New Zealand Pilsner with a fresh lemony lilt. There's also homemade ginger beer and good food (the portions are huge).

The pub sits on top of a hill, with the view a patchwork quilt of greens, patterned by hop bines, orchards, and grape vines. It's a view that probably hasn't changed much since Bensemann first built his house there. Turn toward the building and the structure is also as it was over 150 years ago and, although it feels bright and modern inside, there's something timeless about it. There are always arguments about the oldest pub in a country and there are other Kiwi contenders, though The Moutere Inn seems to be the one that most people consider to be the original and the longest lasting. Don't pass by without stopping in for some lunch and a beer.

The Lowdown

WHAT: The Moutere Inn

HOW: www.moutereinn.co.nz

WHERE: 1406 Moutere Highway, Upper Moutere 7175, New Zealand

Epic Beer in Auckland

TURN YOURSELF INTO A HOP ZOMBIE

Go to a brewery that specializes in Double IPAs and, at some point in the evening, you'll see people in a daze, with a glazed look in their eyes and visibly fuzzy at the edges.

First those big hoppy brews give the enlivening ferocity of alpha acids, their bitterness providing the senses with something exciting to act on (is this bitterness a poison? Will it kill me?), then there's the sweet, booze-bringing malts, that initial rush of alcohol, that rush of excitement at drinking something powerfully delicious, and then the room rises together. But by the third or fourth glass the oils in the hops reveal an older use, that of a snoozy sleep aid, which joins with the eternally hypnotic, tranquilizing effects of alcohol and creates a space filled with hop zombies, stumbling, their initial fast-talking now slow, their movements manual, their minds sedated.

It's hard to associate a hop-brought sleepiness with Epic Beer (www.epicbeer. com). Even their own Hop Zombie—their epically great Double IPA—seems to bring an electricity, a fizz of life and excitement, though inevitably the last bottle or glass you drink will leave you smiling soporifically. It's one of New Zealand's best beers and one of the best beers I drank during the research for this book. It's an oily brew, slick with hops that coat your tongue with tangerines and oranges, but which also keeps the vast bitterness hidden. The body is as lean as an 8.5% ABV beer can be, but also strong enough to give that hop oil something to stick to. It's an intense beer with a full-on brilliance and balance. It shows how hop flavor and oiliness—features that are so often buried beneath a sense-blinding aroma—are integral parts of a beer's composition. That quality is consistent in all Epic's beers. Epic Armageddon IPA is an apocalyptic blast of American hops, rich with all the citrus fruits, and a deep golden body that has a rare kind of malt juiciness, but without sweetness. Epic Thunder is a vicious bolt of American hops. Even the excellent Lager is loaded with lupulin and hop depth.

Epic has been at the forefront of Kiwi brewing since brewer and owner Luke Nicholas started the brewery in 2005. They've always produced bold brews and they are the biggest user of US hops in New Zealand; they also use Kiwi hops, but there aren't enough grown to fulfil Epic's heroic hop needs. The beers are contract-brewed (they always have been) and Auckland is the best place to drink them at their freshest (by the time this book is released, they might have a taproom at their warehouse in town, which, by the way, is where they also have a side-project still for distilling gins under the Hidden World label).

I specifically went to Auckland to drink Epic Beers because I've always craved them and always wanted to drink them fresh, ever since a few stolen sips from someone's holiday haul. If you're in town, then the best places to go to drink the freshest Epic beers are **Vultures' Lane** (10 Vulcan Lane, Auckland) and **Brew on Quay** (102 Quay Street, Auckland). Ease in with a lightning glass of their Lager, move on to Thunder, then into Armageddon, and end up as a Hop Zombie.

New Zealand's First Brewpub

If you're in Auckland, then stop in at **The Shakespeare Hotel and Brewery** (61 Albert Street, Auckland). It's a 100-year-old pub that added a small brewery in 1986 (although brewing ceased for a few years in the 2000s), making it the first brewpub in New Zealand. The brewery is still tucked in behind the bar; there'll be sports on TV and you can play a game of pool or sit by the fireplace. Their Jester is a light, fruity little lager. They also have hotel rooms if you need somewhere to stay. Worth popping into for a quick one.

See a Hop Harvest

A HOP-HEAD'S DREAM

You could go to see the seemingly unending rolling hills of Germany's Hallertau region, with its huge trellis structures like a vast garden metropolis. There are the fields of Kent, England, with their old oast houses peeking above the canopies of hops. You could see the mountain-range backdrop of the Pacific Northwest and breathe in air that's sticky with pungent hops. Or there are the fields west of Nelson, at the north of New Zealand's South Island. Any of these places and more will, for about six weeks of the year, allow you to experience the annual hop harvest and to see how hops complete their journey from bine to brewhouse.

My trip to New Zealand coincided with their hop harvest, so I drove to Motueka, where the majority of Kiwi hops are grown, surrounded by grapes and apples and other orchard fruits, and all backed by steep, verdant hills.

You'll never forget the smell of a hop harvest. It doesn't smell like a glass of beer; instead, it's green, like freshly cut grass on a hot day. It's woody with freshly cut branches, then it's like fresh herbs, minty, and spicy; it's all the shades and smells of green. The bines are cut and dragged onto the backs of trucks or tractors to be processed and passed into huge mechanical pickers, which grab and tug them,

sifting and shaking, ultimately separating the hop flowers from the stems and leaves, with belts and screens and fans of air combining with the weight of gravity to allow only the hops to move forward through the rattling, clanking, grinding, old, rusting machinery.

The hops then travel to large, deep kilns where they are heated and dried, gradually giving out more familiar hop aromas—the leafy greens, the fruits, and florals. Half a day later and they're bundled tightly together into burlap (hessian) sacks. From here they might go to be processed further into pellets, before going onward to a brewery.

Drink Fresh-hop Beers

Hops don't always need to be put through the drying process. Instead, brewers take them from the field straight to their brewing kettles and make "green-hop" or "fresh-hop" beers. Hops begin to degrade and oxidize as soon as they're picked, so these types of beers can only be brewed during the hop harvest and there's a tight timeframe from bine to brewery to maximize the fresh hop flavor—and these flavors are very different to the dried hops we're so familiar with. They are softer and more melon-like; there's cucumber, leafy green herbs, under-ripe fruits; they are a little vegetal. Some say it's the difference between fresh herbs and dried herbs, but I think it's more like fresh tomatoes versus oven-roasted ones—there's a wateriness in the fresh tomatoes or hops that gives them a distinctive taste, whereas the oven-roasted or dried ones are intensified in new ways. You'll mainly find fresh hops and fresh-hop beer festivals in the hop-growing regions. If you're ever nearby at the right time, then look out for them.

New Zealand hops allow brewers to add aromas including tropical fruit, grape, gooseberry, and mango to their beers.

The mesmerizing quality of mechanized processes, combined with the rural setting and fresh green crop, reveals a side to beer that you only usually see in photos and rarely associate with the liquid in your glass. The hop harvest is that rare period of the year when you can get to see beer from the roots and appreciate how the harvest has taken place, with roughly the same processes being undertaken for hundreds of years, to give beer its defining ingredient. Take the time to see the hop harvest one year; you'll gain a new appreciation of how those wonderful aromas and flavors end up in your beer.

Beer in Wine Country

BECAUSE YOU NEED GREAT BEER TO MAKE GREAT WINE

I needed a break from beer. When I landed in New Zealand, I'd drunk in over 80 bars and 80 breweries in 28 different cities in the last eight weeks (beer book research is tough). I headed to two locations in search of wine: Waiheke Island and Marlborough.

Waiheke Island

I was ready for wine and a few days on Waiheke Island. Waiheke, an island of around 25 wineries, is a pleasant ferry ride from Auckland. Although the island seems to be just vineyards ringed by beaches, there are also three breweries. And guess what? I didn't get a break from the beer…

The most impressive of the breweries is comparable with the mighty taprooms of Margaret River, Western Australia (see page 167). **Alibi Brewing** is on the Tantalus Wine Estate (70–72 Onetangi Road, Waiheke Island), a bright and breezy place that's surrounded by grapes and has a fancy restaurant overlooking the vineyards. What I love is how the shiny, stainless brewhouse is right in the middle, set down a floor from the main bar, and surrounded by glass like a goldfish bowl. The Brewer's Lounge downstairs is a dark-wood-and-leather-armchair kind of place and a nice juxtaposition to the light-filled dining room upstairs. As with the wines (which I can confirm are also very drinkable), you can get a tasting flight and try several Alibi beers, where you can expect a peachy Pale Ale brewed with all NZ ingredients, a good Pilsner, and a mix of other interesting brews, including some that use grapes and other fruits. The beers are all as bright and clean as the location in which you drink them.

Wild on Waiheke (82 Onetangi Road, Waiheke Island) is situated next to Tantalus, but the two vineyard venues are total opposites. Where Tantalus is fine dining, Wild on Waiheke is fun dining and outdoor activities. They've brewed beer there since 1998 and you'll find six beers on tap, plus a cider and a ginger beer. Baroona Pale Ale, their Motueka-hopped, Kölsch-style ale, is a light brew with a tropical-fruit hoppiness and just a hint of wine-like fruitiness. The food served is pub grub and backyard barbecue.

Boogie Van Brewing (29B Tahi Road, Ostend, Waiheke Island) is a funky little place producing fine beers for their taproom and is open Friday to Sunday (from 12–5pm). Expect plenty of fruit-forward hoppy beers. Almost everywhere closes by 5pm, including the wineries, so this is an ideal place to grab a growler to take home for the evening.

Marlborough

On the South Island is New Zealand's best-known grape-growing area, Marlborough, famous for its intensely fruity Sauvignon Blancs—the wine equivalent of a big IPA. Base yourself in Renwick, hire a bike, and cycle around for a few days, as you can easily get to over a dozen vineyards, all of which have cellar-door sales and tastings. In the middle of them all is **Moa Brewing Co.** (258 Jacksons Road, Blenheim, Marlborough), which was founded in 2003 by Josh Scott, son of Allan Scott whose well-known winery is across the street from the brewery.

I liked Moa for being so different to the super-smart wineries, for being laid back, with beanbags and bar stools and snacks and pints, instead of standing-up sips of tiny pours of fine wines. You can get a tasting tray, if you wish, or pick a full glass or bottle. You'll drink surrounded by grapes with mountains in the background—it's a beautiful part of the world. Moa make a few beers with wine-links: Pilsner Methode is made with Champagne yeast and zesty Motueka hops, which combine to give intriguing and expected spicy-fruity qualities. There's also Sour Grapes, a beer fermented with their house microflora and with Sauvignon

Stunning vineyards and olive trees growing on the rolling hills of Waiheke Island.

Blanc grapes, which are added during fermentation where they keep the contact while the beer ages in wine barrels. It's tangy and tart, funky and fruity, peachy and grape-like, with complex tannins. It's very good and a fascinating mix of the beers they brew with the wines that are made all around them.

Everywhere in Marlborough is shut by 5pm (although Moa might stay open later, making it the ideal final stop), so drop your bikes off and head to **Cork & Keg** (33 Inkerman Street, Renwick 7204)—they will rent you the bikes for $30NZ a day—for some decent pub food and a good range of wines and beers, including some taps from nearby Renaissance Brewing.

If you're on Waiheke Island or in Marlborough, then you'll be there to drink wine; you wouldn't go there just for beer. You could, but you wouldn't. Chances are that if you like traveling for good beer, then you also want to try local wines and these places are brilliant for that, as you can get to numerous wineries very easily. To be able to have a few beers is a great way to end a day of wine-tasting, in places where beer and wine happily co-exist.

A Wellington Craft Beer Crawl

THE EPICENTER OF NEW ZEALAND'S CRAFT BEER

Wellington is New Zealand's must-visit beer city: the Kiwi Beervana. It's the best place to take in the country's beer scene, to see what's happening now and next, and to visit a few great brewers and many great bars, plus it's a generally excellent city to visit.

Garage Project (68 Aro Street, Aro Valley, Wellington 6021) is the city's big-name brewery attraction. They opened in 2011, wanting to put a brewery in the center of the city and to open it for people to visit—surprisingly, for a place that had a great beer scene, there wasn't a centrally located brewery before Garage Project. They started with a tiny kit and chose always to brew new things, experimental and varied, and that beginning has stuck with them, though they've also added some more refined and consistent beers. They now open the brewery doors for samples, growler fills, and merch, and also have a trendy taproom across the street (at 91 Aro Street) with 20 taps of their beer.

The beers are intriguingly varied. Many have foodie inspirations, including Cereal Milk Stout, which is brewed with cornflakes, or Death from Above, a US-hopped IPA with mango, Vietnamese mint, lime, and chili. Also look for Pernicious Weed, their excellent Double IPA, or Sauvin Nouveaux, a Pilsner base brew with freshly pressed Sauvignon Blanc grape juice and lots of Nelson Sauvin hops on top. The taproom is a cool place; the beers all sounded great—and were largely irresistible to me. They also looked great, and mostly tasted great, though, for me, none quite reached the huge heights of the hype, all just slightly missing a clean preciseness of flavor. But you'll want to go to Garage Project—it's essential in Welly.

Also essential is drinking Kelly Ryan's beers in **Fork & Brewer** (20A Bond Street, Wellington 6011). You go in and upstairs, and the first thing you see is the brewery at the top of the stairs. Walk a full circle around the large central bar and it's a smart brewery restaurant, with around 25 of their own beers always on tap and all brewed with the kit by the entrance. The beer list includes almost every style you might want, from bright, clean lagers to boldly hoppy Pale Ales, to smooth-spicy Wheat beers and a bunch of Sours. They are the best-brewed beers you'll find nearby, always balanced and clean and exceptionally well made.

Tuatara Brewing have a bar called The Third Eye (30 Arthur Street, Te Aro, Wellington 6011) in town, or, if you're driving into Wellington from the north, then you'll pass by the brewery and tasting room—(7 Sheffield Street, Paraparaumu 5032)—

around 30 miles (50km) away. Stop at one of these for good Pale Ales and an excellent Pilsner. There's also **Black Dog Brewery** (17–19 Blair Street, Te Aro, Wellington 6011), which is more scruffy pub than pedigree, but has some good brews. **Husk** (62 Ghuznee Street, Te Aro, Wellington 6011) is a café, bar, coffee roaster, and brewery. It's a funky space with the brewery dominating at the back and producing some interesting beers.

The bars first turned Wellington into New Zealand's best beer city and they continue to be the best places to drink. I really liked **Rogue & Vagabond** (18 Garrett Street, Te Aro, Wellington 6011). It's vibrant and visually interesting, with comfy seating inside and plastic cups so that you can take your pint outside. They have a good range of local brews on tap. **Golding's Free Dive** (14 Leeds Street, Te Aro, Wellington 6011) is on a foodie crossroads, a developed industrial space just off hip Cuba Street, with tasty things on every corner, including a great restaurant called Shepherd, a pizza place, a soda-maker, a bakery, a coffee shop, and Golding's, which has seven well-picked taps and is colorful, fun, and friendly. You can order in pizza from opposite.

Little Beer Quarter (6 Edward Street Te Aro, Wellington 6011) is a cozy, well-worn, old pub with a lively, unfussy, relaxed atmosphere. The 20-odd taps are from around New Zealand and they pour some beers you won't find elsewhere in Welly. **Malthouse** (48 Courtenay Place, Te Aro, Wellington 6011) has the broadest and biggest tap list in town and they pick from all over the country, again including beers you won't find in other local bars. There's also **Hashigo Zake** (25 Taranaki Street, Te Aro, Wellington 6011), which is a "cult beer bar" that feels a little jaded in comparison to other places, as if it hasn't moved on from when it was the must-visit bar, but it's still worth visiting, especially if you want to drink non-NZ beers (it's run by a beer importer).

Wellington is a great beer city. It's a great city full stop. It's a delicious destination, one that's creative and chilled out, with excellent food and drink choices. It's New Zealand's essential beer destination.

Garage Project serve up some of the finest beers not just in Wellington, but in the whole of the country and their taproom is an essential bucket-list tick.

Drink New Zealand Pilsner

THE MOST KIWI-AS BEER STYLE

New Zealand Pilsner has become both a gateway beer and a fall-back favorite. Many New Zealand brewers make one as standard and it's the country's unique entry in beer's style guide, where it takes a body of pale malts and uses lots of the fruity local Kiwi hop varieties to give their famously tropical aromas.

In flavor, these beers are not exact Pilsner clones; hops aside, the base brews are different from their European cousins. In New Zealand Pilsners you get a richer malt base, cookies, and some tangy, chewy grains, rounder but still firm and without chubby sweetness—they're often closer to a Kölsch or Golden Ale than the snap of a German Pils or the caramels of a Czech Pilsner. But it's the hops that make these beers special, giving the grape, gooseberry, tropical fruits, lime, passion fruit, and ripe stone-fruit qualities of Kiwi varieties to add a distinct local accent. It's the combination of clean, rich, pale malts, gentle lager fermentation, and super-fruity hops that make this a favorite Kiwi beer style.

One of the reasons these beers work so well is the parentage of the hops, with many of the lushest, fruitiest hops being bred from European noble hops: Motueka and Riwaka are the daughters of Saaz, while Wakatu, Wai-iti, Kohatu, and Pacifica are bred from Hallertau. The cross-breeds, plus the growing conditions, have allowed these varieties to take on extremely fruity, tropical aromatics, while retaining the kind of clean, focused bitterness of noble hops.

While traveling around the country, I tried to drink as many NZ Pilsners as possible, loving the mix of the lager base brew with the lushness of the hops. I loved Emerson's Pilsner (see page 191), which is the original of the style. Other great examples include Tuatara's Mot Eureka, brewed with a few hop varieties

Three great New Zealand Pilsners. They really do deserve more exposure outside of their home territory. If you see one of these bottles, buy it.

that are all grown in Motueka; Panhead's Port Road Pils was a glass of passion fruit juice with a spritz of Sauvignon Blanc; and Hop Federation, brewed in Riwaka with Riwaka, Motueka, and Nelson Sauvin hops, was mangoes, tropical fruits, and juicy oranges, and, while it veers toward Pale Ale, the taut body pulls it into the shape of a Pilsner.

Just like the locals would say, "The New Zealand Pilsner is Kiwi-as."

Go to Emerson's Brewery

FOR THE ORIGINAL NEW ZEALAND PILSNER

Emerson's Pilsner started as an experiment to try and brew an organic beer, with brewer Richard Emerson deciding to make a lager with all-New Zealand ingredients, producing what he dubbed "the Sauvignon Blanc of beer." That initial brew evolved into what is now one of New Zealand's best and most important beers, because it created the style category.

I love Emerson's Pilsner. There's something intoxicating about its hop aroma and flavor; there's a full lushness, a richness of hop flavor, a slick juiciness, a fresh fruitiness that's tropical and grape-like; there's a peachy creaminess and white-pepper bitterness—and all with the kind of body that means you can drink a pitcher of it and still be thirsty for more. It's the original and it's seen many imitators, or many others creating their own interpretations of it, but it still stands out as one of the best—probably *the* best.

You can visit Emerson's Brewery in Dunedin. They have a large, smart tasting room where you can drink all their beers. They also have some of the country's smartest brewers on staff and are certainly leaders in the industry. Their 1812 should be held up as a modern classic brew, a hoppy amber beer that's orangey, marmalade-y, tangy, and juicy, all with a kind of jammy body that's not sweet, but has a caramelized quality which helps juice up the hoppiness. Bookbinder is a great mix of low-alcohol English ale with the fruitiness of New Zealand hops. And the specials are worth trying too. But always start with their Pilsner.

The Lowdown

WHAT: Emerson's Brewery

HOW: Open daily from 10am (www.emersons.co.nz).

WHERE: 70 Anzac Avenue, Dunedin 9016, New Zealand

New Zealand beer geeks were anxious when Lion Breweries, owned by Kirin, took over Emerson's, but the buy-out has seen the beers get even better.

Chapter 5
Rest of the World

Thailand's (Illegal) Craft Brewers

IT'S GOOD CHIT

Did you know that home-brewing is illegal in Thailand and comes with a maximum penalty of six months in jail? Brewing laws are also so prohibitive that it's effectively illegal to brew beer on a small scale, plus it's also illegal to sell it. Despite this, did you also know that there are possibly over 200 craft brewers in Thailand and a growing number of bars to drink craft beer in?

Wichit "Chit" Saiklao is the man doing the most to challenge and change craft beer in Thailand. His Chit Beer (pronounced "Sheet") is on a small island around 12 miles (20km) from the center of Bangkok and it requires at least three modes of transport to get there (219/266 Baan Suan Palm 11120 Pakkred, Nonthaburi). The bar alone is Beer Bucket List-worthy for its location on the river, but it's more significant because of the restrictions Wichit faces, for how he's standing up against the rules, fighting for better beer from small brewers, and for how he's opened his brewery to teach prospective home-brewers and pro-brewers. The aim is to brew until the law changes and he's recruiting many others to join his craft-beer crusade.

The great news looking forward is that Chit and a collective of brewers applied to open a communal brewpub. This was approved, giving Thai brewers a place to make beer in Thailand (the rules allow beers to be brewed abroad, imported back to Thailand, and then sold as Thai beer). This is a very significant development in changing the laws to make Thai craft beer viable.

The craft beer list at Namtom's House Bar in Chiang Mai.

And from all of this a genuine new beer scene is growing, with the emergence of new breweries and bars (there are even a couple of guys growing hops in Thailand). The hub is in Bangkok, where there are dozens of places to drink decent beer. **Wishbeer Home Bar** (1491 Sukhumvit Road, Sukhumvit Soi 67, Bangkok) is a cool beer hall with 22 taps and a bottle store next door. They have a good selection of Thai craft beers, plus lots of imports. **Hair of the Dog** (they have two bars) has a lucky-for-Thais 13 taps with a nerdy range of imported beers and well-filled fridges. In Chiang Mai, be sure to check out **Namtom's House Bar** (196/2 Chiang Mai-Lam Phun Road, Chiang Mai). It's definitely an intriguing country to watch as beer develops there.

LOCAL TIP: **Mikkeller's Michelin Star**

Not content with dominating the Copenhagen beer scene (see page 160), Mikkeller has opened a bar in Bangkok, just a short 5-minute tuktuk ride from Wishbeer. Even better is the restaurant attached to the bar, imaginitively titled Upstairs at Mikkeller (26 Ekkamai Soi 10 Yaek 2, Ekkamai Road, Phra Khanong Nua, Bangkok). Here you can dine on a top-end, 10-course tasting menu paired with beer. The food is so good Upstairs earned a Michelin star in 2017.

Drink Bia Hoi in Hanoi

VIETNAM'S UNIQUE CHEAP DRAFT LAGERS

Bia hoi is local to Vietnam, specifically to Hanoi, and I think it's one of the world's best beer experiences, where you drink light, cheap beers beside a busy street as the unrivaled, live-action theater of Hanoi life flys past you.

Bia hoi is the name of both the beer and where you drink it—so you go to a bia hoi to drink bia hoi—and the name means the equivalent of "fresh draft beer." You'll find it all around Hanoi, in places that vary from big beer halls to the front of someone's house, and it's something almost exclusively drunk by the prodigiously thirsty Vietnamese.

The French introduced beer (*bière* became bia) into Vietnam at the end of the 19th century. The significant part of the story in terms of bia hoi comes decades later when French-trained Vietnamese brewers started making beer for themselves, using war-rationed local ingredients and incorporating rice. The beer couldn't be bottled or canned because of materials shortages, but it could go into metal barrels, which were delivered daily to street corners where it was drunk by workers involved in the war's background efforts. It was low in alcohol and cheap, and the workers went home when the keg was emptied. A new drinking culture started and draft beer like this became an everyman drink.

Many breweries make bia hoi, but it's possible that you won't know who brewed the beer you're drinking (the yellow and red signage of Bia Hoi Ha Noi is the most common). Regardless of who made it, all are probably 3.0–4.0% ABV; they are lagers brewed with a high percentage of rice, some pale barley, probably some sugar, and very few hops; and they're designed to be brewed and drunk as quickly (and cheaply) as possible,

which means the beer you drink might only be a week old.

Quickness here also equals freshness because another distinctive feature of bia hoi is that new kegs are delivered every morning. Order a cold bottle of local lager and you have no idea how long it's spent baking in the sun before it got into the fridge, but with bia hoi you know the keg was delivered that morning and will be gone by that evening; bars don't order more than they need and they don't have cold storage to keep unpasteurized, light draft beer for more than one day (which is one of the reasons this daily draft delivery is necessary and why it started in the first place).

The beer is typically poured straight from an unpressurized keg; there's rudimentary refrigeration (perhaps a wet towel), no gas, rarely a tap, and usually just a garden hose, and it'll always be poured into a chunky tumbler, made from blue-tinted recycled glass, with cracks and bubbles and an uneven rim. Bia hois are often quite basic spaces and you'll probably be squatting on shin-high plastic stools, with your feet on the street, which isn't always the most comfortable type of seating for big Western butts. (One anecdotal aside: in Vietnam, the higher the seating, then the better the perceived status of a place. Street-side bia hoi stools are the lowest; "quan nhau" restaurants serving bottled lagers and good, cheap food have plastic chairs; nicer restaurants have wooden chairs; craft beers and cocktails lift your high-status bottom onto bar stools.)

While the brewing processes for all bia hoi are essentially the same, the flavors will vary. The best examples are fresh, clean, sometimes a little

Bia hoi is a favorite pastime for the Hanoi locals, but you need to be a serious *bia* drinker to chug from these giant mugs.

creamy, sometimes dryly bitter, with a gentle fizz, and—just like any good Asian light lager—they are perfect in Hanoi's humid heat (FYI: on especially hot days, your beer will come served with some ice in the glass). Others demonstrate the characteristics of immature beer: fruity esters, buttery diacetyl, no carbonation. No bia hoi is necessarily bad; some are just better than others. But when you've only paid 10,000VND (US$0.45) for a glass, then it doesn't really matter. And while the "cheapest beer in the world" tag gets bia hoi some attention, we should instead think of them as the "best-value-for-money" beers because they're cheap, but also fresh and taste good.

LOCAL TIP: **Beer and Status**

The Vietnamese are prodigious drinkers and beer is a key part of local socializing culture. They are in the top 10 of world drinkers and they're in the top 10 of world brewers. Beer is what everyone drinks, and they drink it all the time—particularly in Hanoi with bia hoi. But bia hoi is a low-status drink and status is important—it links with what you're drinking. Most beer is drunk in quan nhau restaurants, which are the equivalent of a standard local bar for the Western drinker. Groups—and it's always groups—drink beer by the case, which is chosen by the person paying the bill, and depending on who you're drinking with, you'll order different brands: the cheapest brand for your family as you don't need to impress anyone; the better beers if it's your friends; the most expensive if it's with your boss. Craft beer is now the next step up in terms of perceived status.

If you read travel guides or anything online about bia hoi, then it'll say to go to Bia Hoi Corner; if you read my book *The Best Beer in the World*, I tell you to go to Bia Hoi Corner. But don't bother now. Not for bia hoi, anyway, as it's changed irrevocably in the last few years, and it looks like Tiger and Tuborg have thundered in, effectively buying the place, branding it with their neons and promotion girls, and making the cheapness of bia hoi essentially worthless, when better bar profits come from buying branded bottles. You might still be able to drink bia hoi on Bia Hoi Corner, but you'll end up in some alleyway away from the action. The corner is still a Beer Corner, and it's still fun on a busy weekend evening (though quieter midweek), but don't go there specifically for bia hoi.

The best place to drink bia hoi near the Old Quarter, where you can find six or seven close together, is the intersection of Bát Đàn and Đặng Thành. **Bia Hoi Ngoc Linh** on that corner is my favorite for its lively atmosphere, for the quality of the beer, and for being on a vibrant, busy street. Diagonally opposite is **50 Bát Đàn**, which has a menu of innards and stuff like sparrows and frogs (plus some more "normal" things). Up Đặng Thành is **Bia Hoi Nam Còi** and continue up there and turn right onto Hàng Vải where you'll find one on that

corner and a few more are two corners over on Bát Sứ, with one in between (which is basically someone's front room). One other place worth visiting is **Bia Hoi 68** on Quảng An, which is a huge, open-air beer hall that looks out onto West Lake in the north of the city. But there are bia hois all over Hanoi. Sometimes you find big beer halls, sometimes you'll see three close together, other times they'll be on their own, and sometimes you'll just see a small silver keg and some glasses on the side of the street or in someone's house.

I love bia hoi for the cool, fresh, tasty, uncomplicated beer. I love that it's so cheap because I can drink a dozen for less than the price of a pint at home. I love it for the busy bars that are lively with a tonal chorus of conversation, laughter, and arguments; for people eating from large communal plates, toasting their chunky beer tumblers, and for how it all happens street-side where the view is of life happening, a constant speeding spectacle better than any sports game or soap opera. It's real life and in Hanoi that's a frantic, fast, loud life where anything could happen next. There's no other world-beer or beer-drinking experience like it.

Craft Bia in Ho Chi Minh City

SAIGON BEER CITY

As a craft beer destination, Ho Chi Minh City (or Saigon as it's still often called) has gone from non-existent to one of the most exciting new beer cities in the world in under three years. We can set day zero in 2014, with early 2017 as a sudden boom for Saigon brewing.

The ignition for this great beer explosion was the opening in 2014 of **Quán Ụt Ụt** (168 Võ Văn Kiệt, Cầu Ông Lãnh, Quận 1, Hồ Chí Minh), an American BBQ and beer joint that was started by Tim Scott and Mark Gustafson. They put in a few beer lines for Mark's home-brew and the extra taps gave other brewers somewhere to sell their beer—before them there was nowhere to sell draft craft beer in the city.

The Ụt Ụt guys (Ụt Ụt, by the way, is the Vietnamese version of "oink oink") also opened a beer bar called **BiaCraft** in District 2 that gave more tap space to the first wave of local brewers. A second larger wave of brewers came a few months after a second BiaCraft opened in District 3 at the end of 2016 (1 Lê Ngô Cát, phường 7, Quận 3, Hồ Chí Minh). This place is special, a world-class beer bar with 50 taps of just Vietnamese craft beer and cider, including the BiaCraft house brews, which are all good and mostly brewed by Phat Rooster Ales. The space is an open, breezy corner bar and, once you've looked at the striking beer board, you'll notice it's mostly young Vietnamese drinking there. Craft beer isn't just for wealthy Westerners in Saigon and is already impressing the locals.

Around the city you can visit many taprooms for these new breweries (most brew their beer in the suburbs). **Pasteur Street Brewing Co.** (144 Pasteur Street, Bến Nghé, Quận 1, Hồ Chí Minh) has two taprooms side by side. The beers are American-inspired, but almost everything they brew uses Vietnamese ingredients. Their flagship beer is Jasmine IPA, which is bright and refreshingly light for 6.5% ABV, with pithy citrus joined by the fragrant, calming elegance of jasmine. In their Passion Fruit Wheat Beer the juiciness of the fruit gives the brew a similar tantalizing tartness and it's the most thirst-quenching drink you might find in the whole of Vietnam. For something special, have Cyclo, their truffle-rich Imperial Stout, which uses Vietnamese cocoa beans, cinnamon, and vanilla—it's incredible (though it is expensive at around 182,000VND/US$8 a glass). For prices in general, 95,000VND (US$4) is where most bars try to top out for 13½-oz (400-ml) glasses of IPA, not wanting to break the psychological barrier of 100,000VND—US$1 is around 23,000VND.

Heart of Darkness (31D Lý Tự Trọng, Bến Nghé, Quận 1, Hồ Chí Minh) make the best IPAs I've tasted in the whole of Southeast Asia—try Kurtz's Insane IPA—and their whole beer range is broad enough to supply the 20 taps in their tasting room near the Opera House. They have the excellent Pizza 4P's in the kitchen (if you want pizza, then this is the best in Vietnam and they also have a few restaurants: www.pizza4ps.com).

East West Brewing Company (181–185 Lý Tự Trọng, Bến Thành, Quận 1, Hồ Chí Minh) is the most impressive of the new brewers. Their brewpub is an extraordinary space, a beer destination that's a huge beer hall with the tanks at the back (it's the only actual craft brewhouse in the city center and is close to Ben Thanh Market) and a rooftop beer garden. There are 10 taps, with all the beers being very good, and the San Diego-style Pale Ale is a great place to start.

Go to **Winking Seal** (50 Đặng Thị Nhu, Nguyễn Thái Bình, Quận 1, Hồ Chí Minh) before or after visiting Marou, a chocolate-maker that uses beans from all over the country (amazing place). The Winking Seal beers are as bright and vibrant as their tasting room. Nam Nam Nam ("555") Cream Ale is good and a refreshing lager-like brew that's a playful riff on the mainstream Ba Ba Ba ("333") lager.

ICE COLD BEER

BC XAOBĂ CÓ SUMMER ALE 50 70 100 FUZZYLOGIC PALE ALE   50 75 115   SG. ORIGINAL APPLE CIDER   65 95 145 HOD VAST COUNTRY N.E. IPA 65 95 145 LAC...IPA   55 85 130
BC ÁO TÙNG CHAO-RYE ALE 50 70 100 FUZZY LOGIC RYE I.P.A.   55 85 130   SG. GUAVA   CIDER 65 95 145 HOD. PHI LESS FOLLY PALE ALE 65 95 145 LAC...RED ALE 55 85 130
BC LÚ MÍ LÀO BLONDE ALE 50 70 100 PSBC PASSIONFRUIT WHEAT ALE 65 95 145 HN. HOPPED APPLE CIDER 65 95 145 HOD. KURIZ INSANE IPA   65 95 145 LAC...EAM ALE 55 85 130
PC DÙNG CHOC LAO PALE ALE 50 70 100 PSBC COFFEE PORTER   65 95 145 HN. MULBERRY CIDER 65 95 145 W.S. BABY FAISO DRY SOUL 55 85 135 30.A.B. KOSMONAVT 55 85 130
PC NGÙ MÁLI AMBER ALE 50 70 100 PSBC JASMINE I.P.A   65 95 145 TÉ TÉ. WHITE ALE   65 95 145 W.S. NÁM NÁM NÁM CREAM ALE 55 85 135 30.A.B. BOHEMIAN BASTARD 55 85 130
BC XÁ LÍ NHÀ CHANH I.PA 50 70 100 PSBC DRAGONFRUIT GOSE 65 95 145 EW. SAI GON ROSÉ   65 95 145 W.S. KAPTAIN KENNY IRISH 55 85 135 HE VERLEE PILSNER 55 65 130
NÀRLIYLIGAL. 55 85 130 PHAT. SAIGON BLONDE   50 70 100 EW. SUMMER HEFE WEIZEN 65 95 145 W.S. MEKONG MASH SUMMER ALE 65 95 145 HE VERLEE BELGIUM WHITE 55 65 ...
BARLEY LEGAL DARK RYE ALE 55 85 130 PHAT. EAR ADOLPH SNR 50 70 115 EW. GOLDEN HARVEST I.PA 75 110 165 F.M. NETHER WORLD DARK ALE 55 85 135 PLATINUM ROOT GINGER 50 75 115
GLEANT, BLONDE ALE 65 95 145 PHAT. GALLO NEGRO   55 65 130 EW. MODI KNHEEL TAN DARK 75 110 165 FURBREW. TÁY PALE ALE 55 95 145 PLATINUM GOLDEN ALE 30 45 ...
        65 95 145 PHAT. SHÍV I.P.A   55 85 130 HOD GLIMMER OF GOLD PILSNER 65 95 145 FURBREW. RUBY I.P.A 55 85 130 PLATINUM PALE ALE 30 45 ...

The taplist at BiaCraft. With 50 taps pouring the best of Vietnamese craft beers, it's the best place to drink in Saigon.

FIVE LESSER-KNOWN BEER DESTINATIONS YOU SHOULD VISIT

- Vilnius, Lithuania (see page 165)
- Warsaw, Poland (see page 125)
- Tijuana, Mexico (see page 62)
- Perth, Fremantle, and Margaret River, Western Australia (see pages 167–173)
- Ho Chi Minh City, Vietnam
- Pilsen, Czech Republic (see page 126)

I liked Chicken Coop in the backpacker district. This is the tasting room for **Phat Rooster Ales** (28/2 Đỗ Quang Đẩu, Hồ Chí Minh), who brew on their own farm outside the city and serve the best Vietnamese food of any of the beer bars, plus some of the best and biggest chicken wings I've ever tasted—try the Saigon Blonde or the American Pale Ale to drink. Around the corner is **Ông Cau** (240 Bùi Viện, Quận 1, Hồ Chí Minh), a smart beer bar with 20-odd taps pouring all the local brewers, such as Lạc—who also have a tasting room in District 7—and Platinum, who were one of the founding craft brewers in the city, along with Fuzzy Logic and Tê Tê. And there are a dozen more bars serving great beer around the city.

Vietnam is the most vibrant, enthralling, delicious of countries, with some of the world's best food, yet until very recently the only beer options were light lagers. Today you could visit Ho Chi Minh City for a week and still not get to every brewery or main beer bar. The quality is also very high in general and the beer ranges are very broad; it might be a new beer market, but it's progressing very quickly, often—although not always—in the image of American craft beer. Vietnam has become a craft beer destination and Saigon is where you can find the most of these beers, bars, and breweries.

Craft Beer is Happening in Hanoi, too…

Hanoi also has a growing number of breweries and bars. **FurBrew** (8b/52 To Ngoc Van, Hà Nội) is the best brewer. Their **100 Garden** is a large outdoor space, behind which the beer is brewed (they also have another tasting room nearby). There are 20 beers on tap and the kitchen cooks excellent bia hoi-style Vietnamese food. Try their Pho Bia, which is inspired by Vietnam's famous noodle soup, or have a Lime Leaf Wheat for a fragrant, refreshingly citrusy wheat ale. **Standing Bar** (170 Trấn Vũ, Trúc Bạch, Ba Đình, Hà Nội), on Trúc Bach Island, is the bar to go to for the best range, with 16 taps of Vietnamese beers and ciders (try Hanoi Cider's dry-hopped cider which is excellent) and a view over the lake. It's a calm little oasis away from the Old Quarter's hectic madness. If you're in the middle of that madness, then just back from Bia Hoi Corner is the **Craft Beer Pub** (26 Hàng Buồm, Hoàn Kiếm, Hà Nộ), which has a few local craft beers on tap, and **The Hill Station** (2T Tạ Hiện, Hàng Buồm, Hoàn Kiếm, Hà Nội), a smarter bar with good food and a couple of taps. Also check out **A Taste of Hanoi**, which runs craft beer tours in the city (No. 34 Gia Ngu, Hoan Kiem District, Hà Nội 10000).

Cracking beers and excellent food at FurBrew in Hanoi make this a worthwhile diversion from bia hoi.

A perfectly formed Czech pilsner served at Hoa Vien in Hanoi.

The Best Czech Lagers outside the Czech Republic?

Vietnam has its bottles of Ba Ba Ba, its cheap glasses of bia hoi, its great craft beers, but did you know that it also has dozens of Czech and German-style brewpubs and microbreweries? The Czech places are distinctly Czech and the German ones very German; the Czech pale lagers are legit Světlý Ležák copies, being caramel-y and bitter, while the German lagers are drier and cleaner. If you visit Vietnam, then just look up microbreweries nearby and you'll find them, with **Hoa Vien** (1A Tăng Bạt Hổ, Quan Hai Ba Trung, Hà Nội, Ha Tay) in Hanoi being one of the best and just like walking into a Pilsner Urquell pub (and there are a few big bia hois on the left as you leave).

LeVeL33, Singapore

THE WORLD'S HIGHEST URBAN BREWERY

The view is of steely skyscrapers and neon signs, lush green trees, a colonial cricket pitch flanked by the squat old City Hall and Supreme Court, the super-modern Supertree Grove of Gardens by the Bay, cargo ships passing by, the three towers of Marina Bay Sands, and lots and lots of clear sky. It's from up here on the 33rd floor, at LeVeL33, the highest urban brewery in the world, that you appreciate what a singular place Singapore is. It's also a singular view from an urban brewery.

It's high-end brewing, literally. It's a smart cocktail bar with a smarter brewkit behind it, a gleaming, copper-covered, thousand-liter (8.5-barrel) brewhouse. The brewhouse is a two-vessel mash kettle and lauter, capable of decoction mashing—a process used in the lager. There are six beers available: Blonde Lager, German-style Wheat, English-ish IPA, Irish-style Stout, House Porter (a blend of IPA and Stout made when it's poured), and a seasonal special, all served from tanks behind the bar. You'll also see big tanks when you walk in from the elevator. These are the fermentation and conditioning tanks, and the beers you'll be drinking next week.

The food is at the high-end of brewpub dining, with a beer snack menu of fancy finger food and many of the dishes using various beers as ingredients. And there's a dedicated list of beer cocktails, which judiciously use the brews in clever ways, and is one of the better applications of cocktails I've tasted—it's also a simple side-step to introduce an emerging nation of craft beer drinkers to come and play

on our side. And that's one important aspect of LeVeL33: this is primarily a cool rooftop bar and most first-time visitors come for the view. Because of this, the beers have to work for everyone, from that coktail crowd to the beer lovers. And they do because the beers are very good, very clean, and very well made.

The IPA was my favorite; it was a love letter to Kent hops. One gulp and I was sitting by the Thanet coast drinking a pint of Gadds No.3, which is one of the best compliments I can give a beer. Gadds brew in East Kent with a fanatic love of East Kent Golding hops and LeVeL33's IPA, brewed in Southeast Asia, on the edge of the equator, is literally half a world away from Ramsgate, yet flavorwise they are next-door neighbors. It's a glass of orangey, tangy floral hops, deeply set within the beer, with a nutty malt character in front of it. Simply wonderful.

The beers are all perfectly brewed in the clean, European style. They give you the feeling of getting into a bed of tightly made fresh sheets in a luxurious hotel. They're not disruptive or destructive; instead, they're classy and classic, and emblematic of smart, west-facing Singapore in general—and they do what they need to do in the best way. But even the most dedicated beer geek won't be there dissecting the decoction mash; they'll be looking out at the best view from an urban brewery anywhere in the world.

The Lowdown

WHAT: LeVeL33 Brewery and Restaurant

HOW: www.level33.com.sg

WHERE: 8 Marina Boulevard, Marina Bay Financial Center Tower 1, Singapore

Whether you're coming more for the beer or the view, you'll definitely enjoy both at LeVeL33.

Smith Street Taps, Singapore

HAWKER FOOD MEETS CRAFT BEER

From high-end and high up at LeVel33 to down and dirty, hot and sweaty hawker centers. This is the perfect counter, showing Singapore as a city of duality, of epic modern skyscrapers and old underground markets, of five-star steak and five-dollar dim sum. The leveler is the hawker center. Sprawling, busy, loud food halls of flashing hot woks with the full stockpot of cuisines—Malay, Chinese, Indian, Thai, Indonesian. You go in and find a seat at a small plastic table, then pick your food from the dozens of stalls—it's served quickly on plastic plates with throwaway chopsticks. It's the great Singaporean food experience, and the growing influence of craft beer in the country has made its way, via the smart stuff, and down to these hawker centers.

In the Chinatown Complex there are three beer bars and many, many food stalls. **Smith Street Taps** (335 Smith Street, Chinatown Complex, Singapore 050335) have a dozen beers on draft, mostly from USA, Australia, and the UK, though there's an occasional local brew (look out for Brewlander, which are made in Cambodia by Singaporean John Wei who then brings them back home and sells them locally—they're some of the best beers in the country). This place is a local beer institution: Singapore's local craft beer bar, with tables and chairs set outside like the food stalls, where you can just drink or bring whatever food you like to go with the brews. **The Good Beer Company**, a few yards away, is a bottle store with USA and European brews, and you can open a bottle and drink it with your food. Also nearby is **On Tap**, with the beers "home-brewed" locally. There were around eight beers on tap when I was there, though the quality varied from bad to barely okay.

Good beer, on draft, with great street food all around.

The beers are expensive—some cost the same as four plates of food—but this is a country that's pummeled with extraordinarily high taxes on beer and even a cold can of Tiger will have you roaring with surprise at the price. Overlook the cost because the brilliance of the hawker and beer experience is in putting excellent craft beers with everyday food; in a dichotomous way, it elevates the new complexities of craft beer to that understandable everyman place, a reversal of smart beer bars serving burgers, and it's bringing it to where everyone meets and eats. This experience is uniquely of Singapore and it's a fun flipside to the fine dining of LeVeL33.

Have a Beer in North Korea

GET ON THE KIM-JONG ALES!

I found a quote from a North Korean chap who said, "There is no other beer in the world that tastes better than Taedonggang." I can't think of a single reason not to believe this bloke. I also can't dispute it, as I've never drunk any of the beers from the Taedonggang Brewery in Pyongyang. But I want to.

"Taedonggang Brewery in Pyongyang" is a pub quiz answer. The question is: "In 2002, Ushers of Trowbridge closed their brewery and sold their brewhouse. Who bought it?" It's a state-owned brewery and we can assume it's popular with the proles, where in a country of working men it makes sense that the ultimate working-man's drink should be widely available and widely drunk, although soju seems to be the knock-it-back, get-drunk-quick drink of choice and beer is emerging in a more middle-class market. When you look further into the limited amounts of information about beer and brewing in the country, there seems to be a nascent scene with beer halls and numerous venues brewing their own beers— bowling alleys, restaurants, a few hotels. There's more to North Korean beer than the state-owned brew.

In 2016 the country hosted its first-ever beer festival, with locals hoisting steins of Kim Jong's finest lagers at the 20-day event in Pyongyang. The venue overlooked the Taedong River, which gave its name to the brewery the festival was set up to promote, and all the brewery's seven beers were available. If you're interested, they are socialistically named: Taedonggang 1, Taedonggang 2, Taedonggang 3, and so on through to 7, with some using over 50 percent rice in the grain bill, while numbers 6 and 7 are dark.

Most western reviewers of the Taedonggang beers are less enthusiastic than the North Korean fella, though most are also a little surprised, making comments such as "Not as terrible as I expected…" and "It's fine." Frankly, that's better than I was expecting. And I'm certainly interested in what beer might be like there, what that festival would be like,

and where else I might be able to find places that make their own beer. To put words in the mouth of that man from Pyongyang: "There's no country in the world with better beer." Probably, anyway, and one day I'd like to find out for myself.

South Korea's Growing Beer Scene

If North Korea is unappealing or inaccessible, then jump south to Seoul for an emerging beer city. It isn't necessarily as Beer Bucket List-worthy as other destinations, yet it's good enough to be of interest to travelers. **Magpie Brewing** (244–1 Noksapyeong-daero, Itaewon-dong, Yongsan-gu, Seoul) was my favorite—a smart little taproom with some top-quality brews, especially their Porter. They also have a few other locations around the city. Turn left out of Magpie and you're right by **The Booth Gyeonglidan** (7 Noksapyeong-daero 54-gil, Yongsan-gu, Seoul), a brightly graffiti-decorated pizzeria taproom for The Booth Brewery, another company with a few locations in town, including one nearby at Itaewon Station, which has a larger tap list than Gyeonglidan's. **Craftworks** (238 Noksapyeong-daero, Itaewon-dong, Yongsan-gu, Seoul) is a few minutes from Magpie and the original South Korean craft brewer. In the north is **Amazing Brewing** (4, Seongsuil-ro 4-gil, Seongdong-gu, Seoul), the new star in the city, which has an impressive 50-plus taps of their own beers and imports in a cool, wooden-roofed, industrial space, with the brewery to one side.

Search for Makgeolii in Seoul

If you're in Seoul and interested in local drinks, look for makgeolii. This is an old style of rice wine, the oldest kind of Korean alcohol, and is gaining new attention. It's a milky, gently carbonated drink that's naturally fermented. It's a little sweet and a little tangy and smooth, like a lightly alcoholic drinking yogurt. There's a lot of variety and additional ingredients are sometimes added. The new focus on this drink is putting it with food.

Taedonggang being served to thirsty locals in Pyongyang.

Elsewhere in Southeast Asia

THERE'S GOOD BEER (ALMOST) EVERYWHERE

Unless they've got their own entry in this book, I don't think many places in Southeast Asia are truly Beer Bucket List-worthy. There are a lot of great places to drink excellent domestic and imported beers, which stand out for being important or interesting locally, but, when compared to the best of the best around the world, they don't yet compete. But that's a little unfair on these emerging, exciting craft beer locations, so here's some useful stuff to know about the region in general.

Hong Kong

Hong Kong is seen as a central spot for craft beer in Asia. There's a range of good breweries and a lot of bars. **Young Master Ales** (Sungib Industrial Center, 53 Wong Chuk Hang Road, Hong Kong) is a brewery getting lots of attention for its classic brews, often with a local accent. Others to look out for include **Moonzen** (www.moonzen.hk) and **Kowloon Bay Brewery** (www.kowloonbaybrewery.com).

Taiwan

Taiwan has a young and passionate craft beer community, and is seeing lots of breweries and bars open. **Taihu Brewing** is at the forefront (www.taihubrewing.com). They have some seriously cools taprooms that would happily fit in in Williamsburg or Vesterbro, including one that's a retrofitted airstream. Watch out for Taiwan.

Cambodia

In Siem Reap, the town you stay in when visiting the life bucket list tick of Angkor Wat, the most famous place to drink is the brash **Pub Street**, a never-ending happy hour of 50-cent draft lagers and US$2 cocktails, which is culturally insignificant in Cambodia's most culturally significant place. Way more fun is **The Local Brew Pub and Guesthouse** (115 Street 20, Siem Reap). There you can stay in one of

A flight of Cerevisia beers served at Botanico Wine & Beer Garden in Phnom Penh.

the world's only brewery guesthouses, where rooms cost around US$15 a night. The beers are brewed on site and cost a couple of bucks each. You can probably skip the **Siem Reap Brewpub**, because the beers and the location are not especially interesting (if you want to go, it's on the corner of Street 5 and Shinta Mani). In Phnom Penh, there is a growing number of expat brewers doing good things. For the best, go to **Botanico Wine & Beer Garden** (Street 29, Phnom Penh) for the Cerevisia beers, while there's also a couple of other breweries in town, mostly German in style.

While the quality of Cambodian beer is often as low as the price you pay for it, a night out on Siem Reap's Pub Street is definitely a lively experience.

The Philippines

Alongside Vietnam, the other country seeing significant craft beer growth is the Philippines. It's spread all around and there are upward of 40 breweries now. The best place to find out more is the Philippine Craft Beer Community page on Facebook (www.facebook.com/craftbeer.ph).

Drink Snow in China

HAVE YOU DRUNK THE WORLD'S BEST-SELLING BEER?

I had to test a simple hypothesis: was the world's best-selling beer the world's best-tasting? This seemed like simple logic, as surely something that accounts for around one-in-20 of every beer brewed and drunk in the world has to taste good. I did the research for a previous book—*The Best Beer in the World,* which covers a few of the entries that are also in *The Beer Bucket List* in greater detail—and you can probably guess the answer to my theory was that it isn't a delicious beer. In fact, far from being the best, it was more like the worst. Regardless, I think it's worthy of a tick for being the biggest-selling brew. I'd also suggest that drinking the other nine of the top 10 best-selling brews is worth doing, if only to recalibrate the palate and realize exactly what the majority of the world are drinking every day while we're hunting out the best hoppy brews. The Top 10 in 2017 were Snow, Tsingtao, Bud Light, Budweiser, Skol (Brazil), Yanjing, Heineken, Harbin, Brahma, and Coors Light.

Chinese Craft Beer

China is the world's biggest beer market by volume and brews four of the 10 best-selling beers in the world. Interestingly, the megabrew and economy side of the industry is contracting and premium and import beers are experiencing growth, where the Chinese middle-class mentality of wanting quality, or perceived quality, has affected drinking habits, with foreign or foreign-style brews and brewpubs having a high-status appeal. If you go to the big cities, you'll be able to find some excellent breweries and brewpubs.

Great Leap Brewing was Beijing's first craft brewery when it opened in 2010. They have three brewpubs in the city, but go to their Hutong location (DouJiao Hutong 6, Beijing), which is hidden down an old alleyway. This is a nice east-meets-west mix of old China and new craft brews that's distinctly local to this part of the world. Great Leap is also notable for using local ingredients, including Chinese hops (try Pale Ale #6, which is made with 100 percent Chinese ingredients). In Beijing, there's also the exceptional **Jing-A** (1949 The Hidden City, Courtyard 4, Gongti Bei Lu, Chaoyang District, Beijing) who use a lot of local ingredients in their exceptional beers. In Shanghai, the well-established **Boxing Cat Brewery** was bought by AB-InBev in early 2017, which tells you how important the big guys think the growing Chinese market is. They have three brewpubs in Shanghai—visit www.boxingcatbrewery.com for details. If I'm in the city, then I'll still be drinking their beers.

Is India the World's Unknown Beer Destination?

100 BREWPUBS AND COUNTING...

Around 20 miles (32km) southwest of New Delhi is Gurgaon. In just a couple of decades it's gone from dusty land to a city of high-rises, shopping malls, and offices for half of the world's Fortune 500 companies. You'd be forgiven for not having heard of this place before. You'd also be forgiven for not knowing that Gurgaon has over 20 brewpubs. Almost all make the Indian standard beer line-up of Wheat beer, Pale Lager, and Dark Lager, and some back these up with other brews, though don't expect to find too many IPAs, as bitterness doesn't work well for many Indian drinkers. Photos of the venues—I've never been—make them all look like smart hotel bars, which is indicative of the way the city is developing.

Gurgaon fascinates me because there aren't many cities in the world with 20 brewpubs. Certainly not outside America. And who has ever heard of Gurgaon's beer scene? I hadn't until I started looking into India's beer scene. And yet this isn't the only Indian city with 20-plus brewpubs because Bangalore is another. This is the center of India's high-tech industry, the capital of the southern state of Karnataka, and the original Beer City in India. Bombay and the relatively nearby Pune add even more brewpubs to the ever-growing list and could be where the next big surge of beers comes from.

A decade ago there were two brewpubs in India. Now there are over 100. With a growing middle-class, a developing taste for drinking alcohol in bars, especially in the Western-leaning bigger cities, and the drive of entrepreneurs opening brewpubs, I think India is a fascinating place to watch out for.

A barman pours a jug of beer in the Mint Lounge, one of the 20 brewpubs in Gurgaon.

Pick from the 70 Taps at Popeye

TOKYO'S LEGENDARY BEER BAR

If you want Japanese *jibirru*—locally brewed beers—then go to Backashu Club Popeye, in Ryōguku, Tokyo (that's Sumo Town). It's the legendary original Tokyo beer bar. They opened in 1985 and have added more and more taps over the years to get to their Sumo-sized 70 draft lines. It's not a big place. You'll be sitting elbow-to-elbow with people; it's boisterous and crowded, and there's so much stuff on the walls you'll be distracted from your drinking, but that's part of its everlasting charm.

Popeye is the best place to get acquainted with Japan's burgeoning craft brewing scene.

The Lowdown

WHAT: Backashu Club Popeye

HOW: www.facebook.com/
70beersontap

WHERE: 2-18-7 Ryōgoku,
Sumida-ku, Tokyo 130-0026,
Japan

The beer menu has the largest range of Japanese craft beers on tap, including many you can't find outside Japan and many you can't get outside of Popeye, plus in 2014 the bar launched its own brewery, Strange Brewing. Drink as many Japanese beers as possible, as there are some exceptional beers available, generally very well brewed, cleanly fermented, and dry. It's in all the guidebooks and must-drink lists, but that's because it's deserving of a place there and, despite this, it's still mostly filled with locals. Just eat before or after you go, as the bar food isn't the best, but when they've got 70 taps of beer to look after they've got other priorities.

Go for the Nomihoudai

There's a little secret in Tokyo when it comes to big drinking. Many bars offer Nomihoudai, which is an all-you-can-drink offer (or challenge, depending on how you look at it), and, for around JPY 3,500 (US$32) per person, you get a couple of hours of drinking along with food delivered to the table throughout the evening. Most of these offers are only advertised in Japanese, so, unless you've been there long enough to figure it out or are lucky enough to have friends to include you in a Nomihoudai, you may never know. Tokyo's craft beer bars also offer Nomihoudai (the catch is that you can only order one beer at a time or may be limited to ordering half pints only). Here's a few places where you can get it (Google for full details): **All Craft Beer Market** locations across the city; **Two Dogs Taproom** and **Ant n Bee** (both in Roppongi); all **Yona Yona** bar locations; **Vector Beer** in Shinjuku; and **Craft Beer Kitchen** in Jiyūgaoka. Just be sure to call ahead to make a reservation and let them know you want the Nomihoudai. And arrive thirsty.

One row of the 70 taps pouring at Backashu Club Popeye.

Hanami and Craft Beer

This is one for the ultimate Picnic Bucket List… You've probably heard of Japan's popular Sakura or cherry blossom scene, but there's a traditional custom called "Hanami," which is the practice of enjoying and viewing the cherry blossoms. This means grabbing a blanket, sitting under your favorite cherry blossom tree (we all have one, right?), and treating yourself to loads of food and drink. With craft beer stores and local convenience stores stocking more craft beers, you can now drink great beer while watching the once-a-year cherry blossom. Bet you didn't expect this in a craft beer book?

Drink Umqombothi

AFRICA'S INDIGENOUS SORGHUM (HOME) BREWS

Not many truly indigenous beers exist now and if you want to find them, then you have to visit places such as Peru, Tibet, and Africa, while remote Scandinavia (see page 156) and Lithuania (see page 165) have their farmhouse beers. Most of these beers are hard to find; they require lots of travel to faraway places that you'd probably not bother going to if it wasn't for some local home-brew (and even that is only appealing to the slimmest minority of booze boffins). Yet the fact that these brews still exist makes me want to drink them and know more about them.

Africa has a few such brews and they're based on local grains, such as sorghum, millet, and maize, and root sources of starch like cassava—these have such a presence that large commercial breweries make their own versions for these markets. Chibuku Shake Shake (so named because you have to shake it before drinking) is one of these brands. It is sold in cardboard milk cartons—appropriate for something that looks like milk when it's poured. This is a commercial version of the home-brew umqombothi. There's a lot of regional variety around the country, much of it still existing as home-brew.

Women brew Umqombothi in Bloemfontien, South Africa.

Little is written about many of these beers. My suspicion is that they have such an ingrained and long-standing tradition that they're just a fact of life there. Made daily or weekly, and consumed locally, people don't write about them just as I don't write about how I make a cup of tea. The fact that these beers are such a part of their lives is what adds interest for me. They are technically "beers," and they're beers that have been drunk for centuries or more, but they're nothing like the beers we know and drink elsewhere in the world. American Pale Ales have only been available since the 1980s, while these ancient home-brews pre-date dates and go back to the origins of civilization.

A Guinness advert on the wall outside a Lagos bar.

Drink Guinness in Nigeria: It's Not the Same as in Dublin…

Did you know that more Guinness is drunk in Nigeria than in Ireland? Guinness was first exported to Africa in the 1820s and, in 1962, the first non-Irish or British Guinness brewery opened in Nigeria's capital, Lagos (Guinness also has breweries in Malaysia, Ghana, and Cameroon). It arrived at the same time as an advertising campaign telling Nigerians that "Guinness gives you Power." The Lagos Guinness is not the same as that brewed in Dublin. Nigerian Guinness Foreign Extra Stout is made with malted, roasted maize and sorghum, and it's 7.5% ABV. It's dense, black, oily, and bitter, with the roast qualities you expect in Guinness—it's a really nice beer. And it's Nigeria's beer; Nigerians drink a lot of it and they drink the stronger, more powerful stuff, too, not that wimpy Irish brew.

South African Craft Beer Experiences

IN A FAST-GROWING CRAFT BEER SCENE

Craft beer is growing rapidly and in exciting ways in South Africa. There are two must-visit breweries in Cape Town: **Devil's Peak Brewing Company** (95 Durham Avenue, Salt River, Cape Town 7925) and **Jack Black's** (10 Brigid Road, Diep River, Cape Town 7945). Devil's Peak basically started craft beer in South Africa and Jack Black's are the cool, progressive new guys grabbing all the brewing awards—they're the leaders in a growing number of great South African brewers and their taproom is a great place to drink.

Also go to **The SAB World of Beer** in Johannesburg (15 Helen Joseph Street, Newtown, Johannesburg). It's owned by SABMiller and has a fun look at the history of beer, both locally and globally. On the tour, you can get a traditional taste of umqombothi (see page 210) from a communal clay pot and also learn about shebeens.

You should try and visit a shebeen. In the 1800s enterprising women opened illegal speakeasy-style drinking dens in their homes. When an apartheid licensing law from 1927 stated that non-white Africans couldn't enter a licensed venue or sell alcohol, these shebeens grew in popularity and became a unifying environment for black Africans, places where they could drink umqombothi brewed by the Shebeen Queens. As rules and society changed, their significance shifted, but today they are returning to fashion and celebrating those famous old bars in a new way.

And here's one you might have missed. In Limpopo, there was once a pub inside the trunk of a huge, old baobab tree—the largest (154ft/47m in circumference) and oldest (at least 1,700 years old) tree trunk in Africa. In early 2017, the **Big Baobab** collapsed and, while parts of it have reopened and you can still drink next to the tree, it's not quite what it used to be (www.facebook.com/SunlandBaobab).

Also near Limpopo is **Zwakala** (Glendennis Farm, Cheerio Road L 10, Haenertsburg), a craft brewery and taproom in a picturesque setting surrounded by the Magoebaskloof Mountains. Try the Limpopo lager, winner of a gold award at the 2016 South African National Beer Trophy.

A worker at Zwakala Brewery, packing up their popular Naked Ale.

Craft Beer in the Middle East

BRINGING BEER BACK TO ITS BIRTHPLACE

The commonly held belief is that brewing began at the dawn of civilization when migratory man stopped moving and, instead of searching for food sources, domesticated his own, with the Fertile Crescent—today's Egypt, Jordan, Israel, Syria, and Iraq—being the first settlements. Wild grasses provided the grains that could produce food, drink, and alcohol, whereby mixing varying amounts of water with crushed grain gave the liquid base for three very important products: bread, porridge, and beer. Allow that liquid to ferment and you get a drink that gives you a pleasant feeling of intoxication and also additional nutrition from vitamins, minerals, and fermentation.

That was 10,000 years ago but, while beer was born in this part of the world, it has effectively been extinct there for millennia, with bread becoming the important staple in an Arab region of alcohol-avoiding Muslims. But, as with everywhere else in the world, craft beer is flowing in the Middle East and it's taking brewing back to its birthplace.

In Jordan, there's the **Carakale Brewing Company** (Fuhays, Amman, 11821 Jordan), the country's first craft brewery. You can drink Palestinian Shepherds Beer from the **Birzeit Brewery** (Basateen Street, Old City Birzeit, Ramallah, Palestinian Territories). In Lebanon, there's **Colonel** (Bayadir Street, Batroun, Lebanon), the Middle East's first brewpub, which is by the sea in Batroun. There's also **961 Beer** (Mallah Building, Industrial Zone, Mazraat Yachoua, Lebanon).

Israel is the craft beer hotspot of the region, with around 30 small brewers. **The Dancing Camel** (HaTa'asiya Street 12, Tel Aviv-Yafo, Israel) was the first to open in 2006—their Tel Aviv brewery and taproom is an essential stop. Tel Aviv, in general, is the place to visit to drink the broadest range of Israeli beer, with the **Beer Bazaar** being a top spot (they have four bars in Tel Aviv and one in Jerusalem; check out www.beerbazaar.co.il). At these you can get 100-plus Israeli bottles and a selection of draft beers. Other Israeli brewers to look for include Jem's, Alexander, Negev, Malka, and Herzl.

One thing to note: these breweries use local ingredients to gain local favors. Fruit is common, as are herbs, and spices; 961's Lebanese Pale Ale includes za'tar, sumac, camomile, sage, anise, and mint; Dancing Camel make beers with pomegranate, date honey, and local herbs; Negev brews with passion fruit; Lela Brewery has a Jaffa orange Wheat. Most breweries have a range that includes a pale lager, a red ale, and a stout, plus other brews.

When we think about beer destinations, we automatically have images of Bavarian beer

Fancy a Beer in Armenia?

Dargett is Armenia's first craft brewery. It's in the capital city of Yerevan, one of the world's oldest inhabited cities, and they brew Central European lagers and Wheat beers, Belgian ales, and fruity brews, plus bolder American hoppy styles. Their tasting room has 20 beer taps and a menu with dishes from all around the world. You might not go there specifically for beer, but if you're in Armenia, then you know you can get a decent drink (Dargett Craft Beer, 72 Aram Street, Yerevan 0001, Armenia).

The Jerusalem Beer Festival

Put the Jerusalem Beer Festival on your go-to list. It's been held annually in late August/early September since 2004 and you'll find over 120 different beers in the open-air festival. Visit www.jerusalembeer.com for details.

Drinking local beers at the Jerusalem Beer Festival.

halls, old British pubs, quirky Belgian bars, and big American brewpubs. But craft beer is happening everywhere, almost always led by determined individuals who want to change local drinking habits. It's now happening where beer was born.

Blumenau's Oktoberfest

THE WORLD'S SECOND BIGGEST (AND FIRST SEXIEST) OKTOBERFEST

It was at the exact moment that thousands of people in lederhosen began singing a German drinking song in thick Portuguese accents that I had to step back and really think about what was going on. There I was, in the sultry south of Brazil, in the middle of a series of trips that took me to five continents in two months, all in the search for *The Best Beer in the World* (I wrote a book about it)—and I couldn't believe what I was seeing.

It wasn't just the Brazilians in German outfits; it wasn't the oom-pah music with the samba beat; it wasn't even that everyone was drinking German-style lagers from tankards while surrounded by subtropical forest. What really struck me was how this town was built to look like a postcard illustration of a Bavarian fairy tale.

The town is called Blumenau and is named after Dr. Hermann Blumenau, a well-connected German chemist who founded it in 1850, bringing with him a small group of immigrants from his homeland. The town gradually grew over the decades, as more Germans arrived and were joined by increasing numbers of Brazilians.

A century later, in an attempt to draw in the tourists, the town decided to market its German-ness and play up to its past, eventually leading to 1984 and an ostensible Oktoberfest, which has since become an annual thing. Alongside the party, they built a replica German village, complete with a small castle modeled on the town hall in Michelstadt, Germany, and lined the streets with stores selling typical—or stereotypical—German clothes, food, and beer glasses, all while encouraging the citizens to embrace the town's German heritage.

Today the locals call their Oktoberfest "The Party." The whole town gets excited about it; they dress up and drink steins of German-style beer. If they didn't do it annually, and they didn't take it so seriously, you'd almost think it was the most elaborate parody you'd ever seen—a trick for the tourists. But it isn't. And it's a big deal: The Party has literally put the town on the map and draws in hundreds of thousands of visitors every year, making it the second or third largest Oktoberfest celebration in the world (there's another in Canada which challenges this for second place behind Munich).

The festival is held in three huge tents, each with different live music and atmospheres (although it all blurs into one by midnight). The beer is good and includes plenty of local craft takes on German styles, plus a few Pale Ales—look out, in particular, for Eisenbahn. But what is quite different from the Bavarian festival is the sexiness—or the promiscuity. Everywhere I looked, people were making out with each other. The Party is exactly that: it's a place to go to let loose, drink lots, and have some fun.

As I stood in the sweaty heat, drinking local Pilsners, repeatedly and drunkenly shouting something like "Zicke Zacke, Zicke Zacke, Oi! Oi! Oi!" and watching people get off with each other, I couldn't help but laugh. This is one of the most surreal and wonderful and unexpected world beer festivals in a town that looks like a scaled-up version of a South German toy town. Blumenau's Oktoberfest is not the easiest or cheapest beer event to get to; it's not the best beer festival either, and you probably won't find the greatest beer you've ever drunk, but you will experience something totally unique.

The Lowdown

WHAT: Oktoberfest Blumenau

HOW: Takes place each year around the middle of October; www.oktoberfestblumenau.com.br.

WHERE: German Village Park, Rua Alberto Stein, 199 - Bairro da Velha, Blumenau, Santa Caterina, Brazil

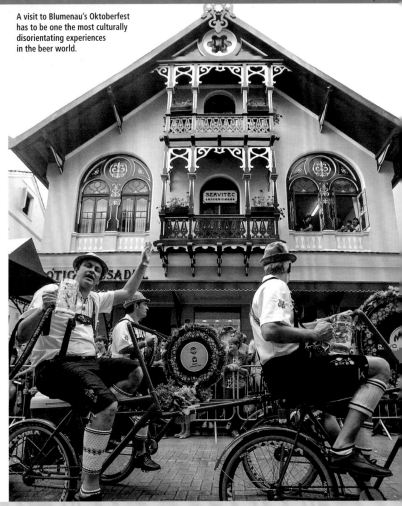

A visit to Blumenau's Oktoberfest has to be one the most culturally disorientating experiences in the beer world.

Don't Fancy Blumenau's Oktoberfest?

Then you should still consider this as an unlikely beer destination because it's effectively the Beer Capital of Brazil. The town has numerous good breweries nearby, plus every March they host the largest beer event in Latin America (aside from Oktoberfest, but that's more of a party, of course). Over 40,000 drinkers attend the Festival Brasileiro da Cerveja; there's a significant trade show and a large beer competition. And it all takes place in the German Village Park. For more information, visit www.festivaldacerveja.com.

A Brazilian Beer Crawl

ENJOY A FEW PINTS WITH THE CARIOCA AND PAULISTANOS

Today Rio de Janeiro, São Paulo, Minas Gerais, Paraná, and Rio Grande do Sul concentrate the largest numbers of breweries, bars, and bottle shops in Brazil, with Curitiba, in the state of Paraná, deserving special mention as some of the highest-rated craft breweries in Brazil are based there.

If you're in Brazil then it's most likely you'll be in Rio de Janeiro and São Paulo, so here are some top suggestions.

Rio de Janeiro

Start on the Rua Barão de Iguatemi in Praca da Bandeira, where you will find **Aconchego Carioca**, **Botto Bar**, and **Hop Lab**. Aconchego Carioca is a proper "boteco," the Brazilian equivalent of a pub, with an extensive beer list and great tropical atmosphere. Botto Bar has 20 taps and is popular among craft beer fans. It pours a lot of Brazilian beers but also American and European brews. Hop Lab probably has the largest number of taps in Rio, with 30 lines. **Pub Escondido** (Rua Aires de Saldanha, 98) has 24 taps in Copacabana so it's a good location. Also in Copacabana is **Melhores Cervejas do Mundo** (loja A, R. Ronald de Carvalho, 154), which has a very diverse stock of bottles and it's a good place to find rare beers. **Hocus Pocus** brewery tap (R. Dezenove de Fevereiro, 186, Botafogo) is a popular place with a rustic deco and classic craft beer set-up of wood and chalk boards.

São Paulo

Empório Alto de Pinheiros (Rua Vupabussu, 305) has the largest range of craft bottled beers in the city—about 500—as well as 33 taps with Brazilian breweries and excellent imports. Also in Pinheiros, one of the city's best areas for food and drink, is **Cervejaria Nacional** (Av. Pedroso de Morais, 604), a brewpub with good beers and sharing platters of food. **Cervejoteca** (Rua Bartolomeu

de Gusmão, 40, Vila Mariana) is a proper bottle shop with small tables for drinking in and shelves packed with beers, with many Brazilian and Belgian beers. **Capitão Barley** (Rua Cotoxó, 516, Água Branca) is away from central São Paulo but worth the visit for its focus on Brazilian craft beers through their regularly changing 15 taps. **Van Der Ale** and **Empório Sagarana** are opposite each other on Rua Aspicuelta in Vila Madalena, the hip district of the city. Van Der Ale brew their own beers and sell them among some guest beers, while Empório Sagarana is a rustic, charming

A burst of color in the famous favelas.

place with a smaller range of bottled craft beers beside an equivalent list of cachaças—perfect if you want to pair beers with cachaças, something that many Brazilians do.

And while on your bar crawl, look out for some the following breweries and beers. **Bodebrown** were one of the original craft brewers and still have a good reputation. Try **Urbana's** Gordelícia, Fio Terra, and A Piscadinha—they are all good. **Júpiter's** American Pale Ale is famous in São Paulo. **Colorado** is now one of AB-InBev's brands but that shouldn't detract from their Brazil-inspired beers, like their coffee-infused Porter. **Tupiniquim** make the impressive Monjolo Imperial Porter; **Coruja** make some super lagers. **Bamberg** beers are based on the best German traditions and are faithful recreations. **Dogma** have some excellent brews, including Cafuza and Touro Sentado. **Synergy Brewing** is highly rated; **Perro Libre** make some good hoppy brews.

Note: Special thanks to Pedro Batalha (follow Guiadecervejas on Instagram) for help with this entry.

Drink Chicha in Peru

LOCAL CORN-BASED HOME-BREW

This is one of the hard-to-get experiences left on my list. I'm fascinated by indigenous beers, beers uniquely of a place and not replicated anywhere else—beers that have been brewed for centuries using recipes and processes passed down through the generations. One such beer is chicha.

Chicha, or *chicha de jora* (as opposed to *chicha morada* which is non-alcoholic), is a fermented drink made from maize. In Peru, chicha has its distant origins in religious ceremonies. It has lesser prominence in other Central and South American countries, which have their own versions. Production varies; some contain additional adjunct sources of starch and sweetness, plus fruits and spices can be used. Some versions are made with germinated maize, some now include malted barley, while other more infamous and ancient versions are (or were) made with ground maize that's chewed by the chicha-makers and spat out in small balls—the act of chewing allows an enzyme in the saliva to help break down the starch in the maize into fermentable maltose (the beer is later boiled, sterilizing any grossness from the chewer's gob).

It's an ancient drink, essentially home-brew, and not a singular thing—there's great variety around Central and South America. In Peru, seemingly the best place to go to drink it is Sacred Valley in the Andean Highlands, not far from Machu Pichu (so, when I do finally get there, it'll be on another doubled-up Bucket List trip). If you end up there, then look for houses with red flags hanging outside—these tell you that you've found a *chicheria*. Today the most likely brewing process includes germinating the corn in water, then drying it out in the sun—essentially replicating barley's malting process. Then it's ground, mixed with water (and often malted barley), boiled, and left to ferment naturally, sometimes with additional flavorings added. It is drunk still-fermenting-fresh and there will probably be a sour edge to the soupy, low-alcohol brew. Sounds delicious, right? Especially if some Peruvian dude has already been chewing on the corn kernels.

Of course, this is all gleamed from desk research and might be entirely wrong, but it sounds wonderful and the idea of a Peruvian pub crawl through small chicherias, drinking local home-brew up in the highlands, sounds like something I need to experience.

BEERS THAT ARE UNIQUE TO THEIR LOCATION

- Farmhouse ales, Lithuania (see page 164)
- Sahti and Maltøl (Nordic farmhouse ales), Finland and Norway (see page 158)
- Kvass, Russia (see page 164)
- Umqombothi, Africa (see page 210)
- Chicha, Peru
- Bia Hoi, Hanoi, Vietnam (see page 194)

Elsewhere in South America…

Peru has over 30 craft breweries. Colombia has over 50 breweries. Chile has over 100 breweries. There are more than 200 in Argentina. Over 300 in Brazil. South America is also the big gap in my beer-drinking travels, having only been to Brazil. There's a serious amount of beer and brewing happening in South America now and it's the next big stop on my on-going Beer Bucket List adventures.

Beer at the Ends of the Earth

A FEW FINAL REMOTE BEER DESTINATIONS

I'll finish my Beer Bucket List with some suggestions for far-flung destinations that you (and I) might just get to one day.

The world's southernmost breweries (and Argentina's hop-growing region)

If Svalbard Bryggeri (see page 158) is on top of the world as the northernmost brewery, then you need to head all the way to the very south of Argentina, to the very south of South America, almost as far south as you can go, to drink at the world's southernmost brewery. There's a surprising amount of craft beer in Patagonia and, at the very bottom of them all, on the Argentinian side, is the **Fuegian Beverage Company** (Heroes de Malvinas 4160, Ushuaia, Tierra del Fuego, Argentina), which makes beers under the brands Cervecería Beagle and Cervecería Cape Horn. Look up the location; you probably didn't realize the world even went down that far. And they brew with actual glacier melt. On the Chilean side (but not quite as far south) is **Cervecería Austral** (2473 Patagona, Punta Arenas, Chile), which was founded in 1916.

If you're in Patagonia, then look up **Bariloche**, a town with around 15 breweries, while 62 miles (100km) south of there is **El Bolsón**, Argentina's hop-growing region. Yes, they have a hop-growing region and most breweries use these local hops—every year, around harvest time, they host a large beer festival in the spectacular surroundings of the hop fields (www.ellupuloalpalo.com).

The most remote brewery in the world

Cervecería Rapa Nui brews on Easter Island, in the middle of the Pacific Ocean, thousands of miles away from any mainland. Their Mahina beers (that's the Polynesian name for the moon) include a moderately strong Pale Ale and a powerful, chocolate-y Porter. To see the famous Moai statues cut from volcanic rock is a lifetime bucket list goal for many people and now it comes with a local brew—probably the remotest local brew in the world (www.facebook.com/mahinarapanui).

Bottles of Monsteiner's house beer, brewed by BierVision, the highest brewery in Europe.

Is there anywhere else that remote? Well, there's **Stone Money Brewing Company**, which is in the Manta Ray Bay hotel on Yap, Micronesia. Or on Rarotonga, the largest of the Cook Islands, there's the **Matutu Brewing Co** (Tikioki, Titikaveka, Rarotonga, Cook Islands).

The highest brewery in the world

Singapore's LeVeL33 is the world's highest urban brewery (see page 200), but that's only around 500ft (150m) above sea level and thousands of brewers can claim to make beer at greater altitudes than that. The highest-altitude brewery in the world appears to be Tibet's **Lhasa Brewery** (Sela North Road, Chengguan, Lhasa, Tibet), which is 12,000ft (3,700m) above sea level. It's brewed with Himalayan spring water and Tibetan barley, which has no outer hull.

While I'm on the subject, Europe's highest brewery is **BierVision** (Hauptstrasse 36, 7278 Davos Monstein, Switerland) in Monstein, a town that's 5330ft (1,625m) above sea level. America's highest is **Periodic Brewing** (115 E 7th Street, Leadville, Colorado 80461) in Leadville, which is at 10,150ft (3,094m).

Index

Acknowledgments

I'm grateful to many people who helped in my search for unusual, wonderful, unmissable bucket list beer drinking destinations. I raise my glass in thanks to the following: Chris Nelson, Merideth Canham-Nelson, John Holl, Jeff Alworth, Stan Hieronymus, Jordan St John, Alessio Leone, John Duffy, Adrian Tierney-Jones, Richard Taylor, Craig Heap, Leigh Linley, Josh Bernstein, Breandán Kearney, Marcin Chmielarz, Rudi Ghequire, Hedwig Neven, Natalya Watson, Olivier Dedeycker, Alex Troncoso, Brad Rogers, Christine Poreca, Lucy Corne, Ken Weaver, Kelly Ryan, Luke Nicholas, Russ Gosling, Brian McDonald, Pedro Batalha, Adam Vlček, Matt Stokes, Mark Charlwood, Chris Perrin, Lee Bacon, and all the brewers and drinkers that I shared a few beers with.

Thanks to Matt Curtis for the great images you supplied. Thanks to Pete Jorgensen for making this book happen (our fifth book together!), it's always a pleasure working with you. Thanks to Caroline for editing, Eoghan for the design, and Cindy and everyone else at Dog 'n' Bone. Thanks to all the breweries, bars, and events that kindly supplied us with images to use in the book.

Emma, you make everything more wonderful and combining our own life bucket-list trip while on the beer-bucket-list search is the best thing that I've ever done. My dad was a brilliant drinking and travel buddy, this time in New York, New England, Lille, Belgium, and Warsaw, where my mum also came on her first ever beer trip. These are some of my favorite memories from the book and show that sometimes the best experiences are the simple things, like sharing beers and moments with loved ones.